Contents

The following Level 1 optional unit is available on the Pearson Education website

www.pearsonschoolsandfecolleges.co.uk/ITQLevel1 using the password IT_user_level1

Credits and acknowledgements

The publisher would like to thank the following for their kind permission to reproduce their photographs:

(Key: b-bottom; c-centre; l-left; r-right; t-top)

Alamy Images: Ben Molyneux 135, Ingram Publishing 60; **Fotolia.com:** bloomua 70, Martin Lehotkay 181; **Glow Images:** OJO Images 11; **Imagemore Co., Ltd:** 255bl, 255br; **Imagestate Media:** John Foxx Collection 54, 59; **Jupiterimages:** Photos.com 62; **Masterfile UK Ltd:** Multi-Bits 2; **Pearson Education Ltd:** Coleman Yuen 255tl, 255tr, 281, David Sanderson 35, Jon Barlow 235; **PhotoDisc:** 253l, 253r; **Photoshot Holdings Limited:** NHPA / Martin Harvey 262; **Shutterstock.com:** artja33 282, AVAVA 5, George Dolgikh 3, Gorilla 260, imagefactory studio 16, Lynne Carpenter 14, n-trash 1, QQ7 268, Valerie Potapova 55

Cover images: Getty Images/Iconica

All other images © Pearson Education

Every effort has been made to trace the copyright holders and we apologise in advance for any unintentional omissions. We would be pleased to insert the appropriate acknowledgement in any subsequent edition of this publication.

The publisher would also like to thank Microsoft® Corporation, Google™ and Skype™. Microsoft® product screenshots reprinted with permission from Microsoft® Corporation.

Bishop
Auckland
College

iTQ FOR IT USERS
USING OFFICE® 2010

LEVEL 1   STUDENT BOOK

Karen Anderson

Alan Jarvis

Allen Kaye

Richard McGill

Neela Soomary

ALWAYS LEARNING

PEARSON

Published by Pearson Education Limited, Edinburgh Gate, Harlow, Essex, CM20 2JE.

www.pearsonschoolsandfecolleges.co.uk

Heinemann is a registered trademark of Pearson Education Limited

Text © Pearson Education Limited 2012
Typeset by Kamae Design, Oxford
Original illustrations © Pearson Education Limited 2012
Illustrated by Kamae Design
Cover design by Andrew Magee Design Limited
Cover photo/illustration © Getty Images/Iconica

The rights of Karen Anderson, Alan Jarvis, Allen Kaye, Richard McGill and Neela Soomary to be identified as authors of this work have been asserted by them in accordance with the Copyright, Designs and Patents Act 1988.

First published 2012

16 15 14 13 12
10 9 8 7 6 5 4 3 2 1

British Library Cataloguing in Publication Data
A catalogue record for this book is available from the British Library

ISBN 978 0 435 07524 8

Printed in Spain by Grafos S.A.

Websites
Pearson Education Limited is not responsible for the content of any external Internet sites. It is essential for tutors to preview each website before using it in class so as to ensure that the URL is still accurate, relevant and appropriate. We suggest that tutors bookmark useful websites and consider enabling students to access them through the school/college intranet.

Introduction

The qualification

The iTQ provides an **up-to-date, 'hands-on' nationally recognised IT user qualification** based on the National Occupational Standards (NOS) for IT Users 2009 that helps people to develop the IT skills they need in their day-to-day life. It is designed to help you improve your IT skills whether you are using technology at work, in education or in your free time. The iTQ is also designed to help you prepare for employment in jobs within the IT industry.

You may be studying the iTQ alongside other qualifications, as part of a Foundation Learning programme, as a standalone course or as part of an IT User Apprenticeship at school, college or in the workplace. Whatever level you are studying at, the iTQ can:

● provide you with **good employability skills** to help you get a job
● allow you to **progress through the levels**, whatever level you start at
● give you the chance to **put into practice the skills you learn**, in your daily life and in the workplace
● equip you with the IT skills you need to help you with a **variety of tasks**, such as book keeping and fundraising for voluntary and charitable work.

iTQ is available at four levels: Entry 3, Level 1, Level 2 and Level 3. At each level the qualification is offered in three sizes: Award, Certificate and Diploma.

You can select units from different levels to make up your qualification. The minimum credit value for each size at Level 1 is as follows:

● Award – 9 credits, 6 of which must be achieved at Level 1
● Certificate – 13 credits, 8 of which must be achieved at Level 1
● Diploma – 37 credits, 20 of which must be achieved at Level 1

Units in the qualification

The table below shows the credit value for each unit at the different levels. The units covered in this Level 1 book have been highlighted, together with their credit value.

	Credit value (E3)	Credit value (L1)	Credit value (L2)	Credit value (L3)
Improving productivity using IT	–	3	4	5
IT communication fundamentals	–	2	2	–
IT software fundamentals	–	3	3	–
IT user fundamentals	2	3	3	–
Audio and video software	2	–	–	–
Audio software	–	2	3	4
Bespoke or specialist software	2	–	–	–
Bespoke software	–	2	3	4
Computer accounting software	–	2	3	5
Data management software	2	2	3	4
Database software	2	3	4	6
Design and imaging software	2	–	–	–
Design software	–	3	4	5
Desktop publishing software*	2	3	4	5
Drawing and planning software	–	2	3	4
Imaging software	–	3	4	5
Multimedia software	–	3	4	6
Personal information man. software	1	2	2	–
Presentation software	2	3	4	6
Productivity programmes	1	–	–	–
Project management software	–	3	4	6
Spreadsheet software	2	3	4	6
Video software	–	2	3	4
Website software	–	3	4	5
Word processing software	2	3	4	6
Computer basics	1	–	–	–

	Credit value (E3)	Credit value (L1)	Credit value (L2)	Credit value (L3)
IT security for users*	–	1	2	3
Optimise IT system performance	–	2	4	5
Setting up an IT system	–	3	4	5
Computer security and privacy	1	–	–	–
Using collaborative technologies	–	3	4	6
Using mobile IT devices	1	2	2	–
Using email	1	2	3	3
Using the Internet	1	3	4	5
Digital lifestyle	1	–	–	–
The Internet and worldwide web	1	–	–	–

Mandatory unit

For the Certificate and Diploma sizes, you must complete the mandatory unit, *Improving productivity using IT*. For this unit, you will be required to demonstrate evidence of planning, evaluating and improving procedures that use IT, to make them more efficient. The evidence can be generated from tasks that you carry out in your day-to-day work, through written scenarios/situations or knowledge tests.

How the qualification is assessed

Assessment is by means of a portfolio of evidence – either paper based or, where possible, as a digital portfolio – that demonstrates your competence. At Level 1, your portfolio will be assessed by an Internal Verifier.

Types of evidence

For each unit you need to gather evidence to include in your portfolio to show that you have successfully achieved the required standard for each of the assessment criteria. This evidence is likely to include:

- observation of your performance by your assessor
- responses to oral or written questioning
- projects that demonstrate your work
- assignments
- personal statements that demonstrate planning and decision-making skills and explain your decision-making process
- Witness testimonies – that can be used to support your personal statements.
  - Witnesses can include your line manager, experienced colleagues in your workplace or customers and clients.
  - The witness needs to be able to testify to your performance.
  - Witness testimonies normally take the form of a written statement about the quality and authenticity of your work and need to be dated and signed by the witness.
- Professional discussion (which may be used for the assessment of the mandatory unit.)
  - You will meet with your assessor (or have a series of meetings with your assessor) and have the opportunity to present a range of evidence for discussion. You will be required to take the lead in the discussion.
  - The discussion can be used to explore and explain situations in which you have used IT, i.e. to demonstrate your problem-solving skills, to explore and explain how you undertook tasks, to explore your reasons for choosing different options, (e.g. selecting the best software for a task and to reflect on the final product or outcome).
- Knowledge tests to assess your knowledge and understanding of, for example, an organisational procedure or the knowledge requirements for units.
- Simulation of work tasks and activities within a realistic working environment – the mandatory unit may be assessed in this way.
  - Scenario-based evidence. If you undertake this type of assessment for the mandatory unit, you will be given a written scenario/situation and you will need to write a response explaining how IT can be used in the situation.
- Recognised prior learning – this allows you to count any other relevant units towards your iTQ. Your assessor can give you further guidance on this.

Collecting your evidence

The main ways in which evidence can be collected include:

- from a current job role – you build an assessment portfolio by gathering evidence of IT skills that you have applied to your day-to-day work in the workplace
- from a learning/training programme – you may be studying at a training centre and produce evidence from a mixture of knowledge tests and scenario-based evidence
- Accreditation of Prior Achievement (APA) – qualifications that you have already achieved and that meet the assessment criteria for the optional units of the iTQ may also be used as evidence – for example, a presentation that you have done as part of a geography project.

A combination of the above methods of collecting evidence can be achieved. Other valid evidence can come from social and voluntary activities (e.g. posters/ websites of a club or society you belong to), enterprise activities (such as creating a business plan or marketing materials) and job searches (e.g. CVs, application forms and emails to potential employers).

ECDL Essentials

The following Level 1 units make up the ECDL Essentials qualification:

- IT user fundamentals
- Using email and the Internet
- Security for IT users.

This book provides complete coverage of the content of these units.

How to use this book

Unit introduction and learning outcomes

These introductions give you a snapshot of what to expect from each unit – and what you should be aiming for by the time you finish it!

The learning outcomes are ways to measure your learning and progress. After completing a unit you should be able to achieve all of the learning outcomes listed. The assessment activity and activities will help you achieve this.

Assessment activity

At the end of each unit you will find an assessment activity. The activity will be broken down into steps and you'll be asked to complete tasks. The tasks will be based on the content you have learned in the unit and will cover the learning outcomes. These may take a variety of forms – but each task will require you to demonstrate the skills and knowledge you have developed over the course of the unit.

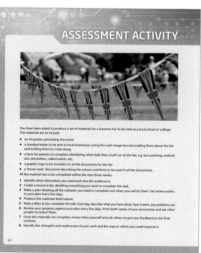

Activities

There are different types of activities for you to do and they will appear at different points throughout each unit. The aim of these activities is to give you a broader grasp of the IT world through the practical application of your skills and knowledge.

How to... activities

These activities run though the steps involved in carrying out an IT task. You will need to be able to successfully carry out these activities in order to complete the assessment activities in this book and to help you in your working life.

How to create a macro

1. Open the **View** menu.
2. Click **Macros** and select **Record Macro**.
3. A dialog box will appear. Choose a name for your macro – this cannot contain spaces or other punctuation.
4. Decide how you want to run your macro – by clicking a button or pressing a keyboard shortcut.
5. If you decide to use a keyboard shortcut, click **Keyboard**. Then press the shortcut keys you would like to use (e.g. **Ctrl + Alt + 6**) and click **Assign**. **Close** the dialog box.
6. Run through the actions you would like your macro to do. For example, if you want to create a macro that saves and then prints your document, click **Save** and then **Print**.
7. When you have finished running through the macro actions, click **Macros** and select **Stop Recording**.

If you assigned your macro to a keyboard shortcut, you can run it by pressing the keys you chose. Alternatively, you can follow the steps below.

8. Open the **View** menu.
9. Click **Macros** and **View Macros**.
10. Find the **Macros in:** drop-down menu and select **All active templates and documents**.
11. Select your macro from the list that appears.
12. Click **Run**.

Figure 1.9: How to run a macro

Case studies

These are extended activities which focus on business cases or real-life working scenarios. There might be one case study used throughout a unit; or there could be more than one case study per unit.

You will be provided with a scenario and asked to weigh up the information, assess the facts and then complete a series of tasks based on the information provided.

Case study: Games console network

In April 2011, a leading games console's online service was hacked. This reportedly resulted in 77 million users' email and password details being compromised (made available to people who should not have access to them). This was one of the biggest and most publicised cases of hacking ever.

Find three different articles about this case and answer the following questions.

1. What was the effect on individual users?
2. What was the effect on the business?
3. What was the effect on the Internet as a whole?

Check your understanding

At the end of some sections you will find a series of questions. They are designed to focus in on some of the key topics and knowledge areas covered in the section. Make sure you can answer these questions before moving on to the next section.

Check your understanding

1. What are icons?
2. Look at the desktop on your computer and list all the icons you can see. You could take a screenshot of your desktop (press the **Print Screen** key) then paste the image into Word® (**Home** tab, **Paste**) and annotate each icon to explain what it does.
3. Why should you always shut down your computer before switching off the power?
4. What do the **Minimize** and **Maximize** buttons do?

Key terms

Technical words or phases you might be unfamiliar with have been placed in **bold font** (black). The terms and definitions can also be found in the glossary at the back of the book.

IT terms

IT terms and functions, such as **Caps Lock** and **desktop** have been made red and are placed in bold so that you can spot them easily. Some of the terms will be explained using the Key terms boxes. However, not all IT terms will be explained. If you're unsure about a word's meaning then ask your tutor.

Did you know?

This feature provides you with additional information about a particular topic or sheds some light on an interesting area that might not have been touched upon in the content.

Remember

In these feature boxes you'll find helpful reminders and top tips relating to the information covered in a unit.

Improving productivity using IT

To complete this unit you must plan, carry out and review an IT project. Your project can be made up of one large task or several smaller but related tasks. For example, you could create your own website or a newsletter as a single large task. Creating a set of marketing materials for a particular event would count as several smaller but related tasks. This unit is mandatory, which means that you must complete it to achieve your iTQ qualification.

Learning outcomes

After completing this unit you should be able to achieve the following learning outcomes.

» **LO1** Plan the use of appropriate IT systems and software to meet requirements

» **LO2** Use IT systems and software efficiently to complete planned tasks

» **LO3** Review the selection and use of IT tools to make sure that tasks are successful

1 Plan the use of appropriate IT systems and software to meet requirements

This section will help you choose and use the right IT systems for a variety of tasks.

Before you begin working on a large task, you should spend time **planning** so that you understand clearly what you want to achieve. This will help avoid problems later and can save a lot of time. You will usually need to complete tasks or projects by a **deadline**. With good planning you should meet deadlines without running out of time.

1.1 Purposes for using IT

In order to plan a task you need to think about the purpose of IT and how it can help improve productivity. Before you start a task, consider the following questions to help you plan effectively.

- Are you completing the task for yourself or for someone else? If it is for someone else, are you sure what the purpose of the task is?
- When does the task need to be finished? You must know the deadline so that you can plan your time effectively (well) and make sure your work is finished on time.
- What information will you need to complete the task? Do you have all this information? If not, where will you get it from?
- How will you provide the content? For example, if you are creating a newsletter, who will write the articles? If you are making a poster advertising an event, who will provide the information you need? You may also need to source photographs or other images.
- Where will the finished outcome be used or how will it be presented? What format will the completed project be in? Will it be printed out, displayed on screen or via a projector, or sent in an email?

Figure 1.1: IT tools will allow you to share and present information more effectively

Activity: Planning a presentation

Your school, college or workplace is holding an Open Day in three weeks' time. You have been asked to prepare a presentation to be shown on the Open Day. It will need to show which courses and facilities the college offers and what types of activity the students take part in.

Answer the questions listed above this activity to identify the nature and purpose of the task.

- Who is your **audience**?
- What is your deadline?
- What information will you need and where will you get it from?
- What IT tools (hardware and software) will you need to complete the task?
- What format will the end result be in?

1.2 Identify methods, skills and resources

In order to complete a complex task successfully you will need to plan. You will do this by identifying the methods, skills and resources required.

Methods and skills

To create a plan, first you need to break complex tasks down into smaller subtasks. This will help you see exactly what you need to do and think about the details of the main task.

Next, you must work out how long each task will take. You can use your previous experience and skills to guess how long you might need. If you have not worked on something similar before, you should ask someone who has. You must be realistic about how long each subtask is likely to take or you will struggle to meet your deadline.

Arrange the tasks into a logical (sensible) order. Most tasks will be related, so you may have to finish tasks before you can start on others. However, if tasks are unconnected you could run them at the same time.

You must be clear about the task you are trying to complete. You should also be aware of the benefits of using IT to complete the task rather than doing it manually.

Resources

You need to consider the resources required to complete each of the subtasks, such as:

- **hardware** – computer, printer (colour or monochrome), scanner, camera, memory card, etc.
- **consumables** – paper, ink cartridges, etc.
- **software applications** – such as word processing, database and spreadsheet software
- **skills** – you will probably have the skills needed to complete some of the tasks, but there may be things you do not know how to do. In this case you should consider how to learn the new skills you need. For example, you could ask people with those skills, use online resources or find information in books or magazines.

1.3 Reasons for choosing IT

In many cases you will have a choice of software for a particular task. For example, if you are creating a simple leaflet, you could use a word processing program such as Microsoft® Word® or a desktop publishing program such as Microsoft® Publisher®. If you need to edit a photograph, you could use the Paint® program that is included in Microsoft® Windows® or specialised image editing software such as Adobe® Photoshop®.

Figure 1.2: You should consider what hardware you will need for the task

Your choice may depend on many factors, including those listed below.

- **Availability**: Software applications such as Adobe® Photoshop® and Microsoft® Publisher® are quite expensive. If a particular program is not available on the computer you are working on, you may have to use an alternative. The availability of certain programs or features may also affect your choice of system. For example, if you need to save files to CDs, you will need to use a computer which can burn files to disk.
- **Suitability**: Some programs may not have the facilities you need. For example, Paint® has a very limited range of image editing tools which may not be up to the task. You should also consider different types of hardware. For example, if you need to produce detailed drawings, you may decide to use a graphics tablet.
- **Knowledge and skill**: You might base your choice on your own knowledge and skills, especially if time is short. A particular application may be most suitable for the task. However, if you do not know how to use it or do not have time to learn it, you will have to use an alternative – even if it is less well suited to the task. This is also true when you are deciding which IT systems to use.

Save time and/or money

The saying goes 'time is money' and every business wants to cut costs. One way of reducing costs is to complete tasks in less time. In many cases, IT systems will allow businesses to do this. For example, database or spreadsheet software can keep track of customer orders to make sure deliveries are made promptly and efficiently.

For more information, see *Unit 8 Database software* and *Unit 11 Spreadsheet software*.

Choose more convenience

This is related to saving time and money. It is often far more convenient to complete a task using IT than to do it manually. For example, if you need to send the same letter to hundreds of customers, you can use the **mail merge** function in Microsoft® Word® to insert each customer's name and address automatically (see page 9). This is much simpler than producing a separate letter for each customer, and more convenient than writing all those letters by hand.

Allow a company to respond more quickly

Efficient customer service is very important to most businesses. In general, the quicker a company can respond to a customer's request, the happier the customer will be. Businesses can usually respond to customers faster by using IT. Happy customers are more likely to stay loyal to a company (keep doing business with it). They may also recommend the business to friends or colleagues.

Enhance communications

For a company to work efficiently (especially a large company), employees, customers and suppliers must be able to communicate well with each other. Electronic communications such as email and video conferencing have greatly affected how businesses work because they allow instant communication between employees, customers and suppliers.

Improve quality

You can use IT in many ways to improve the quality of products. Many applications have facilities (tools) such as spelling and grammar checkers that can help make sure text does not contain mistakes. Programs such as spreadsheets and databases include rules to help make sure you enter data correctly.

Help businesses respond to changing circumstances

In the modern business world, situations can change rapidly, and the most successful companies are the ones that can quickly adapt to these changes. IT and automated systems are often vital to allow businesses to develop new solutions to particular problems quickly. These factors can improve business productivity and help companies become more competitive.

Figure 1.3: IT systems have made it much easier for people to communicate effectively and efficiently

Activity: Benefits of using IT

1 Talk to your tutor about how IT is used in schools and colleges. For example:
   - Do facilities such as electronic registers and spreadsheets for tracking learners' progress make their life easier?
   - How do computerised methods compare with manual methods of completing the same tasks?
   - Do you know what a virtual learning environment (VLE) is? Does your school or college have a VLE?
   - How does using a VLE to access information about your school, college or course compare with manual methods?
   - Can you submit assignment work electronically via a VLE? How does this compare with submitting assignment work manually?
2 Write up your notes to briefly explain how IT can make a tutor's work easier and more efficient.

Figure 1.4: Microsoft® provides a library of ClipArt images, such as the example shown here, which you can use freely in your own documents as long as you acknowledge the company appropriately

1.4 Legal or local guidelines or constraints

There are several issues related to laws, local guidelines and constraints (limits) that may affect your project.

Legal constraints

You must be aware of **copyright** laws when sourcing materials for your project. Unless you have created the materials yourself or they are copyright free, you may break copyright laws if you use them without permission. For more information on this topic, see the section *1.3 Copyright constraints on the use of information* in *Unit 4 IT communication fundamentals*, page 74.

You may also come across issues with software licensing. If you buy a software application, the licence is included in the price. In most cases, this licence will be valid for one user only. This means that you only have the right to install the software on one computer. If you lend an installation disk to a friend so that they can install the software on their computer, you are both breaking software licensing laws.

You can download some software from the Internet for free. These are known as **open source** applications. However, open source software may work in slightly different ways, or include slightly different features and tools from similar software that you pay for and need a licence to use.

You also must be aware of the Data Protection Act 1998. This protects the rights of people whose data is stored on computer systems. You cannot store information about living individuals (for example, in a database) unless you are registered with the Data Protection Registrar. There is more information about the Data Protection Act 1998 in *Unit 3 IT security for users*, page 66.

Local guidelines

Most organisations, including colleges and schools, have guidelines about how you can use their IT facilities and what you can and cannot do on the Internet. This may restrict (limit) what you can do. For example, you may find that sites such as Facebook and YouTube are blocked and you cannot access them. Some of these guidelines are there to help improve the security of the IT systems and help prevent data being lost or other problems caused by viruses, for example.

Many organisations have guidelines about passwords to help keep them secure. They might state that passwords have to be 'strong' (not easily guessed). For example, they may have to be a certain length (e.g. at least 8 characters) and a combination of letters, numbers and symbols.

Many companies also have rules about how their documents are designed. These rules define the company's 'house style' and 'brand'. They may specify how their logo should be used or positioned in documents and which fonts or colours should be used. If you are preparing materials for a company which has a house style or brand then you must make sure that the work you produce follows this style.

1 Find a copy of the IT and Internet usage policy for your school, college or workplace. This should be a written document which lists what you can and cannot do when using the company's IT systems.

2 Read the document and make sure you understand why these rules are in place. Are there any rules which do not make sense to you? If so, you should ask your tutor about them.

2 Use IT systems and software efficiently to complete planned tasks

You need to know how to use IT and software well to complete tasks in time, with the resources you have and within budget.

2.1 Automated routines which improve productivity

In a busy workplace you will be under pressure to complete work quickly and accurately. Many software applications include features that do certain tasks automatically. These will help you complete your work faster.

After you have identified which automated routines you will use in your project, you then need to create and test them to make sure they work. Automated routines can be very useful but you must first spend time and effort to develop and test them.

Shortcuts

You can create a **shortcut** to a file, folder or software application and save it to the desktop or to another convenient location. You can then double click on the shortcut to perform the action. Shortcuts can launch software, open files or display the contents of folders. They are especially useful for accessing documents you use often, as you will not need to click though several folder levels to reach a particular document or folder.

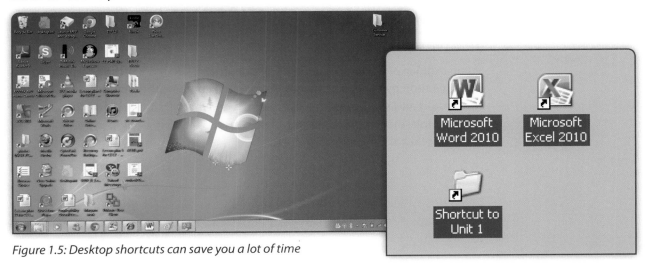

Figure 1.5: Desktop shortcuts can save you a lot of time

Customised menus and toolbars

Many software applications (for example, Microsoft® Word®) will allow you to change the menus and/or toolbars so that the tools you use most often are easy to reach. Figure 1.6 shows the dialog box for selecting tools and shortcuts in Word®.

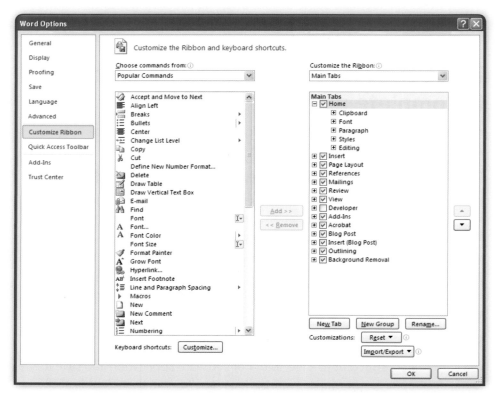

Figure 1.6: Many applications allow you to change the toolbars to help you work more efficiently

2.2 Use automated routines to help plan and improve processes

Templates

If you regularly need a specific type of document, such as a business letter, you can save time by using a template. A template contains the required text and formatting and stays the same every time you create that type of document. For example, a business letter template would contain the company address, a set greeting and signature line, etc.

Activity: Creating a template

Use Microsoft® Word® to create a template that you can use for your assignment task. You should include the following details:

- a footer with page numbers centred at the bottom of the page and your name and student number right aligned
- a header with your school or college name and 'iTQ Level 1' right aligned.

Save this document as a template:

1 Choose **File** and then select **Save As**.
2 In the **Save As** dialog box, choose **Word Template** from the **Save as type** drop-down box.
3 Give your file an appropriate name and then click **Save**.

Mail merge

If you need to send the same letter to several different people, you can use the **mail merge** function to save time. All you need to do is write your letter and create a list of names and addresses. The mail merge function will automatically create copies of the letter and add a different name and address to each copy.

Automated email response

An automated email response is also known as an 'out of office' reply. If you are away from work (for example, on holiday or on a training course) you can set up an automated response to incoming emails to let people know you are away and that you cannot reply to their message until you get back. You can also include details of who they should contact in your absence if they have an urgent query.

Style sheets

You can use style sheets with word processing, desktop publishing and web development software. They allow you to keep all text formatting settings (for example, font or paragraph alignment) together in one place. Then, if you want to change something, you only need to make one change rather than reformat the whole document. Style sheets also make it easier to keep the formatting in a document the same in similar cases.

Macros

Macros are mini programs that can carry out repetitive tasks automatically. For example, you can use macros to format text or add bullet points. Macros save time and are very useful if you have to do the same task over and over again.

Figure 1.7: If you need to send the same letter to many people, mail merge could save a lot of time

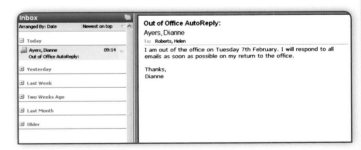

Figure 1.8: An automated email response

How to create a macro

1. Open the **View** menu.

2. Click **Macros** and select **Record Macro**.

3. A dialog box will appear. Choose a name for your macro – this cannot contain spaces or other punctuation.

4. Decide how you want to run your macro – by clicking a button or pressing a keyboard shortcut.

5. If you decide to use a keyboard shortcut, click **Keyboard**. Then press the shortcut keys you would like to use (e.g. **Ctrl + Alt + 6**) and click **Assign**. **Close** the dialog box.

6. Run through the actions you would like your macro to do. For example, if you want to create a macro that saves and then prints your document, click **Save** and then **Print**.

7. When you have finished running through the macro actions, click **Macros** and select **Stop Recording**.

If you assigned your macro to a keyboard shortcut, you can run it by pressing the keys you chose. Alternatively, you can follow the steps below.

8. Open the **View** menu.

9. Click **Macros** and **View Macros**.

10. Find the **Macros in:** drop-down menu and select **All active templates and documents**.

11. Select your macro from the list that appears.

12. Click **Run**.

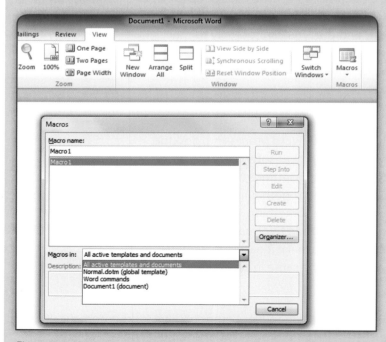

Figure 1.9: How to run a macro

Activity: Creating a chart

You work in a small business. Your boss has asked you to create a monthly sales chart to display on the office notice board. Your boss gives you the sales figures and you need to put them in a spreadsheet, create a chart and then print the chart.

Create a macro which:

- selects the cells with sales data in them
- creates a 3D chart using these figures
- prints the chart.

3 Review the selection and use of IT tools to make sure that tasks are successful

Reviewing what you have done is a good way to develop your skills and will help you carry out tasks more effectively next time.

3.1 Review outcomes

To review your work, you must consider the quality of the information used. You could ask yourself the following questions.

- What information did you collect for the task?
- Was it the right information?
- Was the information up to date?
- Was the information fit for purpose?

For example, for a science project, you may have taken some information from Wikipedia, which might not have been totally reliable. Or you might find that the information you gathered is too complex and you may misunderstand it. This would lead to mistakes in your finished work.

It is important to review your work once it is complete. However, you must also remember to review your work as you go along so that you can correct problems before it is too late. Producing draft copies of your documents is one way to do this. You can ask other people, including the client or intended audience of the task, to review the drafts and let you know if you are on the right track. This is much better than showing them the final version and finding out at that point that you have misunderstood what was required.

You should also review your progress regularly against your original plan. If you fall behind schedule, you could then take action to try to get back on track.

Figure 1.10: It is important to review your work to identify what went well and what you could have done better

3.2 Decide whether the IT tools selected were appropriate

There are many questions you can ask yourself about your choice of IT tools, including:

- Did the tools have the features you needed to complete the required tasks?
- Was the time taken to complete the tasks with the chosen tools acceptable?
- Could you have finished a task more quickly if you had chosen other tools?
- How convenient were the tools you selected? Were they easy to use or did you find some things difficult?
- Did the tools include features that helped to improve the quality of the work? For example, did they have a spelling and grammar check for text or guidelines and rulers to help lay out graphics accurately?

Activity: Review your work

Select one piece of work that you have used IT to complete.

1 Discuss with your tutor or a friend which IT tools you used to complete the work. Explain why you chose those particular tools and whether or not you think they were appropriate for the task and its purpose.

2 Was there anything else you had to consider? For example, would you have preferred a different program which was not available in your school, college or workplace?

3.3 Strengths and weaknesses

You need to review your final work and identify its strengths and weaknesses. It can be quite hard to identify weaknesses in your own work so you might find it helpful to ask someone else to comment on your work too.

When considering the strengths and weaknesses of your work, you should try to answer the following questions.

- Is the formatting you have chosen suitable? For example, have you used fonts that match the style of the document? In a formal document, such as a report or business letter, it is best to use a traditional font such as Times New Roman or Arial. In an informal document (for example, a poster or leaflet), it may be better to use a casual font such as Comic Sans. You should also check that your formatting is consistent. For example, have you always used the same formatting for a heading or subheading? Using style sheets can help you to keep formatting standard.
- Are the layouts you have used accurate and consistent? For example, if you have drawn a diagram, are the lines parallel and straight where they should be? Are lines joined where they should be?
- How well does your work match the original requirements? Look back at what you were asked to do and check how accurately you have met the requirements.

- Could you improve the quality of your finished work? For example, would more time or additional skills have enabled you to complete the work more accurately?
- Is the end result suitable for the intended audience? Is the language appropriate? Is the formatting fit for purpose? For example, a leaflet inviting primary school children to a party should use simple, clear language and bright, attractive colours.

3.4 Improvements to work

You need to be able to identify specific ways in which your work could be improved. It is not enough to simply say it could be made better or more accurate or that the quality could be improved.

Look at each weakness you have identified in the previous section and identify ways to eliminate each one in order to improve the standard of your work in the future. Some ways of improving your work are outlined below.

Correct mistakes

You should proofread written documents very carefully and correct any mistakes. It is often difficult to spot mistakes in your own work, so it is a good idea to ask someone else to proofread it for you as well. As well as checking for spelling and grammar errors, you should check carefully for layout and formatting errors. This also applies to any graphics you have produced.

Avoid affecting other people's work

It is likely that on some projects you will need to work in a team. In these cases the way you work needs to fit in with the whole team. This might include:

- using the same formatting or layout as others in the team
- making sure files are saved in a format which is compatible with (matches) other people's applications
- agreeing on how to manage changes made to a document by different people or making changes to two different versions of the same document.

Although you must avoid affecting other people's work, you should still be able to add to and change documents, depending on your role within the team.

Find better ways of doing things

Although your work may be fine, after completing the task you might identify alternative ways of working which would have been better. Note down anything you would like to do differently next time and refer to these notes if you need to produce a similar piece of work in the future.

Learn new techniques

While working, you may find that you did not know how to do certain things. This may have meant you were not able to complete the task as you would have liked. Once again, note down anything you did not know how to do so that you can try to fill gaps in your knowledge before completing a similar piece of work.

You have been asked to produce a set of materials for a Summer Fair to be held at a local school or college. The materials are to include:

- an A4 poster advertising the event
- a standard letter to be sent to local businesses (using the mail merge function) telling them about the fair and inviting them to come along
- a form for parents to complete, identifying what stalls they could run at the fair, e.g. face painting, mehndi skin decoration, cakes/sweets, etc.
- a graphic logo to be included on all the documents for the fair
- a 'house style' document describing the colours and fonts to be used in all the documents.

All the material has to be completed within the next three weeks.

1 Identify what information you need and who the audience is.
2 Create a resource list, detailing everything you need to complete this task.
3 Make a plan showing all the subtasks you need to complete and when you will do them. Set review points in your plan every five days.
4 Produce the materials listed above.
5 Keep a diary as you complete the task. Each day, describe what you have done, how it went, any problems, etc.
6 Review your progress against your plan every five days. Print draft copies of your documents and ask other people to review them.
7 Once the materials are complete, review them yourself and ask others to give you feedback on the final versions.
8 Identify the strengths and weaknesses of your work and list ways in which you could improve it.

IT user fundamentals

This unit is all about how to use a computer in everyday life, in education, training or in work. It is not about specific software applications such as word processing or using spreadsheets. Instead, it covers the general techniques you will need to run your computer efficiently and deal with common, minor problems. The skills you learn in this unit will make using a computer a more productive and less frustrating experience.

Learning outcomes

After completing this unit you should be able to achieve the following learning outcomes:

» **LO1** Use IT systems to meet needs

» **LO2** Organise, store and retrieve information

» **LO3** Follow and understand the need for safety and security practices

» **LO4** Carry out routine maintenance of IT systems and respond to routine IT system problems

1 Use IT systems to meet needs

This section is about the basic skills you will need to use an IT system successfully to meet your needs and the needs of others.

1.1 Start and shut down procedures

Starting a computer (booting up) is very simple. Press the **power switch** and wait for the computer to start up. Different systems, such as desktop computers or laptops, will have the on switch in different places, which can be confusing if you are using a system for the first time. However, the power switch should look like the one shown in Figure 2.1. If you are using a desktop computer, you will need to turn on the monitor (screen) separately. Smartphones and tablet computers do not always have an obvious power switch, so you may need to check the manual or ask someone for help to find it.

Figure 2.1: A power switch

Log in

When you turn on a computer that has been set up for multiple users, you will see a log in screen. In this case you will need to enter your **username** and **password** to access (get into) the system.

Usernames and passwords

Usernames are not usually **case sensitive**, but passwords are. Check that the **Caps Lock** key on the keyboard is not pressed. The **operating system (OS)** will usually remind you if it is, but you can check the indicator light on the keyboard if you are not sure. Once you have entered your log in details (username and password) correctly, you will have access to the system.

You should then see the **desktop** or **menu** screen, which shows a background and symbols called **icons**. The background and icons will vary according to how the computer has been set up.

For more information on passwords, see section *3.4 Information security* later in this unit, page 38.

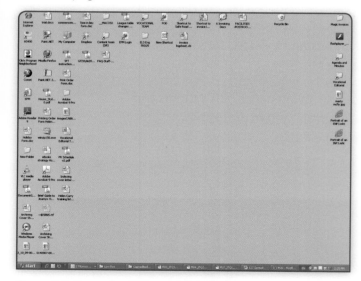

Figure 2.2: Example of Microsoft® desktop

Shut down or log off

When you **shut down** a computer system, you switch off the power completely. It is very important to follow the correct procedure. Turning the power off before the system has shut down properly may cause problems such as files becoming **corrupt**. Sometimes there will be software updates to install. In this case, you must wait for the updates to complete before you turn off the power.

Shut down

It is important to shut down your computer in the correct way.

> #### How to shut down your computer
>
> 1. Save your work and close all the programs you have open.
> 2. At this point, you can choose to **Log off** or **Shut down**. Remember, for security reasons, you should always log off if you need to leave your computer unattended.
> 3. To shut down the system, click the **Start** button in the bottom left-hand corner and choose **Shut down**. Then wait for the system to switch itself off. Make sure that any updates are complete before you turn off the power at the mains or unplug the computer.

Log off

If you do not want to shut down completely, you can log off instead. This ends your session but leaves the computer running so that someone else can log in.

> #### How to log off
>
> 1. Click the **Start** button and then click the arrow on the side of the **Shut down** button.
> 2. From the pop-out menu that appears, choose **Log off** or **Switch User**.

Lock and unlock your computer

If you need to leave a computer for a short time but do not want to close all your applications and/or log off, you can **lock** the computer so that no one else can use it. To lock your computer, press the **Ctrl+Alt+Del** keys together (you will need two hands to do this). From the menu that appears, choose the first option – **Lock this computer**.

> **Key term**
>
> **Corrupt** – programs or files that have become unreliable because of damage, errors or changes.

> **Did you know?**
>
> If you turn off the power without shutting down properly, you may lose the files you have been working on. When you turn the computer on again, it may take longer than usual to boot up as the computer will need to run through a series of checks.

Figure 2.3: Start and Shut down buttons

> **Did you know?**
>
> **Switch User** is a very useful feature because it allows you to leave all your programs open while someone else logs in and uses the computer. However, it is important to save your work before switching users, in case someone else shuts down the computer completely. If this happens, you will lose any unsaved work.

Figure 2.4: The Windows® 7 unlock screen

To unlock the computer, simply click the **User** icon in the centre of the lock screen and enter your password. The screen will unlock and return as you left it. See also the section *Use access controls* in *Unit 3 IT security for users*, page 54.

Sometimes, a software application will stop responding (running). When this happens, you will usually see **Not responding** next to the program name in the title bar. If you click the close button on the program's title bar (the white cross in a red box), a message will ask if you want to close the program. If you click **OK**, the program will be forced to close but you will lose any unsaved work.

1.2 Interacting with IT systems

An IT system is made up of several components (parts). The first is the computer itself. The many different types of computer include:

- desktop computers (the most common), such as home/office personal computers (PCs)
- laptops (portable PCs)
- netbooks (smaller laptops)
- tablets (mobile, touchscreen computers).

Processor

The processor is the 'brain' of the computer that runs all the program instructions. A PC's processor may have several **cores** that can run different programs at the same time.

Key term

Cores – independent processors which read and execute program instructions.

Input and output devices

An IT system also includes various **input** and **output** devices. Input devices allow you to put information into the computer. A laptop has all or most of these devices built in but a desktop computer has several separate devices.

Examples of input devices include:

- keyboard
- mouse
- tracker ball or touch pad (on a portable computer)
- **graphics tablet**
- microphone
- scanner
- stylus (used with personal digital assistants [PDAs or palmtop computers], graphics tablets and tablet computers)
- joystick
- digital camera
- webcam.

The information a computer produces is called 'output' so the devices which receive this information are called output devices. The most obvious output device is the screen or **monitor**, which shows you the information the computer produces. Other output devices include:

- speakers
- printer
- headphones
- plotter (for **CAD** drawings).

Storage media

While the computer is running, programs and data are stored in its random access **memory (RAM)**. This is the computer's temporary internal storage area. Therefore, anything in this memory will be lost when the computer is switched off. To permanently store the work you have done you must save it on the computer's internal **hard drive.** This keeps the information even when the computer is switched off.

You can add **external storage** devices such as **USB** memory sticks or CDs to store data outside your computer system. This type of storage is particularly useful for transferring and/or backing up data. For more information, see the sections *Backups* and *Portable and USB devices* in *Unit 3 IT security for users*, pages 58 and 63.

If your computer is connected to a network, you may also have access to a network drive where files are stored on another computer within the network.

1.3 Interface features

An interface is a program or device that allows you to communicate with your computer. It can also connect items of software or hardware. Windows® software uses a number of user interface features which are common to most programs.

Desktop

When a computer starts up, the monitor shows a coloured background known as the **desktop**. The desktop displays small pictures called icons which represent different programs and folders. Some common icons are **Computer**, **Recycle Bin** (for files you have **deleted**), **Documents** and icons that launch specific programs.

Figure 2.5: Recycle Bin desktop icon

Figure 2.6: Printer shortcut desktop icon

If you click the Start button a menu will show all the available programs and features. From here, you can also access the **Documents** folder or change the computer's **default settings**.

To the right of the Start button is the **Taskbar**, which runs along the bottom of the screen. The taskbar shows an icon for each application you have running. If you move the mouse pointer (cursor) over an application icon, you will see a small preview of the application. You can click on the preview to make the application fill the screen.

Figure 2.7: The taskbar

To the right of the taskbar is the **notification area**. This will show, for example:

- how much battery life is left (on a laptop)
- whether the system is connected to the Internet
- what time it is
- whether the operating system has found any problems.

Windows

All programs run within a window, which is a panel showing an open application. If you have several files using the same application (for example, Microsoft® Word®) open at the same time, each file will appear in a separate window. When you view the application on the taskbar you will see a preview of all its open files.

Each open window can be in one of three states:

- **Maximised**: The window fills the screen.
- **Minimised**: The application window does not appear on the desktop but is shown as an icon on the taskbar.
- **Restored**: You can see the application window on the desktop it but does not fill it. There may be other windows in front of or behind it.

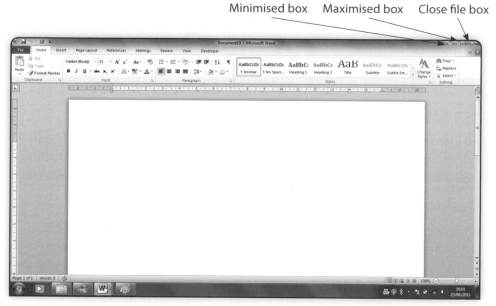

Minimised box   Maximised box   Close file box

Figure 2.8: A maximised window

You can resize a restored window by using the mouse to click on and drag any of its outside borders. You can also move the window by dragging the title bar.

A window that is not large enough to show all its contents will have **scrollbars**. These usually appear on the right and/or bottom edge of the window. They have little arrows at each end which you can click on to move your view of the content. There is also a little box in the scrollbar which shows where you are in the document. You can use the mouse to drag this box up or down (or left or right) to move around the document.

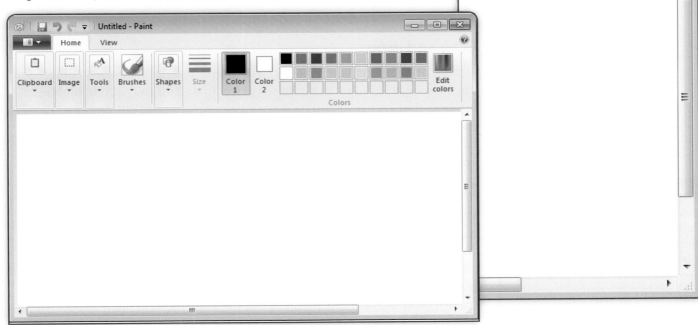

Figure 2.9: The scrollbar

Dialog boxes

Many applications use **dialog boxes** to collect information from you or to allow you to choose different options. These boxes can also inform or alert. For example, if you try to close an application without saving your work a dialog box pops up to warn you. A dialog box appears in its own special window.

Dialog boxes often ask a question, such as 'Do you want to save changes?' Dialog boxes have **buttons**. These are small boxes with a word in them rather than a picture or icon. The most common buttons are **OK/Yes** and **Cancel**. Clicking 'OK' or 'Yes' will confirm any choices you have made and close the box. Clicking **Cancel** will close the box without saving any changes you have made.

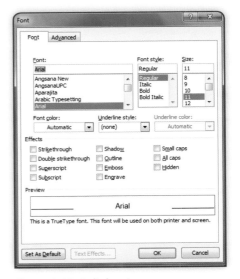

Figure 2.10: A dialog box

21

Menus and toolbars

Many applications have menus**, ribbon toolbars** or both. These are usually at the top of the application window. Toolbars contain buttons or icons that represent different programs, options or tasks. If you hold the mouse pointer over a button, a label will appear to explain its function.

Menus are text based and, when clicked, drop down to show a list of choices. This is called a **drop-down menu**. For example, if you click on the **File** menu in most applications you will see options such as **New**, **Save** and **Open**. Some menu items will open up a **submenu**: a second menu alongside the original menu. You can then click on a choice from the submenu.

Drag and drop

In many applications, you can select a section of text, an image or an object and use the mouse to drag it to a different place. To do this, you need to **highlight** the item, then click on it and hold down one of the mouse buttons as you move the mouse. A right-handed person will click and hold the left-hand mouse button. However, a left-handed person may have to change the default mouse settings and reverse the button functions.

Key terms

Customise – change/modify to suit particular purposes or tasks.
Administrator – someone whose job it is to maintain (look after) and operate a computer or IT system. They will have permission to access most or all parts of the system and make changes if necessary.

Zoom

Many applications allow you to **Zoom** in to take a closer look at your work or zoom out for a wider view of what is on the screen. For example, Microsoft® Word® has a **zoom slider** in the bottom right-hand corner of the application window, while Internet Explorer® has a drop-down zoom menu at the right-hand end of the status bar that runs along the bottom of the application window. There is often also a zoom feature under the **View** menu in many applications.

1.4 System settings

There are many settings you can change to **customise** the way your computer looks and works. Most are found in the **Control Panel**, which you can access from the Start menu. For example, there are options which allow you to:

- change the size of application windows and icons
- alter the screen resolution – see page 24
- change the desktop background
- change the way the mouse works.

However, the computers in your school, college or workplace may be restricted. This means that only someone with **Administrator** privileges (rights) is allowed to change the settings.

Figure 2.11: The Control Panel

Window size

As long as an application window is not maximised, you can adjust its size. Move the mouse pointer over the window border until the pointer changes into a two-headed arrow. Then click and hold down the left-hand mouse button while you drag the mouse to change the size of the window.

Icon size

You can change the size of icons and text. However, if you make items larger, you may have problems fitting everything on the screen.

How to adjust the size of text, icons and other items on the screen

1. Click the **Start** button and then click **Control Panel**.
2. Click the **Appearance and Personalization** icon.
3. In the **Display** section, click on **Make text and other items larger or smaller**.

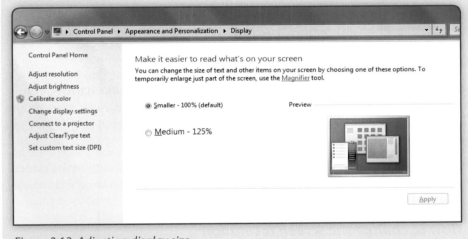

Figure 2.12: Adjusting display size

Mouse settings

You can change the mouse settings in many different ways. For example, you can:

- choose a different pointer/cursor
- change the way the mouse pointer behaves
- adapt the mouse for left-handed people
- adjust the scroll speed of the mouse wheel.

How to change the mouse settings

1. Click the **Start** button and then **Control Panel.**
2. Click on **Hardware and Sound**.
3. In the **Devices and Printers** section, click on **Mouse**.
4. The **Mouse Properties** dialog box will open.

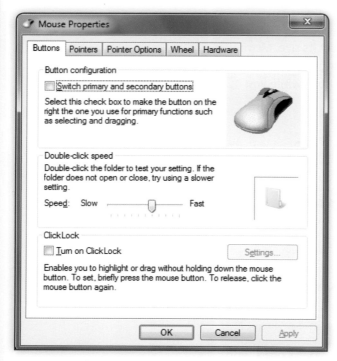

Figure 2.13: The Mouse Properties dialog box

The Mouse Properties dialog box has tabs that allow you to change the mouse settings.

- From the **Buttons** tab, you can adjust the way the mouse buttons work. For example, if you are left-handed you can swap the left and right button functions.
- From the **Pointers** tab you can choose what type of pointer is shown on the screen.
- The **Pointer Options** tab allows you to change how the pointer behaves. For example, you can choose to show a trail behind it as it moves; hide the pointer while you are typing; or change the speed of the pointer.
- From the **Wheel** tab, you can adapt how the mouse wheel behaves (you will only see this tab if you are using a mouse that has a scroll wheel).
- From the **Hardware** tab, you can **troubleshoot** mouse problems.

Screen resolution

Screen resolution determines how much information appears on the screen. A lower resolution will mean there is less information on the screen, so icons and text will be larger and less detailed. With a higher screen resolution there is more information on the screen, so icons and text will be smaller and more detailed.

Adjusting the screen resolution will change the size of everything on the screen. You may want to increase the resolution to make the most of a large monitor or lower the resolution to make small text easier to read.

How to change the screen resolution

1. Click the **Start** button and then click **Control Panel**.

2. In the **Appearance and Personalization** section, click **Adjust screen resolution**.

3. Use the drop-down box in the middle of the window to set the resolution.

Figure 2.14: Adjusting screen resolution

Not all monitors can support all resolutions and you may find that your screen appears distorted (out of shape or focus) at some resolutions. If this happens, just try a different resolution. When you change the resolution, the monitor may go blank for a short while. If you select a resolution that the monitor cannot display at all, it will automatically go back to the previous setting.

Desktop settings

There are options which will allow you to change the desktop's colour scheme or background image. You can choose from several high-contrast themes which may make the screen easier to read. You will find these options in the **Appearance and Personalization** section of the **Control Panel**.

Volume

You can adjust the volume (loudness) of sounds and music played on your computer by using the icon at the right-hand end of the taskbar. If you click on this icon, the **Volume control** will pop up. Drag the **slider** up or down to raise or lower the volume of sounds coming through the speakers or headphones. You can also click the button below the slider to mute (turn off) or unmute all sounds.

Using help

There will be times when you do not know or cannot remember how to do something on your computer. The **Help** function can be very useful in these situations.

Applications running under Windows® also have **Help** functions.

Figure 2.15: Volume control

How to use the Help function

1. Click on the **Start** button and select **Help and Support**.

2. In the window that opens, type the name of the feature you are having problems with in the search box and click the **Search** icon (the magnifying glass at the right-hand end of the box).

3. A list of results will appear below the search box and you can click on the one that seems most relevant.

Figure 2.16: The Help window

Activity: Adjusting your computer

Create evidence for your portfolio by making some adjustments to your computer. Take screenshots and annotate them to show how you made these adjustments.

- Change your screen resolution to 1024 x 768.
- Adjust the volume control to make the sounds quieter.
- Adjust your mouse settings to reduce the double-click speed and choose a different pointer. Add trails to the pointer.
- Use **Help** to find out how to connect your computer to a projector.

Check your understanding

1 What are icons?
2 Look at the desktop on your computer and list all the icons you can see. You could take a screenshot of your desktop (press the **Print Screen** key) then paste the image into Word® (**Home** tab, **Paste**) and annotate each icon to explain what it does.
3 Why should you always shut down your computer before switching off the power?
4 What do the **Minimize** and **Maximize** buttons do?

1.5 Communication services

Internet services are provided by an **Internet Service Provider (ISP)** such as BT or Virgin Media. There are several different ways of accessing the Internet. Most homes and offices will use a **broadband** connection via their telephone, satellite or cable television service. This allows them to connect to the computer's network, usually a **local area network (LAN)**.

An increasing number of desktop computers are now connected to the Internet through a **wireless (WiFi)** connection – see page 27. Alternatively, in areas where broadband is not available, a **dial-up** connection can be used, although this is much slower than broadband.

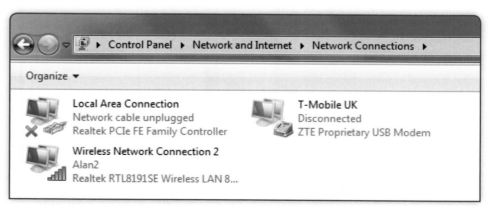

Figure 2.17: Network connections

Broadband

Broadband is a high-speed Internet connection – one that can transfer more than 1 megabyte (MB) of information per second – that uses a telephone or television cable to connect to your house, school/college or workplace. Before broadband was widely available, most people used a dial-up connection.

Dial-up

A dial-up connection uses the same voice connection as your home telephone (landline). Therefore, you need to dial the number of your ISP to connect (just as you need to dial a number to call someone from your home phone).

Dial-up Internet is much slower than broadband and, unless you have a phone line splitter, you cannot use the phone while you are using the dial-up connection. Dial-up connections are now only used in remote areas where broadband is not available.

Wireless connections (WiFi)

A WiFi connection uses a device called a **wireless router** to send data to and from a laptop or other device wirelessly, using radio waves. Many laptops and smartphones have a WiFi interface built into them. WiFi only works over relatively short distances (usually 100 metres or less). In homes, wireless routers are used to avoid the need for cables to a broadband connection.

Mobile devices

When you are out and about, there are two main methods you can use to connect your laptop or other mobile device to the Internet.

- Many hotels, cafes and other public places provide a WiFi connection in a limited area (sometimes called a **WiFi hotspot**). In most cases, you will need a password to use the WiFi connection. You may also need to pay for this password.
- You can buy a mobile network **modem**. This is a device which plugs into a **USB port** on your computer and allows you to send and receive data using your mobile phone network. This means that you can connect to the Internet anywhere there is a mobile phone signal. However, it is slower than WiFi and you will always have to pay for it.

These topics are covered in more detail in *Unit 4 IT communication fundamentals*, page 69.

> **Key term**
>
> **USB port** – a slot in computers and other devices that you can plug a USB cable into to connect the devices. Most PCs will have several ports – for example, to connect printers, scanners, keyboard, etc.

2 Organise, store and retrieve information

It is very important to keep your work organised on the computer, whether at home, school/college or in the workplace. You will need to keep lots of documents and you should be able to find them quickly.

2.1 File handling

Handling files from within an application using operations such as **Create**, **Name**, **Open**, **Save**, **Save As**, **Print** and **Close** is covered in *Unit 13 Word processing software*, page 273.

Organise files and folders

In most applications, the default location for saving work is the **Documents library**. However, it is not a good idea to keep all your documents in one place. You should create new folders within the Documents library and organise your work in these folders.

As with a paper-based filing system, you should structure your folders so that related items are stored together. Remember to make regular backups of your files and store them on a separate storage device such as a USB memory stick, a CD or a DVD. See *Unit 3 IT security for users*, page 58.

To access the **Documents library**, open the **Start** menu and click on **Documents**. This will show all the documents stored in the **My Documents** folder, as well as any other folders you have added to the library.

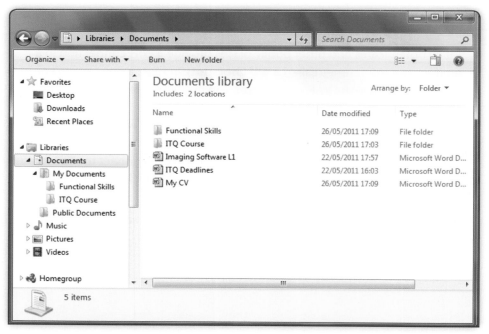

Figure 2.18: Documents library

How to create a new folder in the Documents library

1. Click on the **Start** icon to open the Start menu.

2. Click on **Documents**.

3. In the new window that opens, click **New folder**.

4. This will create a folder called 'New folder', which you can then rename.

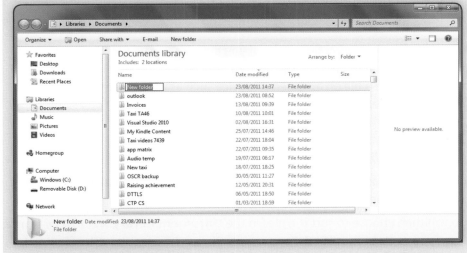

Figure 2.19: Creating a new folder

How to rename a folder or file

You should give each new folder a meaningful name so that you know what it contains.

1. **Right click** on it and select **Rename** from the menu that appears.

2. The existing name will be highlighted. Type over it with a new name and click **Save**.

A folder within an existing folder is known as a **subfolder**. You can create and rename subfolders in the same way as other folders or documents.

To copy or move files from one folder to another, first select the file(s) you want to move or copy in the folder view.

How to copy or move files from one folder to another

1. **Right click** on the file and choose **Copy** or **Cut** from the menu that pops up. Alternatively, click on the **Organize** menu in the folder window and choose **Copy** or **Cut** from the menu that drops down.

2. Open the folder you want to copy or move the file into.

3. **Right click** inside the folder and choose **Paste**; alternatively, choose **Paste** from the **Organize** menu.

Did you know?

- Moving a file to another folder means it will no longer appear in the original folder. The file will have been cut from the original folder.
- Copying a file to another folder means there will be two copies of the file: one in the original folder and one in the folder it was copied to.

To delete a file or folder, click on it and use any of the three options shown in the 'How to' guide below.

How to delete a file or folder

1. **Right click** on the file or folder and choose **Delete** from the menu that appears.
2. Select **Delete** from the **Organize** menu.
3. Press the **Del** key on your keyboard.

You will then see a dialog box asking if you are sure you want to move the file/folder to the **Recycle Bin**. If you are sure, click **OK**; otherwise, click **Cancel**. Note that if you delete a file on an external device such as a USB memory stick**,** it is deleted permanently (it is NOT sent to a recycle bin).

Finding files

There are a number of methods you can use to find files easily.

One method is to **sort** the documents in a folder. To do this, make sure that the folder is set to the **Details** option in the **View** menu.

You can then choose to sort the files in the **Document library** window by **Name**, **Size**, **Type** or **Date modified**. For example, if you choose to sort the files by the **Date modified** this will display the most recently edited (changed) documents first. Clicking it again will display them in reverse order of date modified (and vice versa). If you prefer to see them listed in alphabetic order, click the **Name** heading.

If you know the name of the document (or just a word or phrase within it) you can also use the **Search box** at the top of the **Documents library** window. Type the text into the **Search box** and press **Enter**. A list of documents that contain the text you have entered will appear. Of course, you will need to choose a word or phrase which is not common; otherwise, too many documents will be listed.

Activity: Creating files and folders

You have been asked to set up a computer for a friend and create folders for them to use to save their work.

1 The course your friend is doing has five units. Create a folder for each unit (labelled 'Unit 1', 'Unit 2' etc.) within the **My Documents** folder.
2 Create test documents and save them in each folder to check that the folders are all working correctly.
3 Make a backup of the folders you have created and save it onto a CD, DVD or USB memory stick.

2.2 Storage media

Computers have many different media or devices for storing information. Storage capacity (size) is usually measured in gigabytes (GB). All computers store data in binary format (ones and zeros), called bits: 8 bits are known as a byte.

The size of computer storage media is growing all the time. In the past, computers used floppy disks which had capacities measured in kilobytes or megabytes. Today we use USB memory sticks with capacities measured in gigabytes and the internal hard drive of a modern computer is usually measured in gigabytes or terabytes. Table 2.1 shows the relationship between these measurements.

8 bits	1 byte
1024 bytes	1 kilobyte (KB)
1024 KB	1 megabyte (MB)
1024 MB	1 gigabyte (GB)
1024 GB	1 terabyte (TB)

Table 2.1: The relationship between bits and terabytes

The computer's hard drive stores the operating system, applications and programs and normally has the largest storage space. Removable storage that you can carry around and use on different computers usually takes the form of a USB memory stick.

Many computers have a CD or DVD disk drive. This is also known as an **optical drive** because the disks are read by a laser light. There are various types of disk you can use in an optical drive and some drives can write to disks as well as read from them.

- **Read only** – information is permanently stored on the disk and cannot be changed.
- **CD-R** or **DVD-R** disks can have information written to them once only.
- **CD-RW** or **DVD-RW** disks can have information written to them many times.

It may take several minutes (or longer) to write information to an optical disk, so they are generally used to back up data or move large amounts of information between computers. You can use optical disks to store music, videos and films. Some computers may also be able to read Blu-Ray disks, which are like CDs and DVDs but have more storage capacity.

Many devices such as mobile phones and digital cameras use media cards (or memory cards) for storage. Many laptops and desktop computers include slots which can read these cards so you can copy files to and from them just as you can with a USB memory stick. Media cards come in a wide variety of types and capacities. Common ones include SDHC and microSD cards.

Did you know?

Writing to an optical disk is sometimes called 'burning' because the laser heats tiny spots on the disk to store the information.

Many mobile devices (phones, music players etc.) can be connected to a computer via a USB port. The computer can then use the storage inside the mobile device in the same way as a USB memory stick.

Computers are sometimes connected to a local network (as opposed to just being connected to the Internet), especially in a workplace. Local office networks often have computers called **servers** which provide a shared storage space to all the people on the local network. These shared storage spaces are usually called **network drives**.

2.3 Organise and store information

To complete this course successfully you will need to show that you can save files and find them easily. As mentioned earlier, it is wise to create a number of folders within your Documents folder.

- You should create at least one folder for every unit you are completing.
- Do not forget to make regular backups of your work.
- Remember to give your files/folders meaningful names as this will help you find them later. See section *2.1 File handling*, page 28.
- If you have older files which you no longer use regularly but do not want to delete you can **archive** them by moving them to a CD or DVD. Remember to label the disk with what it contains.
- With removable media such as CDs or DVD it is very important to remove them from the computer's optical drive and label them correctly.
- When creating a backup on a CD or DVD, give the disk a meaningful name when you save it. Also physically write the name on the disk: it can be very difficult to find the correct CD among a pile of unlabelled ones. It is best to use a special CD/DVD marker pen as ordinary pens will not write on disks.

Remember

USB memory sticks are easily lost or broken, which will make some or all of your files unreadable.

3 Follow and understand the need for safety and security practices

It is important to understand the reasons for safety and security practices and why you need to follow these practices.

3.1 Work safely

When using a computer you need to consider how to work safely. You should be aware of a number of health and safety issues.

Risks from hardware

Computers are heavy, bulky pieces of electrical equipment which pose a number of risks.

- **Hardware is difficult to handle:** If you are moving a computer there is a risk you could drop it. In this case you could injure yourself or damage other objects or equipment. You could also injure yourself if you do not follow the correct procedure when lifting hardware. See the section *Handling equipment*, on page 33.

- **Trailing cables:** You should take care when setting up your computer. Make sure that cables are not trailing on the floor – for example, between a computer and a printer. Trailing cables where people walk is a significant trip hazard and could obstruct a safe route to a fire exit.
- **Electrical risks:** Items of electrical hardware pose a number of risks. You can easily prevent one common risk by keeping all drinks and other liquids away from your computer or other hardware at all times. Spilling liquid on them could cause a fire or present a risk of electrocution. See the section *Electrical connection risks and guidelines*, page 34.

Handling equipment

It is important to handle equipment safely, because moving heavy or awkwardly shaped equipment is one of the most common causes of injury in the workplace and at home.

Injuries that can be caused by poor manual handling include fractures (broken bones), trapped nerves and, most commonly, spinal injuries.

When lifting equipment it is important to keep the correct **posture** and to use the correct technique. To get into the correct posture before lifting:

> **Key term**
>
> **Posture** – how you position or hold your body.

How to stand correctly

1. Stand with feet shoulder width apart, with one foot slightly in front of the other.
2. Knees should be bent.
3. Back must be straight.
4. Arms should be as close to the body as possible.
5. Your grip must be firm, using the whole hand and not just the fingers.

How to lift correctly

1. Approach the load squarely, facing the direction of travel.
2. Adopt the correct posture (as above).
3. Place hands under the load and pull the load close to your body.
4. Lift the load using your legs and not your back.

How to stand when lowering a load

1. Bend at the knees, not the back.
2. Adjust the load to avoid trapping your fingers.
3. Lower the load.
4. Release the load.

Electrical connection risks and guidelines

Items of hardware pose a number of electrical connection risks, but you can easily prevent these by following some simple guidelines.

- When using power sockets and extension leads, make sure that the sockets are not overloaded.
- Check that all cables are in good condition, as frayed cables are dangerous.
- It is a good idea to use an extension socket with a surge protector for connecting the computer to the mains electricity. This will help to protect the computer from sudden voltage changes that may occur, for example during a thunderstorm.

Use and disposal of cleaning materials

Most cleaning materials you will use with IT systems (for example, to clean the monitor or keyboard) are harmless. However, you should always dispose of them properly and recycle them where possible.

Risks to self and others from using hardware

Take care of you own health when using computers.

- Sit correctly, with the top of the monitor approximately at eye level.
- Take regular breaks.
- Use a wrist rest if you do a lot of typing.

You should also consider the health risks to you and others from using a computer for long periods. See section *3.2 Minimising physical stress* page 34.

Beware of safety issues too. Keep liquids away from electrical equipment and never try to dismantle (take apart) equipment. If electrical mains cables or plugs are damaged, do not use them. Keep cables tidy to avoid trip hazards.

Some of the risks from using hardware are discussed in more detail on pages 32 and 33.

Organisational guidelines and points of contact

Be aware of your school, college or workplace health and safety and computer usage guidelines. If in doubt, speak to your tutor or supervisor, IT manager or company health and safety officer.

3.2 Minimising physical stress

Using a computer can cause your body physical stress, so you should understand how to minimise this stress.

Adjust seating and lighting

Working at a computer can put strain on your neck, back, arms and hands. You may also suffer from eye strain and general tiredness if your seating and lighting are not adjusted correctly. Therefore correct posture and positioning/adjustment of equipment is very important. Here are some simple guidelines to follow.

- Make sure that your chair is fully adjustable so that you can change the height and adjust the back support.
- Your eyes should be level with the top of the monitor.
- Make sure that the screen is in focus, not too bright or too dark, and that it is not flickering.
- Your forearms should be horizontal (flat) when you are using the keyboard or mouse.
- Make sure that your whole work area (not just the computer) is well lit and well ventilated (has plenty of fresh air).

Screen – should be able to tilt and pivot, and should be 0–20° below horizontal line of sight

Upper back (should be straight and supported)

Lower back (should support lumbar curve)

Feet (flat on floor or on footrest)

Figure 2.20: Correct seating posture when using a computer

Avoid hazards

There are a number of hazards you should avoid with IT or other equipment. Some of these have been mentioned already, such as the trip hazard presented by trailing cables and the electrical hazard posed by leaving liquids near computers. As well as being an electrical hazard, spilt liquid could also damage your computer hardware.

Workspace and working conditions

It is important that your workspace and working conditions are safe and healthy. Adjusting your seating and lighting, as described above, will help ensure your working conditions are healthier for your body.

Keeping your workspace clean will lower the risk of you or anyone you work with getting ill. By keeping things tidy you can avoid trip hazards.

Repetitive strain injury (RSI) – may be caused by repetitive actions such as holding and clicking a mouse or typing on a keyboard. The main symptom is pain in the hands, wrists or arms.

Intranet – an internal Internet which can only be viewed within an organisation such as a company, school or college. For more on intranets, see *Unit 4 IT communication fundamentals*, page 71.

You can protect your keyboard by cleaning it regularly, as dust and debris (for example, biscuit crumbs) can build up and damage the keys. To clean the keyboard, turn it upside down and tap it lightly. You could also use a small, soft brush to sweep away anything trapped between the keys.

Take breaks

Sitting in the same position for long periods puts stress on the body. Therefore, you should take a short break every 40–50 minutes. This will also allow your eyes to relax and so help you avoid eye strain. Make sure you get up and move around during your breaks.

Wrist rests

Make sure your keyboard is in a comfortable position so you do not have to stretch to reach the keys. You should also use a wrist support to help prevent **repetitive strain injury (RSI)**.

Activity: Health and safety

1 Every workplace must have at least one person responsible for health and safety. Find out who this person is in your workplace, college or school. If you have any concerns about health and safety and the use of computers, this is the person you should contact.

2 Does your workplace, school or college have specific health and safety policies or guidelines on the use of computers? If so, find out what they are and where they are kept. There may also be a booklet or **intranet** page giving guidance and advice to computer users in your organisation.

3.3 Minimise risk

Viruses are a constant danger and you need to protect your computer against them as they can cause major problems such as loss of files or theft of personal information. There are many types of viruses and new ones are appearing all the time. Viruses can infect your computer in a number of ways. Some can make your computer unusable; some can infect your computer when you visit a certain website; others may come in emails; or they may get transferred from a USB memory stick or CD/DVD.

Malicious (harmful) programs, viruses, spam and phishing are covered in more depth in *Unit 3 IT security for users*.

To protect your IT system there are several things you must do.

- Install **anti-virus software**. This will scan files to check they do not contain viruses. This includes files you install or download from the Internet or from emails and also files on USB memory sticks and other mobile devices. You will need to keep anti-virus software updated to deal with any new viruses.
- Update your software regularly. Windows® updates are switched on by default. However, you should make sure they are being downloaded and installed. Windows® will warn you automatically if updates are switched off.

- Treat software and attachments from unknown sources with caution. Think very carefully before opening emails from anyone you do not know and certainly do not open any files attached to emails from strangers. Before downloading or installing software think about its source and whether you are sure it is not a malicious program.
- Install **anti-spam software** to block spam or phishing emails.
- Make sure **Windows® Firewall** is switched on. A firewall helps stop Internet hackers gain access to your computer. Windows® will automatically warn you if the firewall is switched off.

How to check the security status of your IT system

1. Open the **Control Panel**.

2. Open **System and Security** and then click on **Review your computer's status**.

3. Clicking the expand arrow next to the **Security** section will show the status of all security settings.

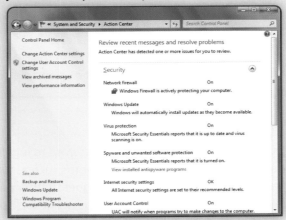

Figure 2.21: Review your computer's status page

1 Carry out a security survey on your computer to make sure it is as secure as possible.
   a Check that anti-virus software is installed and updated regularly.
   b Run a virus scan.
   c In the security centre check that Windows® updates and the firewall are switched on.

2 Carry out routine maintenance on your computer by:
   a running a disk cleanup.
   b cleaning the mouse and screen using suitable materials.

Note: The IT department in your school, college or workplace may not allow you to complete these activities. In this case, write a set of instructions that someone else could follow in order to carry out these tasks.

3.4 Information security

It very important to keep information secure on your computer, so it does not get lost and is also protected from other people. Information held on computers may be commercially sensitive or personal (e.g. customer lists, including bank details). If the information relates to living people it comes under the Data Protection Act 1998.

There are several things you should do to protect personal or sensitive information.

Activity: Data Protection Act 1998

The Data Protection Act 1998 outlines eight principles (rules) for using information about individuals who can be identified (see *Unit 3 IT security for users*, page 66).

- Find out more about the Act and identify three things that its principles would NOT allow you to do.

Passwords or PINs

Did you know?

When you create a password, Windows® will also ask you to create a password hint. This will be shown if you enter your password incorrectly. Be careful what you enter as your hint – if it is too obvious, other people may be able to guess your password.

It is important to have a 'strong' password to log in to your computer. This means one that is not easy to guess. Passwords such as 'password' or 'welcome' are much too easy for other people to guess. Other passwords that are easy to guess are the names of family, friends or pets. The best passwords:

- have uppercase and lowercase letters
- combine words, numbers and other symbols (such as ! or ?)

So a good password might be 'United4thecup' or 'IhateMaths!'. Also see section *1.1 Start and shut down procedure* in this unit and *Make passwords strong* in *Unit 3 IT security for users*, page 55.

Backups

It is essential to back up your files regularly as it can be easy to lose or corrupt important files. Hardware failures – for example, of a hard drive – can mean the loss of large amounts of information.

Make sure you have a copy of important documents on a USB memory stick, CD or DVD. However, remember that these devices can also become corrupt. A virus infecting a hard drive or memory stick can also result in the loss of some or all files. With no backup these files would be lost forever.

Also see the section *Backups* in *Unit 3 IT security for users*, page 58.

Remember

Make sure to back up your data regularly and securely. It is too late to wish you had made a backup once the data has been deleted.

Microsoft® Office® 2010 applications (Word®, Excel® etc.) automatically save your work every 10 minutes (unless you change the default settings). This means that if your computer crashes or there is a power failure, the most you will lose is 10 minutes of work. When you restart the computer and the application you were using, the **recovery pane** will appear. From here, you can open the **autosaved** version of your document.

How to adjust the amount of time between autosaves

1. Click **File** and then select **Options**.

2. In the dialog box that opens, click **Save** from the panel on the left.

3. Change the number in the **Save AutoRecover information every** ____ **minutes** box to increase or decrease the time between autosaves.

Figure 2.22: Save options

Avoid inappropriate disclosure of information

You should take great care when sending emails or using social networking sites such as Facebook. Once you have sent or posted something online (whether a comment or photo), you lose control of what happens to that information, and people may use it in ways you do not want them to.

As well as keeping your own personal details safe, you should also be careful not to give out details about your friends and family.

3.5 Staying safe

The Internet is a very useful resource but it can also be a dangerous place. Take extra care online to protect your personal information or privacy, especially when posting information in public places such as social networking sites.

Here are some suggestions for staying safe on the Internet.

> **Remember**
>
> Take care with distribution lists. You might think it is a good idea to send everyone an email to let them know you have a dining table and four chairs for sale. However, your boss or supervisor is unlikely to agree and you may find yourself in trouble.

Most social networking sites are visible to the general public, so you should be careful about what information you put on them. Do not give out your email address, home address or phone number. Also take care with images you post as these can also be used in ways you do not intend. Posting a picture of yourself drunk on Sunday night might seem like fun but your tutor, supervisor or employer will not find it so amusing if you phone in sick on Monday morning.
People are not always truthful about who they are online. They may lie about their age or intentions. Be very careful before meeting someone in person if you have only spoken to them online. If you do decide to meet someone you have chatted with online, make sure you take sensible precautions: arrange to meet in a public place; tell someone else where you are going and when you will be back.
If you receive abusive or threatening messages or emails, do not reply to them. Instead report them to the company that hosts the site. All chat sites and social networking sites have ways of reporting abuse.
Keep your passwords safe. Do not write them down in a way that can easily be recognised.
Be careful with the language you use: what you find amusing, others may find offensive. You may be banned from the site or, worse still, you may end up in trouble with the police.
In the workplace, use email distribution lists with caution. Employers will not be pleased if you send out non-essential emails to large numbers of colleagues, especially if the messages are not relevant.

As well as taking care yourself you should also respect other people's confidentiality and their views. You can find more details about these issues in *Unit 3 IT security for users*, page 65.

Activity: Facebook privacy settings

Do you know what privacy settings you have on your Facebook account? Check them now.

- Log in to your Facebook account. In the blue bar at the top of the screen, click the down arrow to the right of the word **Home**.

- Click **Privacy Settings** and you will be able to edit the settings that control who can see your account, post on your wall, etc.

To find out more about these different settings, scroll to the bottom of the page and click on **Privacy**.

If you do not have a Facebook account, you can still find out about the range of privacy options available to Facebook users. On the Facebook homepage you will see menu options along the bottom of the page. Click on **Privacy** and you will able to read about the different settings without logging in to an account.

3.6 Guidelines and procedures

Many organisations have guidelines and procedures on computer usage – your college, school or workplace will almost certainly have some. These are called **acceptable usage policies** and are there to protect you and the organisation from the many problems that can happen if IT systems are misused. It is important for you to know your organisation's guidelines or procedures and to follow them carefully. It would also be wise to follow the same procedures at home. See the section *Issue an acceptable usage policy* in *Unit 3 IT security for users*, page 59.

Activity: Internet usage policy

Working with two or three other learners or colleagues, find a copy of your school, college or workplace Internet acceptable usage policy and answer the following questions.

1 Read each point in the policy and discuss why it is important. What problems might arise if you do not follow the rules?

2 What rules does your school, college or workplace have for using copyright materials? See *Unit 4 IT communication fundamentals*, page 74.

3 Which rules would be useful to follow at home, when you are using your own computer?

4 In your group, make a poster to display in the IT classroom, listing the main points of the policy.

---

4 Carry out routine maintenance of IT systems and respond to routine IT system problems

All IT systems need routine maintenance to keep them in good working order. Therefore, you should know how to solve routine IT problems whether at home, in school/college or in the workplace.

4.1 Routine maintenance

In order to keep an IT system running at its best, some routine maintenance tasks should be carried out regularly. Although you will be able to carry out some of these tasks yourself, always ask for help if you are not sure what to do.

What maintenance can be done safely and what should be left to experts? In general you should leave most maintenance tasks to experts. However there are some tools built into Windows® that you can use safely.

What could happen if maintenance is not done? Failure to complete regular maintenance tasks could slow down your computer in the long term. Failure to complete regular backups will mean loss of data if there is a hardware or software breakdown.

Manufacturer's guidelines

Check the maker's guidelines that come with items of hardware for advice on cleaning and maintenance.

Removing unwanted files

From time to time, you should delete unused or unwanted files from your computer. This will speed up the operating system, especially when saving or loading files. Windows® provides a tool called **Disk Cleanup** that does this automatically.

How to clean up the files on your hard disk

1. Click the **Start** icon and choose **Computer** from the menu.

2. In the window that appears, **right click** on the hard disk drive you want to clean up (this will appear under the heading **Hard Disk Drives**).

3. Click **Properties** in the menu that appears and a new dialog box will appear.

Figure 2.23: Disk properties dialog box

continued

4. In the **Disk Properties** dialog box, click **Disk Cleanup**. The cleanup program will automatically check which files can be removed. After a few seconds you will see the **Disk Cleanup** dialog box. This will list all the files you could delete to save space on the hard disk.

5. Click **OK** and another dialog box will appear, asking if you are sure you want to delete the files. Click **Yes** to run the disk cleanup program.

Figure 2.24: Cleanup dialog box

4.2 Cleaning your IT system

As well as routine maintenance it is important to clean your IT system regularly to keep it running well. Although you will be able to carry out some of these tasks yourself, you should always ask for help if you are not sure what to do.

To maintain functionality and appearance

It is important to clean computer equipment to keep it looking good and working well. You should pay particular attention to the monitor, keyboard, mouse and printer.

For different components of an IT system

Monitor

The screen builds up static electricity over time, which will attract a lot of dust. You can use anti-static wipes to remove the dust. If the screen is very dirty (for example, with finger marks), use anti-static wet wipes. If you have a plasma (flat) screen, do not press too hard as you may damage it.

Keyboard

Dust and dirt between the keys may make them stick. You can use a small, soft brush to clean the keyboard.

Mouse

A dirty mouse may not move properly and you may find it difficult to control the cursor. Clean the underside of the mouse with a soft cloth.

Printer

Parts of the printer may need cleaning from time to time, otherwise the quality of printouts may become poor. Check the manufacturer's advice on cleaning.

Printer maintenance

Most inkjet printers will show you how much ink is left in the cartridges and remind you to order new cartridges when they get low. The same is true for most laser printers, but these use a toner cartridge rather than ink cartridges.

Printing - KodakESP7+1085

Black ink cartridge is low. Please take the time to order more ink.

114%

Stop

19:43
02/07/2011

Figure 2.25: A 'low ink' reminder

Replacing ink or toner cartridges is usually quite simple as long as you follow the instructions that come with the new cartridge or with the printer itself. However, you should ask for help if necessary. Modern printers (especially those that are also photocopiers and scanners) can be very expensive, so take care not to damage them.

When aligning the toner cartridge, make sure to follow the guidelines in the printer manual or ask someone for help. After you have replaced the cartridge, you should print a test page to check that everything is working properly (check the manual for instructions).

If the printer runs out of paper you may need to ask for help to refill it, depending on how complex the printer is. When loading new paper, always make sure that it is not creased or crumpled so that it does not jam the printer.

4.3 Expert advice

It is important to understand the limits of your own knowledge and skills: there will be IT problems that you will not know how to solve. For example:

- Do not be tempted to change a lot of settings that you do not understand as you may make things worse.
- If you do not understand how to do something in a software program, there is often a help menu you can use. For example, in Microsoft® Office® programs such as Word® and Excel® you can get help by clicking the white question mark in a blue circle in the top right-hand corner of the document.
- You can also find out how to use equipment in the manufacturer's guidelines. These could come as a printed manual or they may be available online to download.
- Companies, schools or colleges will have an IT support person or department you can contact for help, either via a telephone 'hotline' or by email. In school or college you may need to contact your teacher or tutor first.
- If you have problems with your computer at home, you could ask friends or relatives who have more experience with them for help. Alternatively, you could look for advice or help on the Internet. Software companies usually provide information about their programs. For instance, the Microsoft® website has a range of useful tutorials and videos.

> **Remember**
>
> When faced with a problem you cannot resolve, always seek advice from an expert. For example, it is best not to try to unjam a printer yourself as you could damage it and you may also injure yourself.

4.4 IT problems

If you know how to deal with simple problems that could crop up, you will find computers less frustrating than they can be at times.

Software problems

Software applications sometimes 'freeze' or 'crash'. This means that they will not respond to any input. Apart from being annoying, the main problem here is that you may lose any unsaved changes. However, many everyday applications (such as word processing programs) will automatically save your work, so if the program crashes or freezes you will not lose too much. This is why, as already mentioned, it is good practice to save your work regularly.

If a program freezes you can force it to close down by using the **Task Manager**.

How to use the Task Manager to force close a program

1. To open the **Task Manager**, press the **Ctrl+Alt+Del** keys together.

2. From the screen that appears, choose **Start Task Manager**.

3. A dialog box will appear with a list of all the applications that are running. Click on the program that is not responding and click the **End Task** button.

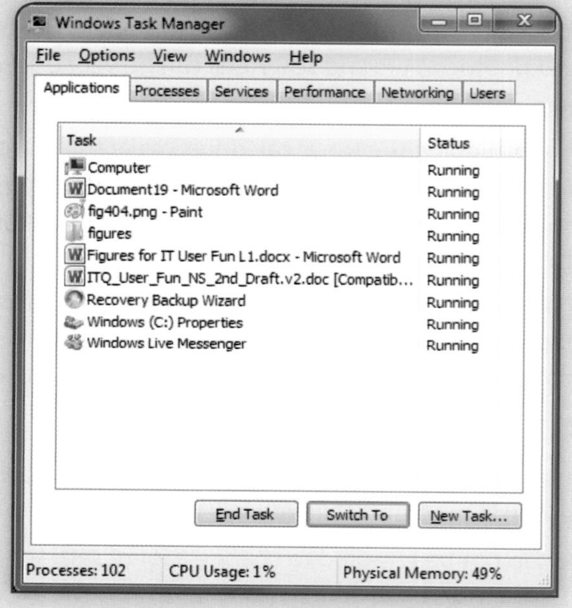

Figure 2.26: The Task Manager

Another common problem is lack of storage space on a computer or on removable storage devices. For advice on how to create more space, see the section *Removing unwanted files* earlier in this unit, page 41.

If you cannot delete unwanted files from removable storage media to make space, you will need to save the new file(s) somewhere else.

If an error message pops up in a dialog box, read what it says carefully and take the appropriate action. If you are not sure what to do, or the messages occur regularly, either note down what they say or take a screenshot and send this information to your tutor/supervisor or IT help desk.

How to take a screenshot

1. Press the **Print Screen** button on the keyboard.

2. Paste the image into a program such as Microsoft® Word® or Paint® and print it.

Hardware problems

Hardware problems might include, for example:

- The computer will not start up.
- The printer does not print.
- The mouse does not work.
- There is no sound from the speakers.

In these cases the first thing to check is the cables and power. Are the connection cables and power cables plugged in? Is the power switched on?

Desktop computers often have a separate power cable and switch for the monitor and base unit, so check both are plugged in and switched on. In some cases switching everything off and starting up again may clear a problem.

Printer problems can be quite common. You should check that the power is on and the cables are connected. Make sure there is paper in the printer and the ink or toner cartridge is not empty. Also check that you are printing to the right printer if there is more than one connected to the system.

If the correct printer is selected but a document will not print, the paper may be jammed inside the printer. In this case, an error message may appear on the screen. You will need to follow the manufacturer's instructions to remove the jammed paper or ask for help if cannot do this yourself. See the section *Printer maintenance* earlier in this unit, page 43.

Figure 2.27: Printer dialog box

Check your understanding

1 Name three input devices and three output devices.

2 State three ways to reduce the physical stress of using computers.

3 Identify three things that could pose a security risk to your computer.

4 What kind of software can you use to reduce security risks to your computer?

5 Give an example of a secure and strong password.

6 State two types of routine maintenance you should carry out on your computer.

7 What kind of maintenance would you ask an expert to help with? Are there any tasks you would ask an expert to do for you?

ASSESSMENT ACTIVITY

You volunteer at a local youth club for children aged 7-10. The club has recently purchased some new IT equipment and the club's Director is keen to start running some computer courses to teach the children basic IT knowledge. The Director has asked you to lead this initiative.

The children who attend the youth club are familiar with how games consoles work but they have very little knowledge of how to operate a computer and basic IT knowledge.

Task 1

Keep a diary for at least a month, recording your use of a computer. You want to capture all the different ways you use a computer – ranging from how you switch it on to personalising settings to what systems and functions you use. Be sure to cover:

- how to operate a computer
- computer components
- system settings
- communication methods.

Task 2

The Director is keen that the children are able to use the computers to store any work they create while attending the youth club.

Create a handout for the children, explaining how to do the following things:

- how to create and name files
- how to create and name folders
- how to search for files
- how to organise and order files.

Task 3

Create two posters, which will be displayed in the computer room, explaining:

- health and safety issues
- potential security risks.

Task 4

Create a step-by-step guide using a series of photographs explaining how to:

- change an ink or toner cartridge
- carry out routine maintenance and cleaning of your IT system.

Ask a friend to take photographs of you completing each of the steps. Then print the photos out and create your step-by-step guides to display in the computer room.

Task 5

Describe any problems you encountered and how you dealt with them. Take screenshots or photographs and use these to compile an FAQ issue log for the children.

IT security for users

You may have heard news stories about computers being hacked or data being lost. You or someone you know may even have been affected by this type of activity.

In this unit you will learn about security threats to your IT system and what you can do to keep your hardware, software and data safe and secure. You will also learn about the laws and guidelines covering the use of IT and data.

For your assessment you will need to demonstrate your skills to keep data safe and organised, with questioning where needed. You should practise these skills to gain confidence before your assessment.

Learning outcomes

After completing this unit you should be able to achieve the following learning outcome:

» **LO1** Use appropriate methods to minimise security risks to IT systems and data

1 Use appropriate methods to minimise security risks to IT systems and data

1.1 Threats to system performance

You need to be able to identify security issues that may threaten a computer system. This section outlines the main threats.

Spam

Spam is similar to printed junk mail but is sent by email. Everyone with an email address now receives spam. The three main aims of spam are usually to:

- advertise
- try to obtain personal details ('phishing')
- spread viruses.

Advertising emails

Not all advertising emails are spam. Some could be from companies you have done business with in the past. You may have signed up to a newsletter or asked a company to send you information about special offers.

Alternatively, a company which has your details may have sold them on to a different company which then sends you more advertising spam. Legally, companies must ask your permission to pass on your details, usually through a tick box when you **subscribe**. You should be able to unsubscribe from these emails at any time.

Advertising spam from a company you did not sign up to is not acceptable, especially as it may sometimes promote inappropriate, dangerous or illegal products.

Key term

Subscribe – sign up for a product or service, for example a newsletter or news of upcoming game releases.

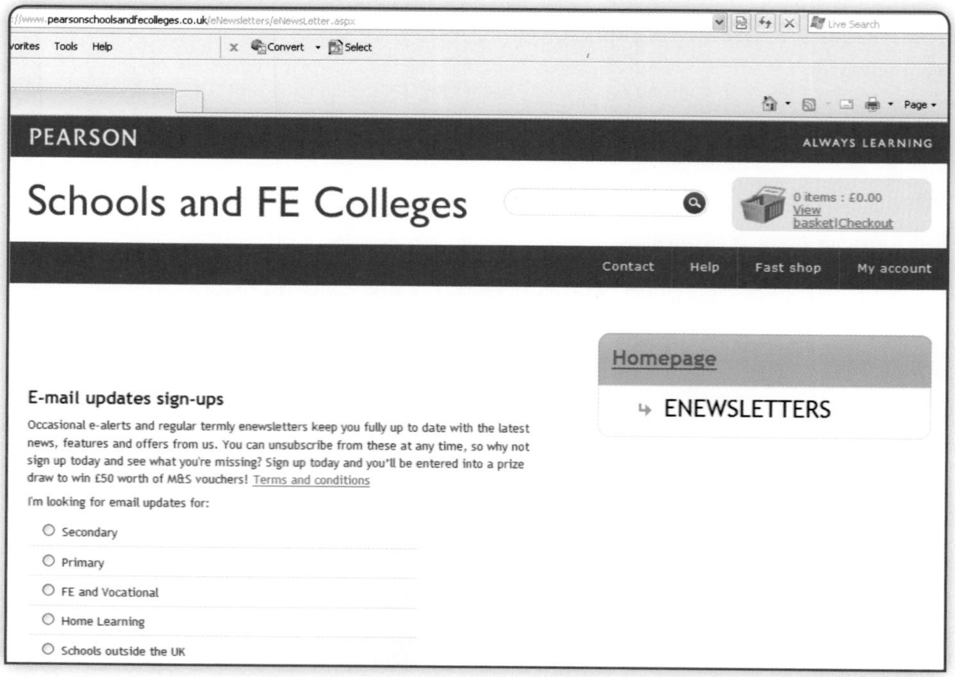

Figure 3.1: You may sign up to a company's e-newsletter service in order to receive information from them

Phishing emails

Phishing emails try to obtain personal details (they are 'fishing' for information). These emails usually appear to come from a real company (such as a bank or credit card company). They might say, for example, that you have won a prize or that goods you ordered are out of stock. The email will then ask you to log on to a website and provide your security details.

You can spot phishing emails by asking the following questions.

- Does the email ask for your password, personal identity number (PIN) or other personal details? A real organisation – especially a financial one such as a bank or money transfer company (such as PayPal®) – will never ask for these details via email.
- Is the sender's address real? If you receive an email which claims to be from Apple but has been sent from a Hotmail account, you can be certain that it is spam. Often the email will look very similar to one from the genuine company. Look for spelling or grammar mistakes in the message.
- Does the sender know your name or has the email been sent to lots of people (e.g. addressed to 'Dear Customer')? Even an email addressed to you personally may still not be genuine, especially if your name is part of your email address. If the sender does not even know your name, it is very likely that the email is spam.
- Have you done any business with the sender? If you get an email saying you have won the National Lottery but you have not bought a ticket, then you can be certain the email is phishing.

Key term

Phishing – this is a technique used to obtain individuals' personal details. Phishing emails are designed to look like official emails (e.g. from your bank) and will ask you to click a link and provide personal information (e.g. your name, address and online banking login passwords). If you enter you details on the fake page then your details will become available to the people behind the phising email, who could use them to steal money from your account.

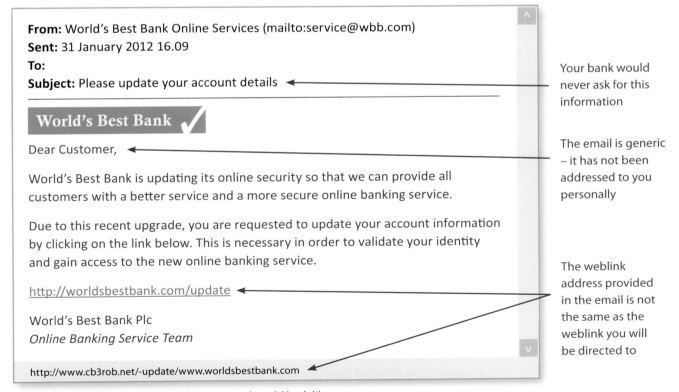

From: World's Best Bank Online Services (mailto:service@wbb.com)
Sent: 31 January 2012 16.09
To:
Subject: Please update your account details

World's Best Bank ✓

Dear Customer,

World's Best Bank is updating its online security so that we can provide all customers with a better service and a more secure online banking service.

Due to this recent upgrade, you are requested to update your account information by clicking on the link below. This is necessary in order to validate your identity and gain access to the new online banking service.

http://worldsbestbank.com/update

World's Best Bank Plc
Online Banking Service Team

http://www.cb3rob.net/-update/www.worldsbestbank.com

Your bank would never ask for this information

The email is generic – it has not been addressed to you personally

The weblink address provided in the email is not the same as the weblink you will be directed to

Figure 3.2: Example of what a phishing email could look like

Anti-spam software

Anti-spam software is usually part of an **email filter**. The filter checks all the emails coming into an account and decides whether or not they appear to be valid (real) messages or are **spam**. If the filter thinks an email is spam, it will either move it to a separate spam or junk mail folder or delete it, depending on how you have set up your email account.

You can check the emails in your spam/junk mail folder. If any 'real' emails have been mistakenly identified as spam, you can then tell the filter that emails from those addresses is not spam. You can also specify certain addresses that are always spam and tell the filter to automatically delete emails from those addresses.

Activity: 419 fraud

419 fraud refers to a very specific type of phishing scam which has become increasingly widespread. There are different versions of this con trick. In general, you will receive an email from someone who claims to have or know about a huge sum of money or valuables such as gold or diamonds. However, they cannot get this wealth out of their country and so they have emailed you for help. They ask you to send money to help them transfer their funds or to send your bank details so they can transfer the money into your account.

This scam works by making the victim believe they will receive a lot of money for very little work. As with most scams, the best way to avoid them is to remember this: if something seems too good to be true, it usually is.

1 Find out how long the 419 scam has been around.
2 What sort of spam do you receive?
3 What is your reaction to it?
4 What do you do about it?
5 Research the things you can do to protect yourself from spam.

Malicious programs

Malicious programs, also known as **malware** (malicious software), are pieces of code or software that are designed to be annoying, intrusive (unwelcome) or hostile (threatening). There are many types of malicious programs that you should be able to identify. They are known by different traits, depending on their purpose.

Viruses and malware

Viruses and malware are unpleasant programs which are at best a nuisance and at worst a threat. Nuisance types of viruses can:

- alter settings on your computer (such as randomly changing letters in documents)
- waste your computer's processing power (making everything run slowly)
- delete files or erase hard drives (these are more extreme types of viruses).

Other cruel types of viruses try to find personal details on your computer and send them back to the virus's owner. These details could be relatively harmless (such as your email address). However, the virus may also seek out your credit card details or online shopping or banking passwords.

Malware tries to do the same as viruses: cause nuisance or steal information. However, malware has another third purpose for its owner: once installed on your computer it allows the owner to access and use your computer (e.g. to attack other computers on a network). Malware may also use your computer to send out massive amounts of spam or attack web pages. In these instances the malware turns your computer into what is known as a 'zombie' computer.

There are several types of malware, including adware (see page 52) and rootkits, which allow someone to have administrator access to the whole computer.

Activity: Viruses

Answer the following questions about viruses.

1   What were Creeper and Reaper on the very early version of the Internet ARPANET?
2   Why is ILOVEYOU considered the most destructive virus ever and which respected American organisations did it shut down?
3   What is Nimda and how did it spread so quickly?
4   Who was the first person to be convicted under the Computer Misuse Act 1990 for creating a virus? What was the virus called, what did it do and how many machines worldwide did it infect?
5   What was Welchia and why was it unusual?

Did you know?

Viruses got their name because they act like real viruses which infect living organisms such as humans. A computer virus can self-replicate (copy itself) and some even mutate (change) so that they can spread from computer to computer – just as a cold spreads between humans.

Remember

The terms 'virus' and 'malware' are often confused – remember this in your research and always try to use the terms correctly.

The main difference between a virus and malware:
- A virus gets onto your computer, runs itself and then tries to copy itself to another computer (e.g. through email). It might then remain on your computer or it might self-destruct.
- Malware installs itself on your computer and stays there, either running continuously or allowing its owner to access or use your computer.

Worms

Worms are viruses that create copies of themselves to spread through a computer network. Unlike a virus, a worm does not need a host program. It can cause trouble simply by travelling through the network or it may have a 'payload' (a cargo of information) which will perform a particular action. For example, the worm's payload might be a code for deleting files or stealing data.

Trojans

Trojans are named after the Trojan Horse from Greek mythology. Trojan files look innocent (like normal image files or programs) but are actually viruses. A Trojan file installed on your computer may open and run a virus or allow the owner to access your computer.

Spyware

Spyware hides on a computer and sends data back to the spyware's owner. For example, some spyware records all the keys you press (including passwords) and sends the information back to the person who created the spyware. Alternatively, it may be used to monitor which web pages you visit.

Denial of service

A denial of service (DoS) attack targets a particular service (such as a web server) and makes it unavailable to its intended users. This is usually done by sending so many requests to the server or website that it slows or stops working altogether. Information is not usually lost or damaged during DoS attacks. However, the attacks can cost organisations huge amounts of money and time.

Adware

Adware displays advertisements on your computer. It may be installed legally if, for example, you accidentally tick a box agreeing to it when installing other software. However, adware is often installed without your knowledge or permission. Adware lets adverts display as **pop-ups**, either at random or when you do a specific action.

Rogue diallers

A rogue dialler is software that automatically re-routes your Internet connection via a premium-rate (expensive) phone line. This may lead to very high phone bills. However, rogue diallers can only affect dial-up connections, so if you have broadband Internet access you cannot be affected. See section *1.5 Communication services* in *Unit 2 IT user fundamentals*, page 26.

Hackers

A hacker is someone who tries to gain **unauthorised** access to computer hardware or software. Hackers strike for a number of different reasons, such as:

- to steal information
- to discredit a company or business (by changing its website for example)
- to cause disruption
- to prove a point (to show up weaknesses in a security system, for example).

It is illegal to hack into a computer or network (refer to the Computer Misuse Act 1990 on page 67) but the Internet has made it increasingly easy for hackers to access systems across the world. Hackers often use malicious programs (such as spyware) to find passwords or to use other weak spots in IT security systems.

Key terms

Pop-ups – online advertisements to attract customers to other websites or to obtain email addresses.
Unauthorised – not having permission or approval to do something, such as access a computer or file.

Did you know?

The words 'hacker' and 'cracker' are often confused. Although hacker is the term usually used, a hacker is just someone who is very good at programming.
A cracker, on the other hand, is someone who tries to break into other people's computers and networks. However, hacker has become so common that now only those in the computer industry use both words.

Case study: Games console network

In April 2011, a leading games console's online service was hacked. This reportedly resulted in 77 million users' email and password details being compromised (made available to people who should not have access to them). This was one of the biggest and most publicised cases of hacking ever.

Find three different articles about this case and answer the following questions.

1 What was the effect on individual users?
2 What was the effect on the business?
3 What was the effect on the Internet as a whole?

There have been several high-profile cases of hacking, with responsibility being claimed by a 'hacktivist' group called Lulz Security. Over a 50-day period, LulzSec carried out a series of high-profile hacks, including:

- making available the contact details of 250,000 people auditioning for reality television shows
- publicising the names of registered users to a large pornography website
- replacing a national newspaper's home page with a story about the owner being found dead (which was untrue)
- targeting US government sites.

LulzSec claimed they were hacking just for the 'lulz'. Then, almost as suddenly as they appeared, LulzSec announced that they were moving on.

Since then police have arrested suspected hackers around the world, including some who may be part of LulzSec. However, at the time of writing, no one has been convicted.

Find three different articles about this case and answer the following questions.

1 What was the effect on individual users?
2 What was the effect on the businesses targeted?
3 What was the effect on the Internet as a whole?

Activity: Hacking in the news

Research WikiLeaks, Anonymous and hacktivists and watch the TED talk by Christopher 'Moot' Poole about 4chan.

Hoaxes

A hoax is a warning sent by email about a threat. Hoax emails will usually warn about a virus which could attack your computer and advise you to forward the warning to as many people as possible. However, the virus often does not exist. Although hoax emails are usually sent to cause a nuisance, they may also carry viruses themselves. By reading the email or following its advice you may end up with a virus anyway.

Activity: Hoax emails

Hoax emails are very common and sometimes they can be hard to spot, as the content looks harmless. If you're not sure, then don't open the email or attachment, or do an Internet search to see whether there are any reports of a hoax email similar to the email you've received. Snopes.com is a website that reports whether information is true or false. It looks at items such as urban legends, rumours and strange news stories.

1 Research three email hoaxes, such as Life Is Beautiful; A (Virtual) Card For You; and Thousand Dollar Bill.
2 What are the key features of an email hoax?

1.2 Security precautions

Security of IT systems is very important and there are several precautions you can take to protect your system and data. Some of these are listed below.

Use access controls

You can control how much access other people have to both hardware and software.

Physical controls

Figure 3.3: It's important to keep equipment safe. Cables are an easy target for damage, whether accidental or intended.

One of the first steps to good IT security is to keep the physical equipment safe. There is no point in installing expensive software protection if someone could simply walk up to the server and damage the actual computer.

As well as protecting the hardware against theft or damage you should be aware that the environment (how and where the computer is kept) could also damage equipment. This could be through:

- fire or flooding
- environmental issues such as high temperatures or damp
- electrical or magnetic interference
- minor faults caused by damage to cables or other components.

To help prevent damage to your system:

- Keep all computer equipment in a locked room, accessible by key or electronic keypad.
- Protect equipment from fire with fireproofing, extinguishers and alarms.
- Fit all equipment with a **surge protector**.
- Remove hazards such as boxes or damaged electrical items.
- Make sure pipes, windows and other fixtures are not damaged.
- Keeping the room clean and tidy.
- Keep the room at a suitable temperature, if necessary using air conditioning.
- Follow laws and regulations.

Key term

Surge protector – a device to protect electrical equipment from voltage surges or 'spikes' (sudden increases), for example in a storm. Power surges can damage or destroy computer hard drives.

Use identity and access control

Some data should only be accessible to certain people. For example, data on a business IT system should be accessible only to people who work in that business. Therefore you should use access controls to make sure that unauthorised people cannot see this data. For example:

- Each user is given a unique (special to them) username and password so that they have to log in before they can see the data.
- Users are given an ID card which can be swiped into the computer. You may have seen assistants in shops using this system to access the till.
- Each user must use a personal identification number (PIN) as needed with debit and credit cards.

Make passwords strong

A 'strong' password is one which is very hard for someone to guess, work out or crack. You should always try to follow these three guidelines when making up a password.

1. Make sure your password is at least eight characters long.
2. Use a mixture of lowercase (small) and uppercase (capital) letters, numbers and symbols.
3. Do not choose a password which is something related to you or an obvious combination such as 'abcd1234' or 'password'.

A 'weak' password could allow someone else to access your data. For example, if you use your pet's name as a password, anyone who knows that name could guess your password.

However, even a strong password can be worked out using a **brute force program**. These programs often begin by testing dictionary words, so it is a good idea to choose a password that is not a word in the dictionary. Given unlimited time and resources, sooner or later brute force programs will find the right combination of letters, numbers and symbols. However, if your password is strong, there is a good chance that the cracker will give up and move on to another account before they gain access to yours.

You should change your password or PIN regularly in case someone has found out what it is. Make sure you never write this information down and do not give your password or PIN to anyone else, not even your friends.

Use a password-protected screensaver

When you walk away from a computer, it can become vulnerable (open to access and/or attack). For example, someone else could send emails from your account, access your personal details or, in a business, try to find company information or alter data.

Figure 3.4: Log-in screen

Key term

Brute force program – a computer program that will try different 'solutions' until it finds the right one; for example, a password.

There are two main ways to protect your computer when you are not there.

- Lock your machine when you are not using it: press the **Ctrl+Alt+Delete** keys together and then click **Lock This Computer** from the menu that appears. You will then have to enter your password to unlock the computer. See also the section *Lock and unlock your computer* in *Unit 2 IT user fundamentals*, page 17.
- Use a **screensaver** that automatically locks the computer as soon as anyone moves the mouse or presses a key to remove the screensaver. This means that anyone wishing to access the computer will need to have the right password to log in again.

Password protect files

Files that contain important, personal or sensitive data might need extra protection. You can add a password to specific files so that no one without the password can open them.

Use file attributes

You can set up individual files with different **attributes** so that you have control over who can access them and what can be done to them. Examples of attributes in Windows® documents include:

- **Read Only** – the file can be opened and read, but the contents cannot be changed or deleted.
- **Read/Write** – the file can be opened and read, and the contents can be changed or deleted.
- **Hidden** – the file will not be visible unless the user has changed their settings to 'turn on' hidden files.

Encrypt data

Encryption is a way of protecting data by turning it into code that unauthorised people cannot understand. Only a computer with the correct 'decryption' code will be able to decode it and access the data. The more complicated the code, the harder it will be for someone to work it out.

Use anti-virus software

Anti-virus software protects computers against viruses. This software uses a data file with details of all known viruses to check whether a computer has been infected. New viruses are appearing all the time, so it is important to update anti-virus software regularly to make sure it can spot all possible viruses.

Key terms

Screensaver – an animated image (or slideshow of multiple images) which will appear on your display screen after a period of no user activity.
Attributes – settings on documents that control what can be done to them and by whom.

Activity: Anti-virus software

Check the computer(s) you work on at home, at school/college or in the workplace.

1 Do they have anti-virus software installed?

2 When was that software last updated?

3 When was the anti-virus scan last run?

Use a firewall

Firewalls are barriers between a computer system and all other technology. This could cover a single computer or a network between the computers inside a business and the Internet. Firewalls monitor (check) all the data coming into or leaving a computer and block anything they think is unwanted (for example, viruses, spam and hacking attempts).

Adjust Internet security settings

The **default** setting on Internet security is usually 'medium'. By changing the setting to 'high' you can reduce the risks from viruses, phishing and other threats. However, with a high security setting you may not be able to see or use features on some websites, since they will be blocked.

Apply content/email filtering

Most email systems automatically filter data. At a low level, they will check for spam or emails containing viruses and filter anything suspicious. At a higher level, they will also look for inappropriate (unsuitable) content or certain types of file (for example, **.exe** files).

Download software patches and updates

You should download software 'patches' and updates whenever they are available. This is especially important for core software such as operating systems, Internet browsers or common software (word processors, email programs, etc.).

Software is often released with **bugs** in it, usually because the publisher does not know about them in advance. Any bugs are often only found after the software has been released and users have begun using it. The publisher then issues patches and updates to fix these problems and improve the security of IT systems. Software patches and updates often contain new functions and tools as well as bug fixes.

Carry out security checks

By checking your IT system regularly you can make sure that its security is still effective. These checks may be simple (checking anti-virus software is up to date) or more extreme. For example, you could try to break into your own system to test its security.

Key terms

Default – a standard setting or option that comes with an IT system but may be changed to suit each user.

.exe – is an executable file, i.e. one with instructions for a computer to carry out. Often this is a program but it could be a virus.

Bugs – errors in the code of a piece of software.

Report security threats or breaches

It is important that you report any threats to security or actual security breaches as quickly as possible. This will allow other security measures to be put in place before things get worse. For example, you may notice:

- a computer behaving strangely, which could be evidence of a virus
- changes to data
- someone viewing data to which they should not have access.

Your anti-virus software should also alert you to any potential security breaches. It should run system scans which check for potential issues. If your system is protected, then you will see a message similar to that shown in Figure 3.5.

Figure 3.5: A status message from your anti-virus software might look like this

Backups

Backups are duplicates (copies) of files and other data. Backups are useful when the original data is no longer available. This could be because:

- it has been corrupted (damaged) – for example, if the hard drive fails
- it has been damaged – perhaps a CD or DVD is scratched
- it has been lost or stolen – for example, a USB stick (see *Backup media* on page 59).

It is vital to back up important data that might be difficult or impossible to replace. Backing up data may seem pointless, but if you lose an important file (which happens to most people at some time) you will be relieved that you took the time to back it up.

Make backups

Backups allow you to retrieve or replace original lost data. However, it is important to back up your files regularly and often so that you do not lose too much data. This will keep your files as recent and up to date as possible.

In order to back up data securely, you should always save backups in a different place from the original file. This might be another drive on a network, although this is risky because if something happens to the server both copies might be damaged. There are also several types of removable (mobile) storage media you can use, especially for personal data. However, it is very important to store these devices securely as they are easily lost, stolen or broken.

Backup media

You could use the following for backing up personal data.

- **Removable hard drives**: These come in a range of storage capacities (sizes) and can store quite large amounts of data. They would be the most suitable for large sets of files.
- **USB sticks** (also known as memory sticks or pen drives): These have fairly limited storage capacity, but sizes are increasing all the time. They are small and convenient to use, but are also very easy to lose or damage.
- **CDs/DVDs**: These are also available with different storage capacities, but again are easily lost or damaged.

Figure 3.6: You can use CDs or DVDs to back up your personal data

In business, it is common practice to back up data to tapes linked to the servers on the organisation's network. There are usually two sets of tapes, sometimes one for each day of the week, and these will be swapped each week. Backups often take place outside working hours (for example, at night) or during quiet times on the network.

Tapes are often stored off-site in highly secure places protected from fire and flood. Very important information, such as financial data that banks store, is often also protected from bombs and nuclear attack. With increasing network power, tape backups are sometimes made remotely so that the backups and the original data on the servers are never in the same building.

Issue an acceptable usage policy

An acceptable usage policy (AUP) is a document given to everyone who will be using a computer network. You (or your parents) may have had to sign one before you were allowed to use your school or college network. It explains what you can and cannot do on the network and what the penalties are if you break the rules.

Activity: Acceptable usage policies

Write an acceptable usage policy for your computer at home. Imagine someone else in your family is going to use your computer. What rules and penalties will you set and why?

Store personal data and software securely

As you have learned, it is important to back up and store personal data and software securely. Refer back to the relevant parts of Section 1.2 – particularly *Use access controls* (page 54) and *Backups* (page 58) – and to Section *1.4 Protecting access to information sources* (page 64).

Treat messages, files, software and attachments from unknown sources with caution

Figure 3.7: Treat email attachments from unknown senders with caution

It is your responsibility, as the user, to be careful about which files and emails you open and which websites you visit. They may not be as innocent as they seem. Using software filtering can be helpful, but it will not catch all suspicious files or emails. See the section, *Apply content/email filtering* for more information on this topic, page 57.

Emails, especially with attachments, that you receive from unknown senders may contain viruses, so you should always treat them with caution. If in doubt about whether an email or file attachment is safe, delete it without opening it.

Case study: Mineral Games

Mineral Games is a company which designs and creates computer games. It sells its products online and also runs servers for people to play the games online. The company is worried about the security of their data, including:

- files on their network about games being developed that it must keep secret from other computer game companies
- financial data, including the company's payroll and finances
- data about its customers, including names, addresses and credit card details
- online game servers where users can sign up and play, including users' email addresses, passwords and game save data.

The company's directors have hired you as an IT security expert to explain and show them how to keep their data safe.

1 Make a list of the security issues that may threaten their IT systems.
2 List five different precautions that they could take to keep information secure.

1.3 Threats to information security

You need to be able to identify threats to information security related to the widespread use of technology.

Physical loss/theft

A major threat to data security which is often overlooked is physical attack on computers or IT systems themselves. Computer hardware that is damaged or stolen is not only expensive to replace, but the data it contains may also be lost if it is not backed up elsewhere.

IT equipment can be insured, which means that if it is damaged or stolen the insurance company will pay to replace it. However, this will probably not take into account the personal or business 'cost' of data that is lost. On a personal computer (PC), you could lose all your school or college coursework, your holiday photos or any digital media you have created or stored.

On a business computer or server, customer details, product designs or other vital information might be lost or stolen. This may mean a loss of profit or a breach of security.

Unauthorised access

Unauthorised access could be physical, such as someone coming onto company premises and looking at things they are not authorised to view. It can also be digital access, where a person gains access to an area of a network or to data which they should not – for example, a company's payroll or customer details.

The person gaining unauthorised access could be someone who does not work for the company or it could be an employee gaining access to information outside their own **privileges**.

Key term

Privileges – the permissions given to users to set their level of access.

Activity: Access and restrictions

1   What level of access do you have on the computer you are using?
2   What restrictions/increased access could be added?

Accidental file deletion

Losing data can be distressing for individuals and very damaging for companies. Accidental loss can range from simply deleting a file by mistake to corrupt hard drives in a server which result in the loss of a large number of files.

Use of removable storage media

As you have learned, removable storage media (USB sticks, CDs etc.) are convenient for storing and transferring data because they are small. However, their size also means they are more likely to be damaged, lost or stolen than a computer system or server. You should password protect sensitive files when storing them on removable storage media. See the section *Password protect files* earlier in this unit, page 56.

Figure 3.8: Keep personal details, items and documents in a safe place to help combat identity theft

Key terms

Impersonate – to pretend to be someone or something else. A person who pretends to be someone else is an impersonator or impostor.
Persona – the part of a person's character that is presented to or perceived by others.

Malicious programs, hackers and phishing

Malicious programs (malware), hackers and phishing can all be a threat to information security. See section *1.1 Threats to system performance* on pages 48–53 for more information on these issues and section *1.2 Security precautions* on pages 54–60 for more information on how to protect IT systems against these threats.

Identity theft

Identity (ID) theft is where someone pretends to be someone else. In order to **impersonate** someone (the victim), a thief must obtain the victim's personal information (i.e. their full name, address, email address, which services/companies they use etc.). Data that confirms the victim's identity – such as credit card details, password/PIN or security question answers – will make the thief's task easier.

The thief may then use the victim's accounts (email, social networking, bank accounts). In more extreme cases the thief may set up a **persona** as if they were the victim. They could then:

- create new bank accounts in 'their' name
- obtain and use credit or debit cards
- even get enough information to obtain a passport.

Offline theft

One common offline method of stealing personal details is to search a victim's bin for documents such as bank statements and utility (gas/electricity/phone) bills. Therefore it is important to always shred letters or other documents containing personal information before throwing them away.

Online theft

Online identity thieves look for personal details which are unsecured on the Internet. They may also use malicious programs or try to get details by hacking or phishing (see pages 50–52).

Activity: To tweet or not to tweet?

Several celebrities have been impersonated on Twitter. This may be considered low-level ID theft (fraud), but it can still be very upsetting to the victims and their followers who are being fooled. It can also be risky if the victim is an organisation and the impersonator is giving out inaccurate or dangerous information.

1 Create a series of tweets written from an impersonator's point of view. Your tweets should be less than 140 characters in length.
2 Then switch and pretend you are the celebrity. How do you feel about what is happening? How would you respond and deal with the situation?
3 You need to find a resolution to the situation. Do you side with the impersonator or the celebrity? Explain your reasoning.

Unsecured networks and public networks

An unsecure network could allow unauthorised access. For example, someone could find a 'hole' in the network security which gives them access to data. The unauthorised access could be someone **piggybacking** onto a network. This means that they see a security hole in a network's **WiFi** and connect to it. They then use the network's own Internet connection (which is often very powerful) as a **portal** to the rest of the Internet.

A public network is not locked and can be accessed by anyone. Some city centres have public networks that allow you to access WiFi connections within specified areas. Users who have signed up and paid for services, such as BT Openzone or Virgin Media, can connect to the Internet anywhere it is available. However, because they provide open access, public networks are more at risk from hackers or others trying to access inappropriate content.

Default passwords and security settings

When you register for an online service you will usually be given a default password, probably sent by email. This is highly insecure, so you should always change a default password as quickly as possible to your own secure password. See the section *Make passwords strong*, page 55.

All users should be aware of security settings on the programs and applications they use. These could be general settings, such as on an Internet browser, or settings that relate to specific websites, such as Facebook. Make sure that all your IT security settings are appropriate and will protect your system from threats. See *Adjust Internet security settings*, page 57.

Wireless networks (WiFi)

Wireless networks connect via radio waves instead of cables (wires). An area where you can access a wireless network is known as a 'hotspot'. Although these are easy to set up and use, they are at risk from intruders as it is easier to piggyback onto the network than with a physically wired network. Therefore wireless networks are often protected by a **Wired Equivalent Privacy (WEP) key**. This is a password to make sure that you are allowed access to a particular network.

Bluetooth

This wireless networking system works over short distances. It is good for connecting two mobile devices or a mobile device to a computer. For example, you could use it to **synch** your smartphone with your home computer.

Portable and USB devices

Portable and USB devices have their own security issues, mainly the risks of damage, loss or theft. These issues have been covered earlier, in the sections *Backups: Backup media* and *Use of removable storage media*, pages 59 and 61.

Key terms

Piggybacking – this term is used to describe several things in computing. Here it describes a situation where someone connects to the Internet via someone else's unsecured WiFi connection.

WiFi – uses radio waves rather than wires or cables to send data to and from a laptop or other IT device. Many laptops and smartphones have a WiFi link built into them. WiFi only works over quite short distances, usually 100 m or less.

Portal – a gateway or entrance.

Synch (synchronise) – updating data in different places at the same time so that files always match: for example, on a home computer and a smartphone.

Remember

If your Internet security settings are set to 'low', your system will be at risk from viruses and other malware, hackers and phishing.

1.4 Protecting access to information sources

You have already learned in this unit that it is important to take appropriate precautions to keep information secure. The following section outlines several ways of protecting data. Some of these have been covered earlier in the unit, so refer back if necessary.

Username and password/PIN selection

Username and password/PIN selection has been covered in detail in section *1.2 Security precautions*, *Use access controls*, *Make passwords strong*, pages 54–60. Review this section and make sure you apply your knowledge to any passwords and PINs you use.

How and when to change passwords

You should change your password regularly – at least every three months, but every month would be better. You should also change your password if you think someone else has found out (or might find out) what it is.

Online identity and profile

You probably have at least one online identity (profile), for example:

- by using email
- on social networking sites such as Facebook or Twitter
- for online games or elsewhere on the Internet.

It is important to remember that YOU can control your online persona. You can choose how much information you put online and who has access to it. In order to do this you need to consider all your security settings and think about your **privacy**.

Remember

Anything you put on the Internet will stay there in some form forever, even if you try to remove it later. Once it is out there, you can never take it back.

Key term

Privacy – not being watched by or disturbed by others; keeping things private.

Activity: Online profiles and privacy

Consider the following situation relating to your security settings and privacy.

- If you put a photo on your profile, who can see it? For example, can friends, family, tutors or employers see the photo?
- Do you want them to see it?
- Would you mind if they saw it?

Although you cannot control what other people put on the Internet about you, you can control what you make available for others to see. Always think carefully before posting anything online.

Real name, pseudonym, avatar

Many people who use Internet services such as eBay™, chatrooms or who play online computer games do not use their real names. Instead, they will use a made-up name or **pseudonym**. They may even create several personas for different activities. For example, they might use one pseudonym for playing games and a different one for posting on discussion boards.

People will often also have an **avatar** that goes with their pseudonym. This could be a square image – such as those on forums – or a whole animated person. Examples include Miis on Wii™ and avatars on Xbox Live®.

What personal information to include and who can see the information

Figure 3.9: An example of an avatar

Each computer user needs to consider their privacy and think about how much information they wish to display publicly and how much they keep private. Usually you can choose whether to make information completely public, accessible only to 'friends' or accessible to no one.

If someone is your 'friend' on a social networking, they could access your personal data if your security settings are too low and allow them to do this. You do not need to be friends with that person directly. In order to maintain your privacy it is important to:

- choose your security settings very carefully
- use settings at the right level for various pieces of your data.

This will ensure that only people you choose can see details about you.

Respect confidentiality

You should always respect the **confidentiality** of information; for example, someone's personal details or a company's financial records. You can keep data confidential by setting suitable security access or just by asking someone to keep information private.

If you come across security settings that stop you accessing folders or files on a company server, you should not try to get through them. Certain files will be restricted for a reason and trying to access them would breach the confidentiality of their owner. This also includes trying to get through Internet filtering systems at school or college.

If you work for a company, you will often have a confidentiality clause in your contract. This forbids you to talk about confidential business matters, especially with people from rival companies.

Avoid inappropriate disclosure of information

You should be careful about what information you put online. Once something appears online, even if it is taken back down again quickly, someone could still have taken a copy of it. The service used could also have made a backup.

> **Key terms**
>
> **Pseudonym** – a made-up or false name.
> **Avatar** – an icon or animated image, which is sometimes movable, that represents a person in cyberspace or on a games console.
> **Confidentiality** – keeping something secret, such as private information.

Always read the terms and conditions before you add any information to a website and make sure you know who will own that information. For example, before uploading photographs to a website you should check whether you are giving copyright of those images to the company that owns the website. See section *1.3 Copyright constraints on the use of information* in *Unit 4 IT communication fundamentals*, page 74.

1.5 Security guidelines and procedures

In order to keep all IT systems and data secure, you should always follow the relevant guidelines and procedures, as outlined below.

Data Protection Act 1998

The Data Protection Act was originally passed in 1984 and updated in 1998. It has eight guiding principles (see Table 3.1). Its purpose is to protect sensitive and personal information about identifiable individuals which is held in databases. It is controlled by the Information Commissioner. Every business that stores data has to register, saying what data they will hold and why. They must then follow the rules of the Act.

1	Personal data shall be processed fairly and lawfully and, in particular, shall not be processed unless (a) at least one of the conditions in Schedule 2 of the Act is met, and (b) in the case of sensitive personal data, at least one of the conditions in Schedule 3 of the Act is also met.
2	Personal data shall be obtained only for one or more specified and lawful purposes, and shall not be further processed in any manner incompatible with that purpose or those purposes.
3	Personal data shall be adequate, relevant and not excessive in relation to the purpose or purposes for which they are processed.
4	Personal data shall be accurate and, where necessary, kept up to date.
5	Personal data processed for any purpose or purposes shall not be kept for longer than is necessary for that purpose or those purposes.
6	Personal data shall be processed in accordance with the rights of data subjects under this Act.
7	Appropriate technical and organisational measures shall be taken against unauthorised or unlawful processing of personal data and against accidental loss or destruction of, or damage to, personal data.
8	Personal data shall not be transferred to a country or territory outside the European Economic Area unless that country or territory ensures an adequate level of protection for the rights and freedoms of data subjects in relation to the processing of personal data.

Table 3.1: The eight guiding principles of the Data Protection Act

Activity: Data Protection Act 1998

Design a poster explaining the eight principles of the Data Protection Act 1998 in simple terms. For each principle, give an example of when it might apply.

Computer Misuse Act 1990

Although the original Data Protection Act (1984) protected data held on computers about identifiable individuals, there was no law to protect computers from threats such as hackers, crackers and viruses. Therefore, the Computer Misuse Act 1990 was introduced. This Act has three principles:

1. It is an offence to gain unauthorised access to computer programs or data.

2. It is an offence to gain unauthorised access with the intent to commit further offences.

3. It is an offence to make unauthorised modification of computer material (e.g. programs or data).

Security guidelines set by employers or organisations

Companies will decide the level of security required for their systems and also the rules that their employees and security systems must follow. They will usually have policies that define exactly how this is done, how often they are reviewed and updated and what happens if the rules are broken.

An acceptable usage policy is usually written into staff contracts and covers how employees can use the company's computers. Some also state how or whether employees can use certain IT systems or services. For example, a company might ban employees from accessing social networking sites at work. A company might also specify that employees should not say anything negative (bad) about the company on social networking sites, even in their private life.

Companies will also have a privacy policy that states how employees must handle company data.

Activity: Mineral Games

The directors of Mineral Games have asked you to discuss the following with their staff:

● Why it is important to back up data securely?

● How can you ensure personal data is backed up to appropriate media?

Prepare answers to these questions. Make notes on these topics as evidence for your portfolio.

Check your understanding

1 Briefly describe the purpose of the Data Protection Act 1998 and the Computer Misuse Act 1990.

2 Why are backups important?

3 Name three storage media which can be used for backups.

ASSESSMENT ACTIVITY

1   Give a brief description of the following:

   a   spam

   b   viruses

   c   spyware

   d   adware

   e   hackers.

2   You have completed a project for your ITQ course and you now need to back up your work. It is a large folder of approximately 2 GB of data.

   a   Give examples of two suitable media that you would use for backing up your work.

   b   Why is it important to back up your work and how frequently should you do this?

3   A friend has come to you for help with setting up usernames and passwords. Her name is Jo Brown.

   •   Give two examples of a secure username and password that you suggest she use.

4   Your friend is concerned about security risks to her computer and has come to you for advice.

   a   Explain what data theft is and how to avoid it.

   b   What are the dangers from email attachments and how can you avoid them?

   c   Give some useful tips on how to spot hoax emails.

5   Find out which anti-virus software is installed on your computer. Is it up to date?

IT communication fundamentals

This unit is about using IT to find and pass on or share information using the Internet, intranets, email and other communication systems. The Internet is a vast information resource, but you need to learn how to search for information effectively and how to be selective and identify useful and reliable information.

Besides using the Internet to find information, you can also use it in your daily or working life to check train times and book tickets, for example. IT also provides methods such as email and instant messaging to allow people to communicate with each other (family, friends and colleagues).

Learning outcomes

After completing this unit you should be able to achieve the following learning outcomes.

» **LO1** Use a variety of sources of information to meet needs

» **LO2** Access, search for, select and use Internet-based information and assess its fitness for purpose

» **LO3** Select and use IT to communicate and exchange information

1 Use a variety of sources of information to meet needs

There is a wide variety of sources of information. You should be able to use and select the right source of information for your needs at any given time.

1.1 Sources of information

When we think of IT-based sources of information the Internet is the first to come to mind. However, there are some others you should also be aware of; and of course there are many sources of information which are not IT based.

Newspapers

Newspapers are now available in print and online. Some are published daily and some only at weekends. Newspapers are a good place to find news, plus information on the weather, sport or what is on television, for example. They are also an excellent source of job advertisements and career information.

Books and ebooks

Books can be fiction (they tell a made-up story) or non-fiction (they give factual information or represent true events). Books are for relaxation, information and reference. Some books are now available in an electronic format as ebooks. You can download these from the Internet and read them on an **ebook reader** such as Amazon Kindle®.

Images

Images include photographs (both digital and traditional film), paintings and digitally created graphics. Images can be:

- purely artistic, such as paintings in a gallery
- informative, such as photographs or drawings showing how to do something
- factual, such as a photograph of the president of the USA on a state visit to London.

Maps

Road maps and street atlases are traditionally used to help people find their way to places. However, drivers nowadays increasingly use global positioning systems (GPS) devices. These store electronic road maps and find the user's current location and destination by using information transmitted (sent) via satellites. There are now many different satellite navigation (Sat Nav) devices available.

Websites such as Google™ Maps provide searchable online maps which you can print out rather than using traditional printed maps. Some websites – including Google™ Maps and the Automobile Association (AA) – also have route planners which will suggest a route from one location to another and give directions to follow.

Figure 4.1: An ebook reader

Conversations

You can always find out lots of information simply by talking to people. Conversations may take place in person, over the phone or online (for example, by using instant messaging or video conferencing). Think about people you know who might know more about certain subjects than you. You could ask them for help or advice. If you need specific information, such as train times, you can often phone a special helpline.

CDs/DVDs

CDs have traditionally been used for music, but encyclopaedias and other information sources such as manuals and directories have also been issued on CD. Most of these have now been replaced by updateable resources on the Internet.

CDs can also be used to store data and computer programs. If you buy software in a shop it will usually come on a CD or DVD.

DVDs were traditionally used for films or television programmes but they have become more widespread. DVDs can store more information than CDs and can also be used for software or storing backups of files.

Text messages

Text messages are a very popular way of communicating on a mobile phone and also a useful way of getting information while on the move. Some services will reply to questions sent by text (for example, directory enquiries).

Podcasts

Podcasts are sound recordings. The name originally related to the Apple® iPod® music player. Many radio broadcasts and other audio recordings are available via iTunes® for download onto an iPod®. However, the term podcast is now used to refer to any sound recording in MP3 or other format which can be downloaded from the Internet. Podcasts are available on all sorts of topics, from comedy to cooking. For example, some BBC Radio programmes are available to download as podcasts.

Internet

The Internet is a vast source of information. In fact it contains so much that it can be difficult to find the information that is **relevant** to particular needs. Search engines such as Google™, Yahoo!® or Bing™ will help you find what you need on the Internet. See *Unit 5 Using the Internet*, page 99.

Intranet

An intranet is an internal Internet which can only be viewed within an organisation, such as a company, school or college. Most medium and large organisations have an intranet which contains information about the

Key term

Relevant – closely connected/ linked to a specific matter in hand.

organisation. A typical organisation's intranet might contain:

- details of company policies and procedures
- information for different parts of the business
- information for employees about benefits such as pensions
- news about the organisation
- any other information that employees may need to do their jobs.

Web logs

Web logs, usually called **blogs**, are sites created by individuals or groups to discuss certain topics or interests. The person or group that runs the blog can update it by posting (putting on the site) text, pictures, videos, links etc. People who subscribe to (register with and/or follow) the blog can add their comments to the updates. There are also **microblogging** sites such as Twitter™.

Web-based reference sites

There are many websites that provide reference information about all sorts of subjects. Wikipedia is a well-known encyclopedia site, with a vast range of articles about almost every imaginable subject. It has almost 4 million articles in English alone. Another popular site is HowStuffWorks, which, as the name suggests, contains thousands of articles about how all sorts of things work.

Key term

Microblogging – social networking on websites where people can discuss any topic or update people on what they are doing. Posts are limited to short messages. For example, on Twitter™ a message (known as a 'tweet') is limited to 140 characters.

Activity: Internet research

A friend is having a birthday party and has asked you to help with some of the travel arrangements. The guests coming by car or train will need driving directions and train times. Your friend would also like you to find out what the weather will be on the day of the party.

For each of piece of information, find both Internet and non-Internet sources and make a note of them. With Internet sources, you can bookmark or print relevant web pages. For non-Internet resources, you should create a table in a spreadsheet (such as Excel®), listing the different resources you found.

1.2 Identify different features of information

Information is a very broad term which covers almost anything we find useful. There are several types of information and many things you need to consider when finding and using information.

Types of information

Broadly speaking, information can be divided into four main categories: factual; opinion; fictional; and creative work.

Factual

This is information based on fact (something that has actually happened). For example, a textbook or a history book will contain factual information. Radio and television news programmes also contain factual information. Factual information is an example of **objective knowledge** and it should be up to date. Out-of-date information is often useless and possibly misleading, so it is important to check the **currency** of your sources.

Opinion

Opinions are what someone thinks about something. For example, you might have a friend who says, 'My laptop is the best!' This is their opinion and other people might think that a different laptop is the best. Another friend might say, 'My laptop has 2GB of **RAM**.' This (if true) is a fact, not an opinion. Opinions are an example of **subjective knowledge**.

Fictional

This type of information is not based on fact – it has been made up. In many cases it is obvious whether information is fictional or not. However, sometimes people may try to pass off fictional information as fact. Fiction books may contain pieces of factual information (that are true about the real world), but the people and events in the stories themselves are not based on fact.

Creative work

This includes music, photographs, paintings and sculpture. This kind of artistic material is usually produced for pleasure, but it might sometimes have a political or ethical message. Fiction books – containing a combination of factual, opinion-based and fictional information – are also examples of creative work.

Information that is continually updated (or live)

Some types of information are constantly updated or 'live'. For example, breaking news stories may be reported via a live news feed, which means that the web page will be updated as soon as any new information is available. Most of the information posted on these websites will tell you when it was put up (the date and often also the time) so that you can check how current it is.

Many airport websites provide live information about flights. For example, you can check Heathrow Airport's website for live updates on when flights are expected, whether there are any delays and whether a particular flight has landed. This type of information is sometimes called real-time data.

Audio or video content which is presented live over the Internet is often referred to as **streamed**. For example, you can stream BBC Radio and News 24 live.

Many organisations hold vast amounts of information and need to make backups to avoid losing data. Therefore, some information may need to be archived. Archived information is usually older data which is not needed on a day-to-day basis but is too important to delete. You cannot access archived

Key terms

Objective knowledge – factual information that can be verified (confirmed). For example, 'This hard disk has a capacity of 500 GB' can be confirmed.

Currency – how up to date something is.

RAM – or random access memory is a form of computer storage.

Subjective knowledge – information based on opinion that depends on different people's thoughts and feelings about different things. For example, 'That is the most beautiful painting I have ever seen' might be one person's opinion, but another person might think the same painting is really ugly.

Streamed – audio or video content which is presented live over the Internet.

material (sometimes called offline data) immediately but it can be retrieved when needed. It is stored using media such as magnetic tapes, CDs or DVDs. Many news and magazine websites also have online archives.

Static information

Some types of data (such as mathematical and historical information) do not change very often, if at all. This is known as static information. For example, if you use the Internet to find out about the Apollo moon landings, it will not matter too much whether or not the information is up to date. However, you still need to make sure that the information is accurate.

Case study: Customer reviews

Many websites (such as Amazon, eBay™ and TripAdvisor®) contain factual information about products and services. They also feature customer reviews, which give voice people's opinions. For example, eBay™ relies heavily on feedback from purchasers, which is used as a guide to how trustworthy (honest and reliable) the sellers are. However, it is important to remember that feedback and reviews are only opinion and some hotel owners, for example, have complained that reviews of their hotels are unfair.

1 Look at review-driven websites and find some reviews of any hotels you have stayed in, restaurants you have eaten in or attractions you have visited.
2 Do you agree with what people have said?
3 Do you think any of the reviews are unfair or even factually incorrect?

1.3 Copyright constraints on the use of information

When using information you have not created yourself you need to be aware of copyright restrictions.

Effect of copyright law

The Copyright, Designs and Patents Act 1988 protects the rights of people who create almost any kind of material, including works of art, music, photographs, film or video and text (including books, magazines and newspapers). Unless you have created the material yourself or are sure they are copyright free, you should not use material you find on the Internet or elsewhere. Do not assume that because something is on the Internet it is copyright free; in many cases it will not be.

For educational purposes only (such as coursework), you can quote short sections from books, newspapers or websites, and use images or data, as long as you acknowledge (identify and give credit to) the source of the material you have used (see below).

For any commercial use (where you would make money or if you are advertising or displaying something publicly), you will need to get the copyright owner's permission to use their material.

Copyright law protects people who work hard to produce something from having it stolen. Of course it would be nice if films and music were free. However, the actors or musicians who have put time and money into creating these films or music depend on the income they get from people paying to watch or listen to their work. These people are not just rich film stars and famous musicians. They are also ordinary people such as recording engineers, carpenters who make film sets and so on. When people steal copyright material they put ordinary people's jobs in danger.

Acknowledgements

When you write a report for school, college or work, it is quite acceptable to quote from a book, magazine or website to back up what you are saying. However, it is wrong and not acceptable to claim that this work is your own. Instead you must identify the quote by enclosing it in quotation marks and acknowledge its source.

Here is an example of how you might quote from a book in your own work.

> *I have been researching how businesses use data, and one way they use data is to help them decide on things, for example:*
>
> *"Information systems support decision making when a problem arises and management needs to take action to resolve it." (Anderson, K. et al. 2007, page 87)*
>
> *But there are lots of other ways in which businesses can use information.*

The name of the author is put in brackets after the quotation ('et al.' means there were several authors of this book). At the end of your work you should include a bibliography listing in full all the books you used, like this:

> Anderson, K. et al. (2007). *BTEC National Information Technology Practitioners Book 1* 2nd Edition, Oxford, Heinemann.

In this example, Oxford is the place where the book was published and Heinemann is the name of the publisher. You can find all this information inside every book.

Plagiarism and permission

If you try to pass off someone else's work as your own, this is known as 'plagiarism'. As already mentioned, if you include quotations from books, websites or other sources you must not claim them as your own. Equally, you must not copy another learner's work and claim it as your own. Your school or college will have a policy which states the penalties for plagiarism. At the very least you should expect to have to do the assignment again if you are found to have plagiarised someone else's work or used sources that you have not acknowledged. You should also take care to ensure others do not plagiarise your work.

- Make sure you do not leave copies of your assignment work lying around.
- Promptly collect any printouts of your work from the printer.
- Never give electronic copies of your work to other learners.

If you need to use copyright material for non-educational purposes you must get written permission from the copyright owner(s). However, they do not have to give permission and they may charge you to use their material. See the section *Legal constraints* in *Unit 1 Improving productivity using IT* for more information about copyright, page 6.

Activity: Information sources

Keep a record of all the different types and sources of information you use over the next couple of days. Include sources such as bus timetables, books/magazines, music, radio or television programmes and so on. Sort each source of information using the following table (two examples have been completed for you):

Information	Source	Subjective or objective	Is it copyright?
Bus times	Internet	Objective	No
Article on fashion	Magazine	Both	Yes

Check your understanding

1 You are planning a holiday. What sources of information will help you plan all parts of your holiday?
2 Explain the difference between objective and subjective information.
3 What does the term 'streamed' mean when applied to information on the Internet?
4 What is archived information? What is it used for?
5 What is a bibliography?

2 Assess, search for, select and use Internet-based information and assess its fitness for purpose

You need to be able to assess whether the information you are using is fit for the purpose you are using it for.

2.1 Assess, navigate and search

The Internet is so vast that it can be difficult to find the information you need. You will usually access the Internet using a software application called a web **browser**, such as Microsoft® Internet Explorer®, Google Chrome™ or Firefox®.

Once you are connected to the Internet, you can navigate (move) to a website by typing its address in the bar at the top of the browser window and pressing the **Enter** key. Alternatively, you can browse (look around) the Internet using a **search engine** by entering a topic to search for.

To learn about more accurate ways of searching on the Internet, see section *2.2 Use appropriate search techniques*, page 77.

Home page

When you launch your Internet browser, the page that loads up first is called the **home page**. It makes sense to choose a page you want to visit often as your home page. For instructions on how to set your home page, see section *2.2 Browser settings* in *Unit 5 Using the Internet*, page 96.

Bookmarks

It is also useful to bookmark web pages or sites that you visit regularly or that are particularly useful or important. In Internet Explorer® bookmarks are known as **Favorites**. If you add a web page to your Favorites you will be able to access it easily from the Favorites menu. This means that you do not have to remember and type in the web address each time. To add a website to your Favorites see *Unit 5 Using the Internet*, page 102.

How to use the Favorites menu

1. Open the **Favorites** menu.
2. Scroll down until you find the web page you wish to go to and click on it. This will open your selected page in the browser.

> **Remember**
>
> American spelling is usual in computing – e.g. 'favorite' and 'dialog' rather than 'favourite' and 'dialogue'.

History

If you forget to add a useful page to your Favorites and are struggling to find the page again, you can use your **browser history** to view all the pages you have visited. Click in the **address bar** to see a list of sites visited recently or press **Ctrl+H** for a full list of all the websites you have visited since your browsing history was last cleared. These techniques are covered in more detail in *Unit 5 Using the Internet*, pages 100–102.

> **Key term**
>
> **Sponsored links** – companies that have paid Google™ to put their websites at the top of the search results list.

2.2 Use appropriate search techniques

Before you can search the Internet, you will need to use a search engine such as Google™ or Bing™. You can then enter the search terms (a word or words that describe what you are looking for) and click the search button. You will see a results page, which is a list of web pages that contain your search terms. If you are using Google™, the first three or four results in this list will be **sponsored links**. The websites listed in your search results list will usually be relevant to your search.

See *Unit 5 Using the Internet* for more on search engines page 99.

Table 4.1 (page 78) lists some of the key features of Internet searches.

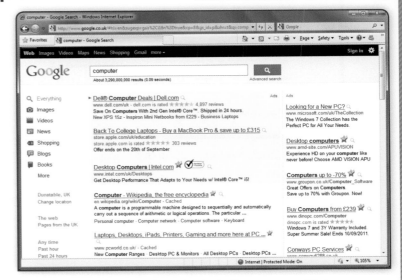

Figure 4.2: Google™ search results, including sponsored links

Key words	These are the words you type into the **search box**. Try to be as specific as possible with key words otherwise you may get lots of irrelevant results. For example, words such as 'computer problem' may not be useful; but 'text on my screen is too small' might be better, as it is more specific.
Quotation marks	Putting double quotes around a set of words tells the search engine to look for those exact words in that exact order. For example, "British Olympic 100m swimmers".
Search within results	You can refine (narrow down) the results by asking to see only certain types of content (such as images or maps) or only results which have been updated recently.
Relational operators	You can include 'OR' in your search to make sure the pages that are found contain either of the search criteria. So, 'FA Cup 2007 OR 2009' will show pages about the FA Cup in either of those years. You must put 'OR' in capitals for this to work.
'Find' or search tool	Many websites have their own find or search tool which allows you to search within that website only.
Turn questions into key words for an online query	If you are looking for an answer to a question, then often just typing in the question will get the right results: such as 'Who won the FA Cup in 2006?'

Table 4.1: Features of Internet searches

Refine your search

Figure 4.3: Google™ Advanced Search

Try to be specific about what you enter in the search box, otherwise you will get too many matches and you will not be able to tell which sites are relevant and which are not. For example, you can ask the UK-based version of Google™ (the one ending '.co.uk') to only show pages from the UK rather than the whole world. To do this, select the 'Pages from the UK' link on the left.

This is often useful when buying goods, as it is usually cheaper to buy something from a supplier in the UK than to pay for it to be sent from abroad. If you do not want Google™ to exclude (leave out) pages from outside the UK, select 'The web' instead.

Clicking the **Advanced Search** link will open a page with many more options – for example, for combining words or excluding sites which include certain words. Internet searching is covered in more detail in *Unit 5 Using the Internet*, page 100.

1   Use two different search engines to look for the same things. Compare the facilities and search results from each engine.
2   Are the results of the searches different?
3   Which search engine seems to provide the more useful results?

2.3 Evaluate information

Before using any information you find on the Internet, you will need to **evaluate** it. You need to remember that if you use information from the Internet then it needs to be appropriate and that it is fit for purpose (i.e. the information is reliable, it comes from a trustworthy source and it is suitable).

Remember that the Internet is open to anyone, anywhere in the world. There are very few checks on information put on the Internet. Therefore, you need to take care and consider the following issues.

What is the intention and authority of the information provider?

You should consider the intention of the website where you found the information:

● What is the purpose of the website and the information it is giving?
● Does the website aim to entertain, advertise or inform?

For example, if you are looking for information about a new laptop, you could look on the manufacturer's (maker's) website. Here, you should find accurate technical information about the laptop (such as weight or battery life). However, opinions from this site may be **biased**. The manufacturer will say that the laptop is really good because they want you to buy their products.

Alternatively, you could look at user reviews on a site such as Amazon. A problem here is that reviewers are generally not experts and their comments are only opinion. This is a question of **authority**. In this case, a laptop manufacturer's website is likely to be an authority on the product. However, you must be aware that they will be biased towards their product. User reviews may not have authority – especially about technical specifications – but they may highlight real advantages and disadvantages.

See also the section *1.2 Identify different features of information* earlier in this unit, page 72.

The websites of well respected companies such as the BBC should be reasonably authoritative. They will have accurate and well researched information which is relatively free from bias. However, even newspapers are not totally objective. For example, read the same news story in different newspapers and see if you can spot differences in the way the story is told.

Key terms

Evaluate – work out how useful or worthy something is.
Bias – liking or prejudice for or against something or someone.
Authority – a reliable and trustworthy source of information.

Remember

You should always be aware of the possibility of bias, especially when researching issues such as politics or religion.
Make sure you question the intention and authority of any information you find online.

Is the information up to date?

You need to know the currency of information you find on the Internet, as not all of it is up to date. This is becoming more of a problem as newspapers make their archives available online. You may find a news story which seems relevant but which is in fact so out of date that it is of no use.

Check whether the information you find has a date on it. If it is not dated, you should **cross-check** the information.

Is the information relevant?

The Internet is a vast international resource and not all the information you find will be relevant to the UK. Therefore, you need to find information that is relevant to you. See the section *Refine your search* earlier in this unit, page 78.

Is the information accurate?

Anyone can put information on the Internet, but not all of it is accurate. If you have any doubt about information on the Internet, you should check it by looking at other sources. Factors to consider include authority and currency.

What level of detail do you need?

Some sources on the Internet may provide more detail than you need. Wikipedia, for example, often has very detailed descriptions of technical subjects which may be difficult for non-experts to understand. On the other hand, some information may not have enough detail for your purpose.

> **Key term**
>
> **Cross-check** – use different sources or methods to check information or details.

Case study: Wikipedia

How accurate is the information on Wikipedia? Unlike a traditional printed encyclopaedia, anyone can write and edit articles on Wikipedia. This means that some information may not be accurate. However, studies show that although some articles contain errors and may not be complete, Wikipedia as a whole is about as accurate as a traditional encyclopedia.

The best approach is to use Wikipedia alongside other sources of information. Do not use it as your only source and consider the factors covered in this unit when evaluating information from the site.

Activity: Finding a course

A friend has asked you to help them find a course at a college. They would like to study:

- full time
- at Level 1
- a hairdressing or sports course
- at a college within 10 miles of your home town.

Search the Internet to find a suitable course for them. Create a list giving details of the possible courses they could study.

3 Select and use IT to communicate and exchange information

Using IT to pass on and exchange information has many benefits and this section will cover the main types of IT-based communication.

3.1 Using email and other IT-based communication

Email is a very popular method of both personal and business communication. It is covered in detail in *Unit 6 Using email*. However, there are many other IT-based communication methods with different facilities, such as instant real-time communication and information sharing. These will be outlined below.

Text messaging

Text messaging (texting) is a very popular method of communication. You can send and receive short text messages almost instantly. Texting is mainly used for social purposes (for example, contacting friends). Some businesses use texts for marketing and customer support (for example, to remind customers of appointments).

Instant messaging

Applications such as Yahoo!® Chat or Windows Live® Messenger are also used mainly for social purposes. These applications allow people to exchange typed messages and share photographs. Some versions allow voice chatting. Instant messaging is also used in business applications. For example, many software companies use it to provide technical support to their customers.

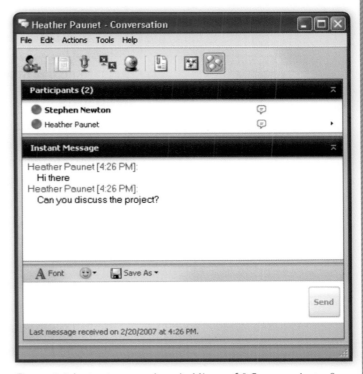

Figure 4.4: Instant messaging via Microsoft® Communicator®

Figure 4.5: Video calling on Skype™

Video calling/web conferencing

Several applications – including Skype™ and Apple® FaceTime® – support video calling. Like other IT-based communication methods, you can use it for personal and business purposes.

Web conferencing allows people to communicate over the Internet as if they were having a meeting. This is being used more and more for business meetings because it can save time and travel costs – especially when the people who need to meet are geographically far apart. One of the most popular web conferencing applications for business is WebEx®. Web conferencing can be also be used for purposes such as online training.

Forums

There are forums on the Internet covering almost every possible topic or interest. If you join a forum site you can post messages, ask questions or make suggestions that other members can then reply to.

Web logs

A web log (usually blog) is just like a website about you or your interests. Blogs are similar in some ways to forums. Anyone can create a blog. You can make posts to your blog whenever you like. People who follow your blog can comment on your posts.

Many blogs also include features of social networking. For example, Twitter™ is a combined blogging and social networking service. These services are known as microblogging sites. See *Web logs* in section *1.1 Sources of information* earlier in this unit, page 72.

Social networking

Social networking through sites such as Facebook is also very popular, particularly with young people. Users can:

- create accounts and include personal details and photos
- add other Facebook users as 'friends', who can then share their information

- update their status with what they are doing or other information (including links to other websites, videos etc.) which is then shared with all their friends, who can comment on the updates.

Many businesses use Facebook to promote their products or services. Facebook also supports text and video chatting.

See section *1.4 Access to information sources* in *Unit 3 IT security for users*, pages 64–66 for information on how to keep your personal information safe online.

Activity: Group communication

Set up a team activity with a group of friends – for example, arranging an outing or party. Use a variety of IT-based communication methods to make all the arrangements for the activity, including text messaging, instant messaging (chat) and video calling.

3.2 Using IT tools to schedule activities

Most email applications (for example, Microsoft® Outlook®) include facilities such as a calendar and other features you can use to schedule (arrange) tasks and meetings.

Using an address book

Using an email address book, including adding, amending and deleting contacts, is covered in section *1.5 Address book* in *Unit 6 Using email* pages 120–121.

Task list

Microsoft® Outlook® includes a **Tasks** tab in the bottom left of the main screen. You can use this feature to create a list of things you need to do. This might include pieces of coursework you need to complete; a surprise party you need to organise for next month; what you need to buy at the weekend. You can include details about each task and when it needs to be completed by. You can sort different types of tasks and you can also set a reminder so that you do not forgot to complete the task.

How to add emails that contain useful information to your task list

1. **Right click** on the email you wish to add to your task list; or from the **Home** tab, click on **Tags**.

2. From the drop-down menu that appears, select **Follow Up**.

3. From the next drop-down menu, select **Add Reminder**.

4. In the dialog box that appears, you can change the **Flag to:** option. For a reminder, set it to **Follow Up** and then set the **Due Date** (when the task needs to be completed) and a time and date for a **Reminder**.

Figure 4.6: The Follow Up drop-down menu

Calendar

Microsoft® Outlook® includes a calendar for scheduling events. To view it click on the **Calendar** tab on the bottom left of the main Outlook® screen.

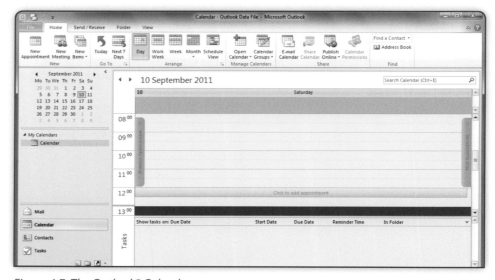

Figure 4.7: The Outlook® Calendar

The default view is the current day, but you can also view by week or month by clicking the icons in the **Arrange** section of the **Home** tab.

How to add a meeting appointment

1. Go to the day of the appointment, using the forward or back arrows at the top of the main calendar display or use the small month calendar at the top left of the main window.

2. Then **double click** on the day and time you wish to schedule the appointment for. This will open the **Appointment** dialog box.

3. Enter a subject for the appointment and a location if required.

Figure 4.8: The Appointment dialog box

Inviting people to a meeting

You can invite people to meetings using your email program.

How to invite people to meetings

1. Click the **Invite Attendees** icon.

2. This will open up a **To...** box above the meeting subject. Click this button and select the people from your contacts you want to invite.

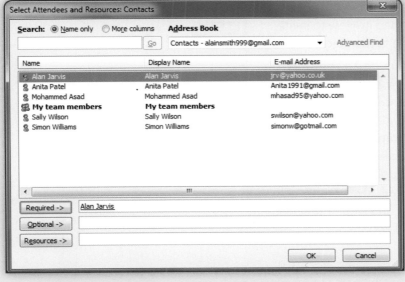

Figure 4.9: Inviting attendees

continued

3. You can make their attendance required or optional by selecting their name(s) and clicking the appropriate button. You can also type email addresses directly into the box.

4. Once you have added all the people you want to invite, click the **Send** button to email the invitations.

5. Click the **Save and Close** icon and the appointment will appear in your main calendar.

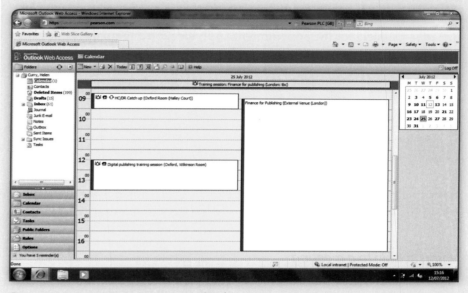

Figure 4.10: Appointments in your calendar

If you have an appointment or meeting which happens every week, month or year you can create a recurring appointment.

How to create a recurring appointment

1. Create an appointment as explained in 'How to invite people to meetings' page 85.

2. While in the **Appointment** window, click the **Recurrence** icon. This will display the **Appointment Recurrence** dialog box where you can set how often the appointment takes place (daily, weekly, monthly or yearly) and when the series should end.

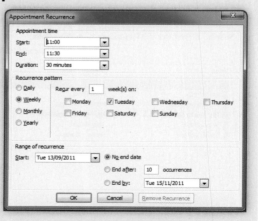

Figure 4.11: Appointment Recurrence dialog box

Responding to an invitation

When you receive an email invitation to a meeting it will look similar to Figure 4.12.

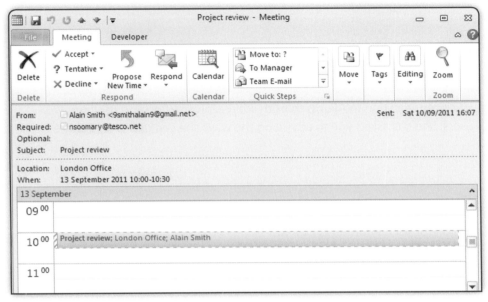

Figure 4.12: Respond to an appointment request

Icons in the **ribbon (bar)** at the top allow you to definitely accept the meeting, accept it provisionally (if you are not sure) or reject it. Clicking on any one of these icons will drop down a menu where you can choose to send the response, edit the response before sending (so you can add comments or questions) or not send a response. Any response you send is emailed back to the person who invited you. Your response is then updated in their Outlook® Calendar.

Activity: Contact lists

Set up a contact list in Microsoft® Outlook® and use the calendar to schedule appointments such as a meeting with your tutor and lessons over a period of weeks. Refer to section *1.5 Address book* in *Unit 6 Using email*, pages 120–121, for help with this activity.

Check your understanding

1   What is the difference between text messaging and instant messaging?
2   List the benefits of web conferencing compared with traditional meetings in person.
3   Explain what a web log is.
4   What are the benefits of arranging a meeting using Microsoft® Outlook®?

ASSESSMENT ACTIVITY

Your friend, Lena, is setting up a new website to do with your town. She plans to feature profiles of local businesses, reviews of restaurants, recommendations for local attractions, topical news stories and articles, and maps linking to relevant places.

Lena plans to use a wide range of communication mediums to both source information and to share information with the website's users. She has asked you to advise on the ways she can gather and share information.

Task 1

Create a list of the different information sources you think would be useful for gathering information for Lena's website. Provide one pro and one con for each information source.

Task 2

Lena would like some guidance on how to search for and evaluate information on the Internet.

1   Create a step-by-step guide for Internet searches. Use a mixture of screenshots and photographs to illustrate the steps and types of information returned by search results.
2   Create a checklist listing all the things Lena needs to consider when evaluating information sources.

Task 3

Lena is keen to explore the different ways she can use email and other IT-based communication methods to gather and exchange information.

Identify six different ways Lena can do this. For each method, create a fact sheet explaining the following points:

- How it can be used to exchange information
- The advantages of using this method
- The disadvantages of using this method.

Illustrate your fact sheet using screenshots and photos, where relevant.

Using the Internet

You have probably already used the Internet many times. However, this unit will boost any knowledge you have and help you master some of the skills and techniques that IT professionals use all the time.

You will learn how to connect to the Internet and how to make the most of browser settings to surf the Internet easily, effectively and safely. You will learn how to use powerful search techniques such as multiple search criteria and logical operators. This unit will also show how you to bookmark pages so that you can return to them later.

You will use social networking sites to share information, download files, use online forms and publish material on the Internet.

Surfing the Internet may expose you to certain online dangers, so you need to be able to identify threats, reduce risks, surf responsibly, keep personal information secure and stay within the law.

Learning outcomes

After completing this unit you should be able to achieve the following learning outcomes.

> **LO1** Connect to the Internet

> **LO2** Use browser software to navigate web pages

> **LO3** Use browser tools to search for information from the Internet

> **LO4** Use browser software to communicate information online

> **LO5** Follow and understand the need for safety and security practices when working online

1 Connect to the Internet

There are many terms to describe the Internet and its use. Table 5.1 outlines some of the key terms you will need to understand for this unit. You may have heard them before but do you really know what they mean?

Internet	The global system of connected computers that allows the worldwide web to work.
Worldwide web (www)	The massive collection of web pages and sites that link (**hyperlink**) together using mouse clicks. Without the www, you would need to type the address of every website you want to visit.
Internet service provider (ISP)	The company you pay for your Internet connection.
Uniform resource locator (URL)	The address of the website, such as **www.pearson.com**. Every website and page has its own **URL**.
Hyperlink	A connection to another document or web page. Links are often underlined or shown in a different colour so that you can spot them easily. Clicking on a link will take you directly to that document or page.
Web browser	A **browser** (such as Internet Explorer®, Firefox® or Google Chrome™) is used to surf the Internet and to see web pages.
Search engine	A **search engine**, such as Google™, is used to find information on the Internet.
Really simple syndication (RSS) feed	An RSS feed can be used to bring regularly updated live information to a web page, such as from a news channel.
Podcast	A download containing a television programme or other recording that you can play later.

Table 5.1: Using the Internet – key terms

1.1 Connection methods

A connection method is how you can connect to or get access to the Internet. The most common connection method in schools, colleges and workplaces is via a **LAN**. The LAN uses cables (wires) to connect computers to the Internet through a router and a modem. See the section *Hardware requirements*, page 92.

Nowadays, most homes, workplaces and public places with Internet access (such as coffee shops or libraries) use a **WiFi** connection. WiFi uses a wireless radio signal to connect a laptop to the Internet through a router, without the need to plug it into a network cable.

Key terms

LAN – a local area network (LAN) connects computers so they can share information and use resources such as printers and the Internet.
WiFi – uses radio waves rather than wires or cables to send data to and from a laptop or other IT device. Many laptops and smartphones have a WiFi link built into them. WiFi only works over quite short distances, usually 100 m or less.

Your mobile phone may connect to the Internet via your phone operator's network (a **cellular network**) or via a local WiFi connection.

Some organisations use a **virtual private network (VPN)** to connect their computers in different places. A VPN provides a secure connection even though it uses public network connections. Anyone wishing to and allowed to use the VPN will first have to prove who they are (for example, by providing a password).

Today, most Internet connections use **broadband** technology. This is a high-speed connection method (over 1 MB of information can be sent every second) that uses either the telephone cable to a house or office, or a cable television connection. Before broadband was widely available, slower dial-up connection was used.

Dial-up access uses the same connections as your home telephone (landline). It is much slower than broadband and you cannot use the landline while connected to the Internet via a dial-up connection.

See also section *1.5 Communication services* in *Unit 2 IT user fundamentals*, pages 26–27.

Windows® can display the network connections you have available.

> ### How to view available network connections
> 1. Open the **Control Panel** and type **Network Connections** in the search box.
> 2. From the list of results shown choose **View network connections**.
>
>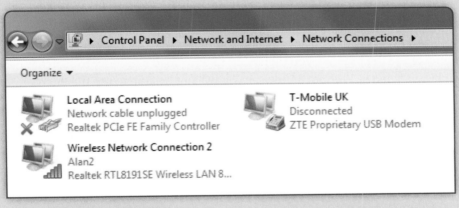
>
> *Figure 5.1: Network connections*

Check your understanding

Identify and describe three IT connection methods.

Key term

Cellular network – a mobile phone system. It is called 'cellular' because the country is divided into cells. Whichever cell you are in will automatically connect to your phone.

1.2 Access the Internet or intranet

You will need a variety of hardware and software to allow you to access the Internet.

Hardware requirements

Modem

This is a device that allows IT systems to connect to the Internet and send/receive information via a telephone line or similar connection. The line could be an Internet-enabled phone line or an optical connection (for example, a television cable) from a company such as Virgin Media, Sky or Carphone Warehouse.

Router

This device splits the connection to the Internet so that you can connect several computers to the same modem. Most modern routers have a built-in modem.

Routers often have WiFi providing a wireless connection to laptops or other devices. If the router is not WiFi, you will need a network cable connecting each IT system to the router.

The **modem** and **router** must be set up so that they can connect to the **Internet security provider (ISP)** and, therefore, to the Internet.

Software requirements

Your ISP (for example, BT, O$_2$, TalkTalk or Virgin Media) will provide the Internet connection software you need (probably on a disk).

Most people using WiFi will set a username and password using WPA2 (WiFi Protected Access 2) to stop anyone else connecting to their system. Once you are connected to the Internet, you then need to download a browser to search for and display web pages. Without a browser, you will not be able to use the Internet.

Intranet

An intranet is like the Internet but is set up and operated by a particular organisation – for example a school, college or company. An intranet can be described as a 'private Internet' where the web pages are controlled and only authorised people can see them.

Activity: Public WiFi

Many hotels now commonly provide Internet access for their guests (through both LAN and WiFi). The LAN connection will be to a public computer (often with a printer) that guests without laptops can use. For WiFi connections guests are given a password to use with their own laptops in their rooms. The hotel may charge for Internet access.

1 Find three examples of public places with WiFi.
2 What are the advantages and disadvantages of public WiFi connections?

2 Use browser software to navigate web pages

You will need to know how to use browser tools and settings to make surfing the Internet more productive and enjoyable.

2.1 Browser tools

There are several key browser tools that you can use to search for and move between web pages (navigate). See Table 5.2 for a full list of these.

Back	This button at the top left of the browser window will take you back to the last page you visited.
Forward	(Top left of the browser window.) This button will let you return to a page you have jumped back from.
Refresh	This button updates the page you are visiting. This is often useful on sites such as eBay™ if you want to see new listings or bids.
Stop	This button stops the current web page from loading. This is useful if a page has frozen or if it is taking too long to load.
Home	This button takes you back to the web page you have set as your **home page**. See section *2.2 Browser settings* for more information about home pages, page 96.
History	The browser keeps track of all the sites you have visited, so you can quickly and easily return to a web page if you need to.
New window	You can choose to open a new web page in a new window rather than in the current window, so that you can have more than one page open at the same time. This tool can usually be found in the **File** menu.
New tab	This is similar to **New window** but allows you to open a new page in a tab within the same window. Tabs are simpler for moving between open web pages.

Table 5.2: Key browser tools and features

You can also use the keyboard to perform certain actions with a browser. For example:

- If you are performing a search, pressing the **Enter** key after you have typed in the search terms (instead of clicking the search button) will run the search.
- Press the **Esc** key to stop the current web page loading (instead of using the Stop button).
- Hold down the **Shift** key while clicking on a link to open the link in a new window.
- Holding down the **Ctrl** key while clicking on a link opens the link in a new tab.

Back button – allows you to move backwards through pages you have previously viewed

Forward button –allows you to move forward through pages you have previously viewed

Address bar – to type in a web address using the keyboard

Refresh button – to reload the current webpage

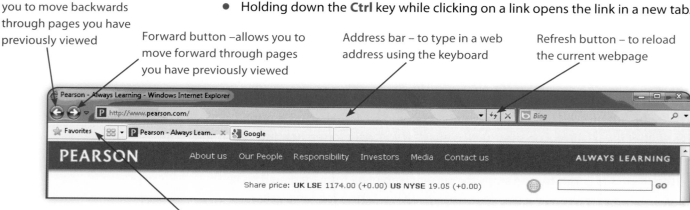

Favorites – allows you to store websites so you can easily find them again

Figure 5.2: Navigation using Internet Explorer®

Click to add a website

Click for options of how to view your Favorites

Examples of Favorite websites

Figure 5.3: Navigation using Internet Explorer®
(History drop-down menu)

Toolbars

Browsers normally provide several toolbars to help you surf the Internet. You can **customise** them from the **View** menu so that you only see the toolbars you use regularly.

- **Search bar**: The search bar will let you search the Web for anything you type into it. The search bar is normally connected to a particular search engine such as Bing™, Yahoo!® or Google™.
- **Address bar**: The address bar can be used to move directly to a specific website. Every web page has an address known as a URL. To go directly to a web page, simply type the URL into the address bar and press **Enter**.
- **Go To**: This option in the **View** menu shows some of the recent web pages you have visited. It allows you to move backwards or forwards to one of these pages or jump to your homepage.

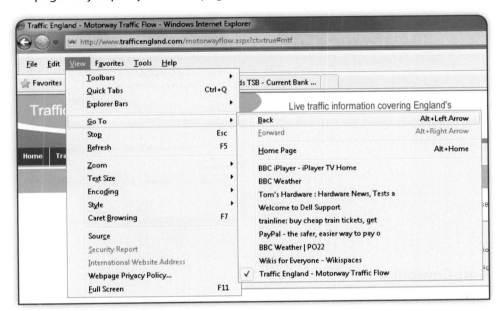

Figure 5.4: Toolbars in a web browser

Activity: Searching the Internet

The Internet offers many opportunities to find a job.

1 Use a search engine and various browser tools to find some job possibilities close to where you live.

2 Produce screenshots to show an example of:
- an agency with job vacancies in your area
- a job that this agency is advertising.

2.2 Browser settings

You can change your browser settings to allow you to use the Internet more easily.

Home page

Your home page is the one that loads automatically when you launch your browser. Therefore, you should choose a website you use a lot or one you like to read first as your home page (for example, MSN®, eBay™, Google™ or an email provider).

How to set your home page

1. Navigate to the website you want to set as your home page.

2. Open the **Tools** menu and select **Internet Options**.

3. In the dialog box that appears, open the **General** tab.

4. Click the **Use current** button and then click **OK** to save your choice.

Next time you open your browser, you will see this website first.

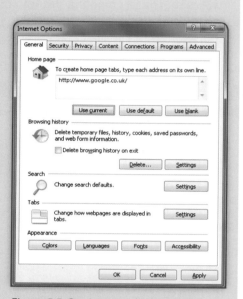

Figure 5.5: Setting your home page

AutoComplete

If the **AutoComplete** option is switched on, your browser will make suggestions every time you type into a web page, listing words you have typed before. For example, it might suggest:

- web addresses when you are typing something in the address bar
- previous search terms when you are typing in the search bar
- your name, address and telephone number when you are filling in a form.

This reduces the amount of typing needed to complete forms. If you are using a public or shared computer to complete a form online, it is a good idea to turn off the AutoComplete option, otherwise whoever uses the computer next may be able to see your details.

How to change the AutoComplete settings in Internet Explorer® 8

1. Open the **Tools** menu and select **Internet Options**.

2. In the dialog box that appears, select the **Content** tab.

3. Below the heading **AutoComplete**, click on the **Settings** button.

4. Change the options to suit you and then click **OK**.

Security

The security settings on your browser should help protect your system from viruses, malware and other online threats.

How to adjust your computer's security settings

1. Open the **Tools** menu.

2. Select **Internet Options**.

3. Click on the **Security** tab and adjust the settings to suit your needs.

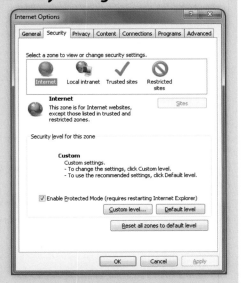

Figure 5.6: Changing your browser security settings

Security settings are covered in more detail later in this unit (page 106) and in *Unit 3 IT security for users*, page 57.

Pop-ups

Pop-ups are windows that open automatically when you view a website. Many websites use pop-ups for advertising or to ask you to complete a survey, but they can be annoying. You can block pop-ups (stop them opening) by selecting the **Turn on pop-up blocker** checkbox in the **Privacy** tab of the **Internet options** dialog box.

Appearance

You can control some aspects of your browser's appearance, such as the toolbars or how web pages are displayed.

How to change the appearance of Internet Explorer®

1. Open the **Tools** menu and select **Internet Options**.

2. At the bottom of the **General** tab is a section headed **Appearance** where you can alter various settings.

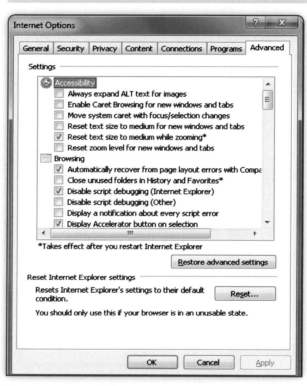

Figure 5.7: Accessibility options

In particular, you can change the **Accessibility settings**, which is very useful if you have trouble seeing the mouse cursor on some web pages. You can specify font sizes, styles and colours, and change the foreground and background colours of web pages. You can set Internet Explorer® to use the colours and fonts you specify in Accessibility settings, your default Windows® colours and fonts, or the settings you have specified in your own style sheet.

Privacy

The privacy options in your browser allow you to control how **cookies** are handled. Most cookies are harmless: they simply remember your preferences on a specific website so that you do not have to reset them or log in again the next time you visit the website.

However, some cookies will send information about you and the websites you visit back to the website owner or to someone else. This information could then be used against you. For example, someone could find out your online banking details and transfer money out of your account. For more on online security, see *Unit 3 IT security for users*.

You can use the privacy settings to **enable** or **disable** cookies, depending on how much you trust the websites you visit.

How to adjust the privacy settings

1. Open the **Tools** menu and select **Internet Options**.

2. Click on the **Privacy** tab.

3. Use the slider to adjust the privacy level or select/deselect the checkboxes to allow or disable pop-ups or cookies, etc.

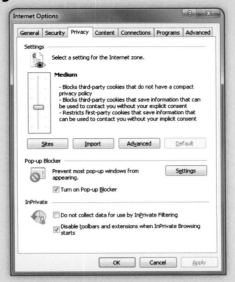

Figure 5.8: Changing browser privacy settings

Search engines

A **search engine** is a program that looks for information on the Internet within a browser. The search engine will show a list of web pages, images and other types of files that use or contain the key words you type in.

One of the most popular search engines is Google™. However, there are many others, including Ask™, Yahoo!® and Bing™. Different search engines may produce different results, so it is a good idea to try more than one, especially if you are struggling to find the information you want.

Zoom

The zoom function makes web pages appear bigger or smaller. To change the zoom setting, go to the **View** menu and select **Zoom**. You can then zoom in (make bigger) or zoom out (make smaller).

You can also select **View** then **Text size** to change the size of the text. However, this may not work for all websites.

Activity: Different search engines

Do you think every search engine gives the same results? Complete the following activity to find out.

1 Open two different search engines, such as Google™ and Ask™.
2 In each search engine, type the same search phrase (e.g. British Prime Minster).
3 Take a screenshot of the results from each search engine. Paste the screenshots into a Word® document and annotate them, pointing out where they are the same and where they are different.
4 Repeat this exercise with two more search phrases. Can you see any similarities in the way each search engine handled the other phrases?

Check your understanding

1 What is a browser?
2 Identify six ways to navigate between web pages.
3 What is a cookie?
4 What is the difference between using zoom and changing the text size?
5 Can you find a website where changing the text size makes no difference?

3 Use browser tools to search for information from the Internet

3.1 Search techniques

Key term

Criterion – a rule or standard used to judge or decide on something (**criteria** is the plural).

Did you know?

Google™ used to show a box after a search where you could type something to search within the results you already had. Now you can search within your results just by typing more words and your search results update themselves as you type. This feature is called Google™ Instant.

The information you find is only as good as the search techniques you use. You must be able to search efficiently to find useful information. Key words are what you use to search for information. The skill here is choosing key words that will find you the most relevant information and improve your searches.

A single search **criterion** is when you type in key word(s) for one thing, such as 'weather forecast', 'holiday' or 'ITQ'. Multiple search **criteria** are when you search for something using two or more sets of key words. For example, if you want to search for a car for sale with a particular engine size you would use the key words 'Car for sale 1.1'. This will bring up cars for sale which also have '1.1' (a 1.1 litre engine) in the web page listing.

To learn more about search techniques, see section *2.2 Use appropriate search techniques* in *Unit 4 IT communication fundamentals*, pages 77–79.

Logical operators

Some search engines allow you to use **operators** such as **NOT** and **OR** to refine your search. The engine will search for every word you type either side of 'OR'.

If you are looking to buy a car with a 1.1 or 1.3 litre engine, typing *Car for sale 1.1 1.3* will show pages where all these words are all present.

If you type in *Car for sale 1.1 OR 1.3* then you will see a lot more individual adverts for cars that have 1.1 or 1.3 litre engines (both engine sizes).

NOT means you are excluding something from your search. Google™ uses a minus symbol – for NOT, which must be positioned immediately infront of the first character of the word you do not want in the search.

For example, if you do not want to see any Ford cars in your search results you can type in *Car for sale 1.1 OR 1.3 –Ford*.

Remember

Operators such as 'OR' or 'NOT' only work if they are in capital letters (uppercase).

Key term

Operators – describe a calculation or comparison. Arithmetical operators such as + work with numbers. Logical operators such as OR work with words. Relational operators – such as > (greater than) – work with both numbers and words.

Activity: Customised searches

1   Create a document with screenshots to show you can search for something you want that is for sale, such as a musical instrument or mobile phone.
2   Start the search with a single word search, then use the techniques you have learned here and in section *2.2 Use appropriate search techniques* of *Unit 4 IT communication fundamentals*, pages 77–79, to refine your search to show the best buys for your chosen item.

3.2 Information requirements

You must be selective about information you find and use and be able to explain how it meets the requirements you are set.

- You need to know where the information comes from and be able to recognise the intention and authority of the provider.
- You should also know the currency of the information, along with how relevant and accurate it is.
- Try to be aware of any bias in the information and whether the level of detail is good enough for your purposes.

To learn more about information requirements and these points, see section *2.3 Evaluate information* in *Unit 4 IT communication fundamentals*, pages 79–80.

3.3 References

If you need to return to a web page, you can look through your browser's **History**. However, this list may be very long and it might be difficult to find the website you want.

If you know you will need to visit a web page again, it is a good idea to save it as a **Bookmark** or **Favorite** (the term used will depend on your browser). When you bookmark a website or add it to your Favorites, your browser will save its URL so that you have a direct link back to that web page.

You can create folders within your Bookmarks or Favorites to store similar links together. For example, if you are looking for a new car, you can make a folder called 'Cars' and save any useful websites in there.

How to add a website to your Favorites in Internet Explorer® 8

1. Navigate to the website you want to save.
2. Open the **Favorites** menu and select Add to favorites.
3. In the **Add a Favorite** dialog box, give your link a name.
4. Select a folder to save the link in or, if you want to save the favourite in a new folder, click the **New Folder** button.
5. The **Create a Folder** dialog box will appear.
6. Type in a name for your new folder and click **Create**.
7. Now click **Add** in the first dialog box to save your link to that folder.

Figure 5.9: Creating a new Favorites folder using Internet Explorer®

3.4 Download and save information

The Internet allows you to **download** and save different types of information from a website or page. If you download and save information, it is very important to use **meaningful filenames** so you can find files easily later.

Before you download or use any information from the Internet, you must be aware of copyright laws. Always look for the © symbol and copyright line identifying the copyright holder. You should also ask permission from the copyright holder where necessary.

You can download:

- images – photographs, artwork, logos, diagrams or anything graphical (usually copyright)
- text – documents about any topic in a number of formats, such as a Word® document or **PDF** files (usually copyright the author or website owner)
- numbers – statistics or financial details of a company etc. (often copyright)
- sounds – ring tones, sound clips or podcasts etc. (usually copyright)
- games – small trial downloads may be available free, but full games cannot usually be downloaded legally without payment (games will always be copyright)
- video – instructional videos, educational videos, news reports (often copyright). It is possible to post videos that are not your copyright to a website such as YouTube, but this is illegal and they will be removed as soon as a copyright issue is identified.
- television – programmes are available from sites such as BBC iPlayer for personal viewing and are usually free to watch or download (always copyright). See also *Information that is continually updated (or live)* in *Unit 4 IT communication fundamentals*, pages 73–74.
- music – it is often free to listen to a song online, but you cannot usually download a song legally without payment (usually copyright).

If you use the Internet to research a project or assignment, you should create a table (similar to Table 5.3) to acknowledge all the sources you have used. Also explain why you chose to use (or not use) the information from those sources. Every source should have a full reference: it is not enough to just put 'the Internet' or 'Google™' as the source.

> **Key term**
>
> **PDF** – stands for Portable Document Format and was developed by Adobe® Systems®. PDF documents use a standard format that any system can read, no matter what hardware, software or operating system it uses.

Information type	Description	Source/location	P/S*	Permission needed if used	Why used/not used?
Text	Definition of 'Upcycling'	Give the full URL	S	None needed	Used to help me understand what upcycling is
Image	Picture of domestic recycling bin	Give the full URL	S	Likely to be protected by copyright; permission needed from supermarket or manufacturer	Project timescales too short to get permission
Image	Photo of recycling bin	Took photo myself	P	None (own photo)	In my web page to advertise my recycling point

Table 5.3: Sources
*P = primary source, S = secondary source

See section *1.3 Copyright constraints on the use of information* in *Unit 4 IT communication fundamentals* for more information on copyright and referencing (acknowledgements), pages 61–63.

Check your understanding

1 Look at work you have previously saved. Can you find any examples of document names you have used that are not meaningful?

2 Can you find an example of material that you are sure is copyright free?

4 Use browser software to communicate information online

You will often want to communicate information over the Internet. For example, you could be creating a podcast; completing an application form; reviewing a film; or discussing your favourite band on a music forum.

4.1 Tools and technique to communicate information

You can share and communicate saved and real-time information in many different ways.

Saved information

- Many radio stations save programmes as **podcasts**. You can download these and play them on an MP3 player (such as an iPod) or using software such as Windows® Media Player®. This means you need not miss any of your favourite programmes.
- **Wikis** are websites that anyone can add to. They provide information and links to related websites. Perhaps the most famous is Wikipedia. You must be careful when using information from a wiki because it may contain mistakes or be incomplete.

Real-time information

- Voice over IP (VoIP) allows you to make phone or video calls using the Internet. For example, you may have used Skype™ to make telephone calls to family abroad.
- Many companies now use **web conferencing** for meetings between people in different offices or even different countries. Each person uses a computer with a webcam and a microphone to talk to the other people in the meeting.
- Social networking sites such as Facebook allow you to keep in touch with friends and get to know new people.
- People might use a **blog** to tell others about themselves and what they have been doing. For example, on a gap year you could set up a blog to describe your travels and share photos or videos.

- Twitter™ is another social networking and microblogging website. It allows people to share their thoughts and ideas in very brief posts of no more than 140 characters.
- Many websites provide real-time information. For example, you may be able to track a parcel to check where it is and when it is likely to be delivered.
- Some people use **peer-to-peer networks** to share music, television shows and films. However, this is illegal if copyright is breached on any of the shared material.
- Many people use **instant messaging** to send short messages to each other. MSN® is a very popular Internet messenger that you may have come across.

For more information on these topics, see section *3 Select and use IT to communicate and exchange information* in *Unit 4 IT communication fundamentals*, pages 81–87.

4.2 Share information sources

There are many ways of sharing information sources with others, for example as links and web pages. You can include a web link in an email or a document by copying the link from the browser address bar and then pasting it into the email or document.

> ### How to send a web page or link using Internet Explorer®
> 1. Select the **Page** button in the toolbar.
> 2. A drop-down menu will appear.
> 3. Select **Send Page by E-mail** or **Send Link by E-mail**.

4.3 Submit information online

When using the Internet, you will almost certainly need to submit (send) information to a website at some point. For instance:

- You may need to fill in and submit a form to set up a new service, such as an email account.
- When buying something online you need to give personal details and payment details.
- You may wish to add a rating, review or recommendation to a shop website.
- You may want to add information to a wiki such as Wikipedia.
- You may wish to join a discussion forum (chatroom) or interactive site to ask for information or advice from people with similar interests.

Netiquette

Whenever you submit information on the Internet, you must consider the proper **netiquette**. For example, you should:

- use the same standards of behaviour online as you would in real life
- respect other people's privacy (for example, do not share information on a social networking site that someone might want to keep private)
- respect other people's opinions – not everyone will agree with you about everything, but that does not make their opinions wrong.

> ### Key terms
>
> **Peer-to-peer networks** – this is when computers in a network work together to facilitate shared access to files and services without the need for a central server.
>
> **Instant messaging** – or IM is a form of communication which involves sending and receiving short text-based messages in real time.
>
> **Netiquette** – guidelines on how to be thoughtful and polite when using email and other IT communication methods; general good behaviour online. For example, typing in capitals is considered to be SHOUTING, which is impolite and should only be used to make something stand out when really needed.

5 Follow and understand the need for safety and security practices when working online

When working online it is important to stay safe and protect yourself and your IT system from any number of threats. Your safety, your personal details or confidential company details could be at risk if you do not take the proper safety precautions.

5.1 Safety precautions

You should be able to identify threats to your safety so you can work responsibly online. The Internet is a fun and interesting world. However, you should be aware of the risks it poses to computer hardware, the security of your personal information and identity – and to you personally.

Use a firewall

Firewalls are designed to stop viruses or other potential risks entering your IT system.

- The firewall checks all the data the computer sends/receives and blocks anything that might be a threat.
- A firewall is the first line of defence against online attacks, so you must make sure it is enabled at all times. Windows® will show a warning if the firewall is turned off.
- Firewall settings can be changed in Windows® or on the router itself.

Use Internet security settings

Internet security settings are in the **Tools** menu of your Internet browser, under **Internet Options**. You can use these settings to control how cookies are stored, whether pop-ups are allowed and how websites can interact with your computer.

The default security level in Internet Explorer® is 'Medium-High'. This means that websites cannot automatically download information or run certain types of content without your permission.

Report inappropriate behaviour and security threats or breaches

When using the Internet, you must report any inappropriate behaviour, especially on social networking sites. Many websites have a tool that allows you to do this. For example, every comment posted on the BBC News website includes a link you can use to report the comment if you think it is inappropriate or offensive.

- You should also follow the rules of netiquette and make sure that your own behaviour online is appropriate. (See *Netiquette* in section *4.3 Submit information online*, page 105.)

- Report any suspected security threat or breach to whoever controls your IT system as soon as possible so that the threat can be removed before too much damage is done.

Use content filtering

Internet Explorer® includes several tools that can filter the content of websites and prevent access to harmful or offensive sites. For example, parental controls restrict which sites children can visit.

Every website is rated according to the language it uses and whether it shows nudity, violence, sexual images, drug abuse or other types of content. You can then choose to allow or block sites according to their rating.

How to enable content filtering

1. Open the **Tools** menu and select **Internet Options**.

2. Open the **Content** tab.

3. Click **Enable** under the heading **Content Advisor** and choose the most appropriate settings.

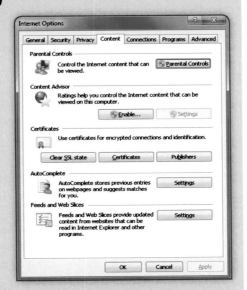

Figure 5.10: Content filtering

Avoid inappropriate disclosure of information

Anything you post on the Internet is open to abuse, so you must be very careful about putting personal information online. This topic is covered in more detail under section *1.4 Protecting access to information sources* in *Unit 3 IT security for users*, pages 64–67.

5.2 Threats to user safety

The Internet is a 'cyber' world and communication online is very different from face-to-face communication. The Internet allows you to communicate with people from all over the world, but it is important to be aware of the risks involved.

Abusive behaviour

Unfortunately, bullying is just as common online as it is in the real world. Online bullying is often referred to as cyber bullying. Cyber bullies may use the Internet to send out embarrassing or personal information about someone. For example, they could post private photographs on social networking sites. Alternatively, they may send abusive or threatening emails or text messages to someone.

Activity: Cyber bullying

1 Have you been affected by cyber bullying, or do you know someone who has?

2 What can be done to prevent online abuse?

3 Does your school, college or company have a 'cyber bullying' policy? If so, find a copy and read it carefully. If not, come up with some guidelines for Internet users in your school, college or workplace to follow.

False identities

Another danger of online communication is that it is very easy for people to lie. This is a common problem on dating sites and in chatrooms. People may create false identities and lie about their name, age, gender, height, weight, occupation, interests and so on. Alternatively, people might try to steal your identity by pretending to be you. This is known as identity theft.

5.3 Information security

You should always keep personal information (such as bank account number, PINs and passwords) secure so that no one else can use them. Make sure your passwords are as strong as possible and never write them down.

For more information on passwords and other online safety topics, see section *1.2 Security precautions* in *Unit 3 IT security for users*, pages 54–60.

5.4 Minimise risk

You can minimise Internet risks in several ways.

- Use email filtering and anti-spam software to block unwanted emails. Millions of emails are sent and received every day and many carry potential threats such as viruses.
- **Anti-virus/spam software** will help protect your computer from viruses. However, it is very important to update anti-virus software regularly.
- A firewall will help protect your system against viruses and hackers.
- Parental controls can check and restrict Internet usage to stop children accessing certain websites.
- Update your operating system and browser software regularly to keep the security tools as up to date as possible. New viruses are being developed and released every day and hackers are constantly looking for new ways to access computer systems.

- Keep away from websites you do not trust and delete any suspicious emails without opening them. Always treat attachments from unknown email sources with caution.

Check your understanding

1 Explain three threats when working online.
2 What do you think are the three best ways to minimise risks from the Internet?
3 How do you think the copyright laws affect your web research and browsing?

5.5 Laws, guidelines and procedures

You should always follow the relevant laws, guidelines and procedures for using the Internet. All organisations (including schools, colleges and workplaces) provide guidelines on safe Internet use. These will outline what learners or employees must and must not do (for example, NEVER open an attachment from an email address you do not recognise).

Activity: Guidelines and procedures

1 Find out what your school, college or workplace guidelines for email and Internet usage are.
2 If you were going to start your own small company, what guidelines would you put in place for your employees relating to Internet security and health and safety?

Relevant laws

As mentioned earlier in this unit, you should be very careful when using material that may be subject to copyright. According to the Copyright, Designs and Patents Act 1988, it is illegal to use the following types of material without permission:

- literary written works (books)
- artistic works, including photographs
- sound and film recordings
- television and radio broadcasts
- cable programmes
- published work.

The Copyright and Related Rights Regulations 2003 is based on the European Union (EU) Copyright Directive of 2001. It modifies the 1988 Act and allows you to use copyright material for educational use if it is for non-commercial purposes (not to make money). However, it is still illegal to download software, music and videos covered by copyright.

ASSESSMENT ACTIVITY

Your friend owns a cafe and would like to set up wireless (WiFi) Internet access for her customers. She has asked you to help her:

- Carry out an Internet search to find out which connection methods she could use. Make a list of the possible methods.

- Carry out an Internet search to find all the cafes and hotels within a 5-mile radius of your home that provide Internet access for their customers. Do any of these cafes or hotels have a Facebook page?

1 Summarise the information you have found for the two requests above and reflect on how relevant and helpful it is. Is it up to date? Is it easy to read and understand? How many searches did you have to do?

2 During your research, make sure you can do the following:

  a use browser tools to navigate between web pages (e.g. **Back**, **Forward**, **Home**, **Refresh**, **Stop**, **History**, etc.)

  b change your browser home page to a website you use regularly

  c experiment with different browser settings (e.g. security, privacy, accessibility)

  d add any useful websites to **Favorites** and create folders within Favorites to organise them

  e send yourself a link to a particularly useful website (send it to your personal email address).

3 As you are working through this question, take screenshots or print out the pages you have viewed as evidence. When adjusting browser settings, you can take screenshots to show the changes you made or ask someone to provide an observation or witness statement describing what you did.

4 Visit a local cafe that provides Internet access and find out how to use this service. Make notes as evidence for your assessment.

5 Advise your friend about potential problems and threats to their customers, including abusive or inappropriate behaviour, identity theft and security threats such as viruses.

6 In a small group, discuss these security issues and decide how your friend could warn her customers about potential risks.

7 Create a code of conduct for your friend's cafe, with at least eight guidelines for users to follow when using the Internet. The guidelines should mention security and legal issues.

Using email

Email is now an essential tool in business and is also widely used for personal communication. Using email is therefore an essential skill that means more than simply being able to send and receive messages.

In this unit you will learn how to use several software tools and techniques to compose and send emails successfully. You will also learn how to stay safe when using email by avoiding risks.

In addition, you will learn how to manage incoming email and responses and how to organise and store emails.

Learning outcomes

After completing this unit you should be able to achieve the following learning outcomes.

» **LO1** Use email software tools and techniques to compose and send messages

» **LO2** Manage incoming email effectively

1 Use email software tools and techniques to compose and send messages

There are two basic ways to access an email account.

Webmail

These systems use an Internet browser to access and manage email. Your emails are stored remotely on the computer servers of the email providers. Examples of webmail systems include Microsoft® Hotmail® and Google Mail™.

Email client

This is a program that runs on a local computer and downloads all emails to a local system. The best known example is Microsoft® Outlook®. You can also use Outlook® to access webmail accounts.

As most businesses use email client, this is the system the unit will focus on.

1.1 Compose and format email messages

When you open Microsoft® Outlook® the main screen shows a list of folders, including **Inbox** (where all incoming emails are stored) and **Sent Mail** (where copies of all the emails you have sent are stored).

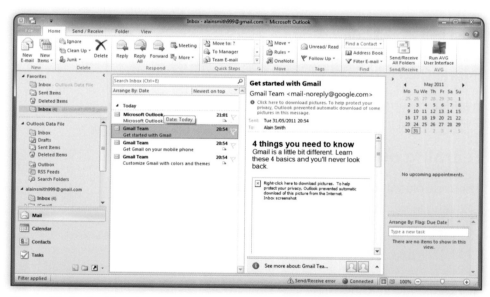

Figure 6.1: Outlook® main screen

A pane next to the folder list shows the contents of whichever folder you have chosen. The **preview pane** shows a preview of the currently selected email.

Composing a new email

The process of composing a new email is very simple.

How to create a new email

1. Click the **New** email icon on the **Home** tab of the toolbar in the top left-hand corner of the main screen. This will open a new message window.

2. Type the email address of the person you are sending the message to in the **To…** box.

3. Enter a subject in the **Subject** box. The subject line should explain briefly what the email is about (e.g. Meeting on Thursday).

4. Then type the main text of the message in the box below.

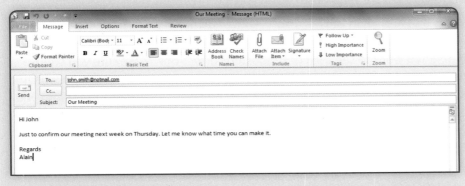

Figure 6.2: New message window

Format text

You can format your emails in many ways to change how they look. The toolbar at the top of the **New** message window has a section with icons for choosing **font** and size. You can make the text **bold**, <u>underline</u> it and/or put it in *italics*. You can also change the text colour and **alignment**.

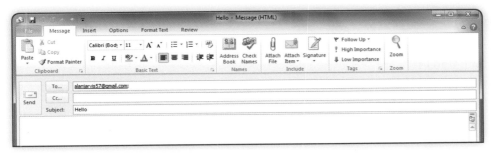

Figure 6.3: The New message toolbar

To change the text format, simply select it with the mouse as you would in a word processing program and click one of the icons on the toolbar. For example, the **B** icon will make the selected text bold. You can choose different fonts from the font drop-down box and change the size from the drop-down box next to it.

Format paragraphs

You can also modify paragraph formats.

- To align a paragraph, put the cursor anywhere in the paragraph and click the left, centre or right alignment icons.
- To add bullets or numbers to a paragraph or list, select the relevant section of text and click the appropriate icon above the alignment buttons.

Spell check

As with any piece of writing, you should make sure the spelling and grammar in your emails are correct. Many word processing programs have a tool (such as Outlook® Spelling) which checks spelling and grammar. You should always use this feature before sending an email you have written.

Words that are not in the Microsoft® Office® dictionary or are spelled incorrectly will be underlined in red. You can use the **Spelling** tool or right click on each underlined word to see a list of suggested corrections. Make sure you choose the correct word from the list. If the word is a name or a technical term which does not appear in the dictionary, you can add it. Make sure that any word you add to the dictionary is spelled correctly, then right click on it and choose **Add to Dictionary** from the dialog box which appears. The word will no longer be shown as a spelling error.

Grammatical mistakes are underlined in green. Again, use the Spelling tool or right click to see suggested corrections.

Activity: Formatting emails

1 Create an email to a friend telling them that you are learning how to use all the formatting features in Outlook® (or other email program). Format different sections of your email to show what you have learned. For example:
   - change the font
   - change the font size or colour
   - make sections of text bold, italic or underlined
   - use different paragraph alignments
   - add a bulleted or numbered list.
2 Take a screenshot of the email you have created and annotate it to show the different styles of formatting you have applied.

1.2 Attach files to email messages

You can send files along with text in an email. For example, if you are applying for a job, you could attach the application form or your CV.

How to attach a file to a message

1. Click the **Attach File** icon in the toolbar to open the **Insert file** dialog box.

Figure 6.4: Insert File dialog box

2. Choose the file you want to attach and then click **Insert**. The attached file will be shown under the subject box in the email window.

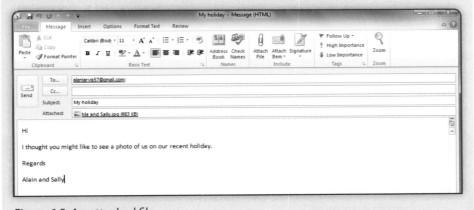

Figure 6.5: An attached file

You can add more files by clicking **Attach file** again. However, you should be aware that some files (for example, digital camera photographs) may be very large. An email with many or large attachments will take a long time to send and a long time for the **recipient** to download.

Email providers may set limits on the size of attachments. If you try to send too many large files, the message may not get sent at all. For example, with Google Mail™ the largest attachment you can send in a single email is 25 megabytes (MB).

1.3 Send email messages

To create a new email, see *1.1 Compose and format messages* earlier in this unit, page 112.

Once you have written your message (including formatting the text and attaching files if necessary), you can click the **Send** button to send the email. This is the basic way to send an email, but there are some more advanced options.

Cc is used to add people who will receive a copy of the email. The message is not addressed to them directly, but it is relevant to them and they need to see it. To enter multiple addresses in the **To…** and/or **Cc…** boxes, separate each address with a comma.

If you have emailed someone before and you are in their address book or contacts list your name will appear next to **From** when they get your message.

Replying to emails

You can click the **Reply** icon to send a reply to the sender of the email.

Clicking **Reply All** will send a reply to everyone the original email was sent to (including people the message was copied to using Cc). However, you should make sure that you do actually want everyone to see your reply before you use Reply All.

When you click **Reply** or **Reply All** a new window will open, complete with the address (or addresses) of whoever you are sending the reply to. The subject will be the same as the incoming email, but with **Re:** (which means 'Reply') at the beginning. You should write your reply at the top of the email, leaving the text of the original email underneath.

The **Re:** will appear when you reply to an email

You will type your email here

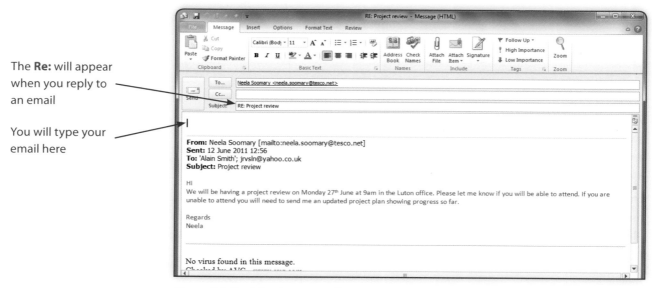

Figure 6.6: Replying to an email

As well as replying to an email, you can also pass it on to someone else. To do this, click **Forward**. You can then enter the relevant email address(es) in the To… box. This is just like sending a new email, so you can also use Cc… if you wish.

- The text of the original email is shown in the lower part of the window and you can type more text above.
- The subject of the forward email will be the same as the original, but with **FW:** added to it.
- When you send a reply, the original email will have a purple arrow next to it in the inbox to show that you have replied.
- When you forward an email, the original email will have a blue arrow next to it.
- The preview pane will show the date and time of your reply or forward.
- Your reply or forward will be saved in the **Sent Items** folder.

Purple arrow will show that
you have replied to this

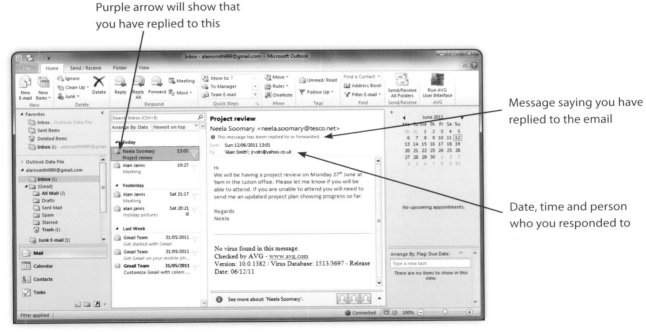

Message saying you have
replied to the email

Date, time and person
who you responded to

Figure 6.7: The 'replied' icon

Activity: Sending and replying to emails

1   Write an email and send it to a friend. Copy in at least one other person (add their email address to the Cc box).
2   Open an email you have received and reply to it.
3   Open an email you have received and forward it to someone else.

Keep copies of the emails you have sent or take screenshots to show that you have completed these three tasks.

1.4 Stay safe and respect others when using email

Email may be a great way to communicate, but it also has its dangers. Email is often used to spread computer viruses, and some people also use it to bully and threaten others. There are also many email scams that try to con people out of their money.

To avoid unnecessary risks, try to follow these guidelines at all times.

1	Be wary of emails from people you do not know. Never open an attachment or follow a link in an email unless you are absolutely sure who the message is from and what the attachment or link is. These attachments or links might contain malicious programs.
2	Be careful also of strange emails (perhaps unexpected or with an unusual subject) from people you know. Some viruses attack email accounts and send messages to all contacts. These emails will often ask the recipient to follow a link to a web page. Check with the person who (it seems) sent the email before following any links or downloading anything. Also make sure your computer's anti-virus software is kept up to date.
3	Beware of emails offering money in return for some service or other. Many scam emails ask you to send your bank details or a fee in order to claim a large prize. If you were to do this it is likely that the person running the scam would then use your details to steal money from your bank account.
4	Beware of emails that ask for your personal details. Phishing emails often appear to come from your bank or credit card company and will ask you to follow a link and provide (or change) your security details. A real financial organisation will NEVER send an email like this. These emails are sent by criminals trying to obtain your personal details so that they can steal money from you.
5	If you receive an abusive or inappropriate email, do not reply to it. Instead, block the sender's address and report the message. See the section *Blocking senders* (page 119).
6	Be very careful before sending photographs of yourself via email and make absolutely sure you can trust the recipient. Once you have emailed a photograph to someone else, it is out of your control. You will not be able to stop them posting the photo to a website or sharing the email with other people.
7	Use language that is appropriate to the purpose of the email. For example, when writing a work-related message you should avoid using slang or inappropriate language.
8	Respect other people's confidentiality. Try to avoid sending your own or other people's personal details via email. Even if you trust the recipient, a hacker may be able to access your account and read your messages.

| 9 | Use **distribution lists** with care. Many organisations provide distribution lists which allow you to send messages to large numbers of people at the same time. (This could mean everyone in a department or everyone in the company.) However, you should not use these lists for personal reasons (for example, to advertise events or items for sale) as you may find yourself in trouble. If you are using a distribution list for work purposes you should consider whether it is appropriate to send the email to everyone on the list. |

Table 5.4: Guidelines

Online security issues are covered in more detail in *Unit 3 IT security for users*.

Blocking senders

It is useful to be able to stop certain people sending you email by blocking their messages.

How to block someone's emails

1. **Right click** on an email in your inbox from the unwelcome sender.
2. Select **Junk** from the menu that appears.
3. Select **Block sender** from the new menu that appears.

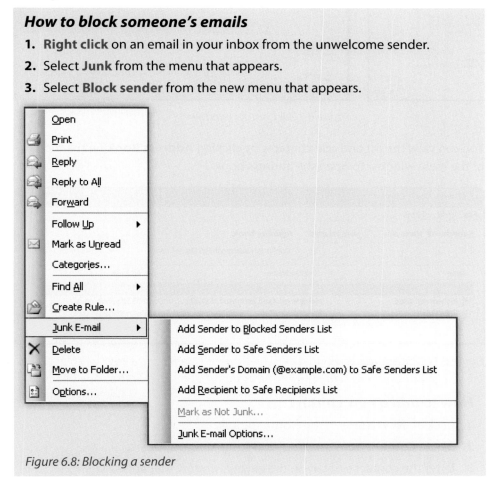

Figure 6.8: Blocking a sender

A message will tell you that this sender has been added to your blocked email list and that the email has been moved to your **Junk E-mail** folder. All future messages from this person will now automatically go in the Junk folder.

1.5 Address book

Using an address book is a good way to keep track of the email addresses of your friends and work contacts. Outlook® calls its address book **Contacts** and there are several ways of adding to it.

The simplest way is to choose an email in your inbox, right click the address in the preview pane and choose **Add to Outlook Contacts**. This will open a **Contact** window where you can add edit (change) the details and add more information about the contact if needed. You can then click **Save and Close**.

Figure 6.9: Adding a contact

Figure 6.10: A Contact window

You can view the list and add contacts by clicking **Address Book** on the toolbar of the main window to open the address book.

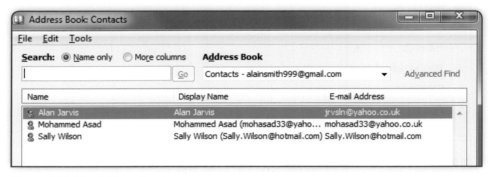

Figure 6.11: The Address Book

How to add a new contact

1. Click on **New Items** in the **Home** toolbar.
2. Select **Contact** from the drop-down menu that appears.
3. Enter the contact's details in the empty window that appears.
4. Click **Save and Close**.

How to amend the details of an existing contact

1. **Double click** their entry in the **Address Book** to open their **Contact** window.

2. Make the changes as needed, then click **Save and Close**.

3. Alternatively, to delete the contact, right click and select **Delete** instead.

If you have a long list of contacts, you can quickly search for someone by typing their name in the **Find contact** box on the main window. (Typing their first name will do, or even just the first few letters of it.) Then press **Enter** and if a match is found, the window for that contact will appear.

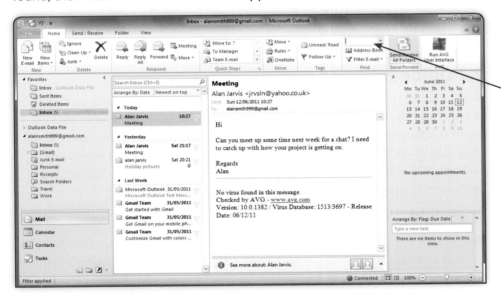

Find contact box

Figure 6.12: The Find contact

How to use a contact when creating a new email

1. Click the **To** button in the **Message** window to open your address list.

2. Find the contact you want to send the email to, click on their name and then click **To** or **Cc** to add their address to the box in your email.

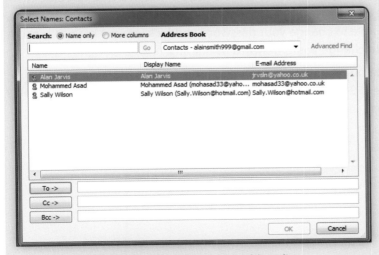

Figure 6.13: Selecting a contact from your address list

Activity: Using contact lists

Create a contact list for everyone in your group doing this course. Practise adding, editing and deleting contacts. Use your contact list to send a welcome message to everyone else doing the course.

2 Manage incoming mail effectively

In this section you will learn how to manage incoming emails effectively by following guidelines and procedures such as netiquette. You will consider how to respond to emails, how to organise and store them and problems you might come across.

2.1 Guidelines and procedures

Most organisations and all schools and colleges will have guidelines on the use of email and the Internet. These outline what you should and should not do when sending emails and explain what is considered inappropriate use of email. They also cover security precautions. For more information these topics, see sections *1.2 Security precautions* (pages 54–60) and *1.5 Security guidelines and procedures* (pages 66–67) in *Unit 3 IT security for users*.

Copyright

Never claim ownership of material (whether text, a photo or video, etc.) that you send as an email attachment. You can use and share content for educational purposes but you should not email the content for non-educational purposes unless you have permission from the copyright owner. For information on copyright, see section *1.3 Copyright constraints on the use of information* in *Unit 4 IT communication fundamentals*, pages 74–76.

Password protection

It is important to keep the password to your email account secret and make sure it cannot be guessed easily. Anyone who knows your password will be able to send and receive emails from your account, which could cause many problems. They will also be able to change your password and lock you out of your account. It is a good idea to change your password frequently.

For more information on password protection see sections *1.2 Security precautions* (pages 55–56) and *1.4 Access to information sources* (page 64) in *Unit 3 IT security for users*.

Netiquette

Be aware of netiquette, which covers behaviour when using not only email but also other electronic forms of communication, such as Internet chatrooms. The rules of netiquette include:

- Do not abuse or insult people.
- Do not send spam (unwanted advertising emails).
- Remember that what you say in an email can be forwarded to other people, so do not say anything you would not want repeated.
- Do not type in CAPITALS (this is considered to be shouting).

Netiquette is also covered in section *4.3 Submit information* of *Unit 5 Using the Internet*, page 105.

2.2 Email responses

Dealing with incoming email involves reading and responding to emails, filing and, if necessary, deleting them. Incoming mail is placed in your inbox. If it is unread it will be shown in bold. The number next to the inbox shows how many unread emails you have.

The number of new emails in your inbox

New email in your inbox

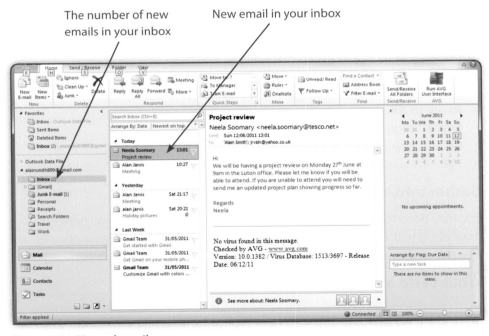

Figure 6.14: Unread emails

Clicking on a message in the inbox will show a snippet of it in the preview pane. Double clicking on the email instead will display it in a new window.

Figure 6.15: Email in a new window

Prioritising emails

You will need to assess and prioritise incoming email. This means you must decide whether you need to reply to it and, if so, how quickly. For example, important emails may need an immediate response but others may just be providing information and will not need a reply.

Decide when and who to copy in

If a message does need a reply, you should consider who needs to see it. For example, if the email was sent to a group of people, you can choose to:

- **Reply to All** – reply to everyone the message was sent to
- **Reply** – reply just to the person who sent the email
- **Cc...** – copy your reply to someone else
- **FW:** – forward the original email to someone else separately from your reply.

Gather information needed to respond

You may need to gather information before responding to an email fully. For example, if you are invited to a meeting you may need to check your diary for a free day or time.

What to do about attachments

If you receive an email with useful or important attachments, you should save them in the **Documents** folder on your computer. If you are forwarding the email, you can choose whether or not to include the original attachments.

Before sending your reply

Before sending your reply, check that:

- you have included everything you need to
- you are sending the email to the right person or people
- you have not made any spelling or grammatical mistakes (use the spell check).

2.3 Organise and store email messages

You should organise and store your messages so that you can easily find them again.

Folders and subfolders

If you receive a lot of emails, folders can help to organise them. For example, you could create separate folders for work-related emails and personal emails.

How to create a folder in your inbox

1. **Right click** on **Inbox** in the column on the left of the main screen.

2. Choose **New Folder** from the menu that appears. This will display the **Create New Folder** dialog box.

3. Type the name of the new folder you want to create in the **Name** box

4. Check that you have the **Inbox** selected in the list of folders and then click **OK**.

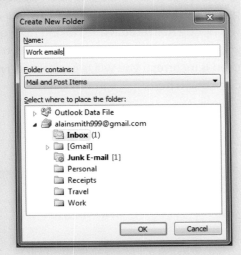

Figure 6.16 Create New Folder dialog box

You will see your new folder listed under the inbox. You can create as many folders here as you want, and also in **Sent Items** and other folders.

To move emails from the inbox, use the mouse to drag them onto the folder you want to put them in on the left of the main Outlook® window.

You can also create subfolders within folders you have created. Just right click on the existing folder and choose **New Folder** again.

Delete unwanted email messages

As mentioned earlier in this unit, you should delete abusive, scam and phishing emails without replying to them. From time to time you should also delete old messages that you no longer need.

How to delete an email

1. **Right click** the message you wish to delete in the list on the main screen and choose **Delete**.

2. If you have the message open in its own window, click the **Delete** icon on the toolbar.

Before they are deleted permanently, messages are moved to the **Deleted Items** folder. If you are really sure you do not want any of the emails in the Deleted Items folder you can empty it by right clicking on the folder and choosing **Empty**.

Remember

Once you empty the Deleted Items folder any emails in it are permanently deleted, so check carefully first.

Address lists

See section *1.5 Address book* earlier in this unit, page 120.

Backups

See section *1.2 Security precautions: Backups* in *Unit 3 IT security for users*, pages 58–59.

2.4 Email problems

The most common problem you may come across when using emails is getting the address wrong. The recipient's email address must be right or the message will not be delivered. When taking note of someone's email address, make sure you write or type it correctly and check it with the person. If an address you have used is incorrect, you will probably receive a notification message similar to the one shown here.

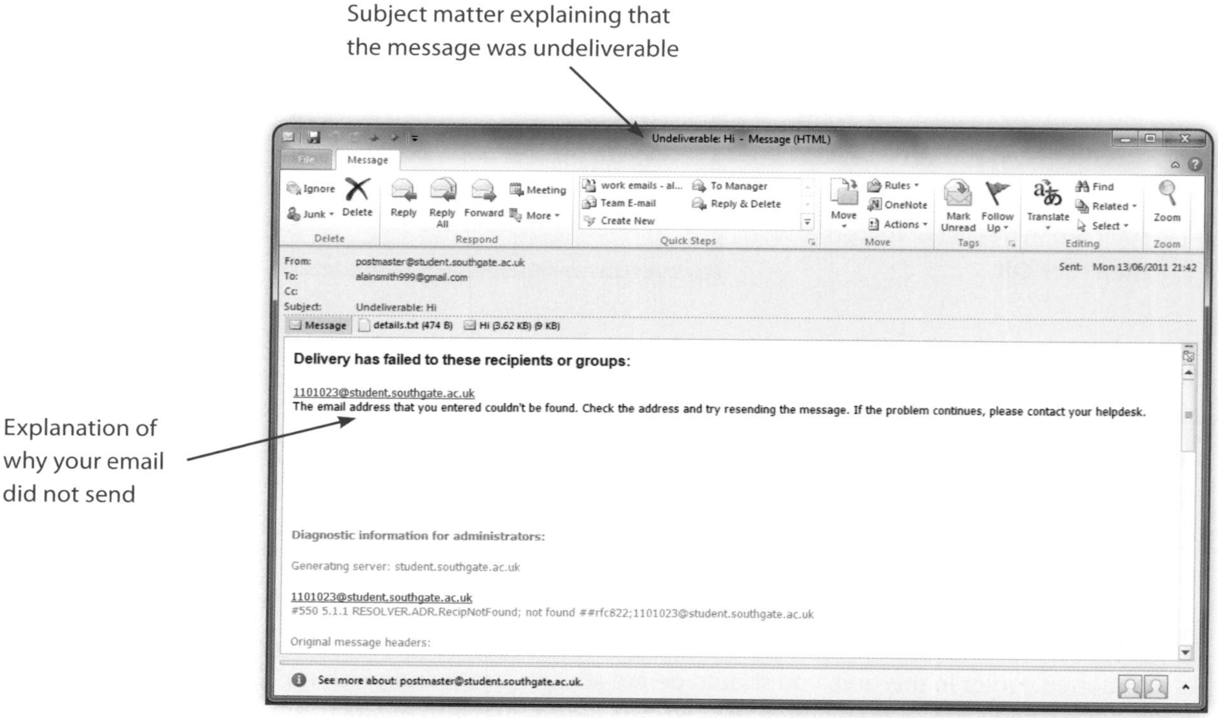

Subject matter explaining that the message was undeliverable

Explanation of why your email did not send

Figure 6.17: Return email notification from an incorrect email address

Email message size or number of attachments

Different email providers have different limits on the maximum attachment size you can send. Therefore, if you are sending several high-resolution digital photos (maybe 2–5MB each) you will need to send several emails with two or three photos attached to each. You should also avoid sending too many attachments at the same time.

Messages from unknown users and viruses

Many advertising and promotional emails include images within the message itself (rather than as an attachment). These can be used to send viruses, so many email programs will hide them, which may make the email look odd.

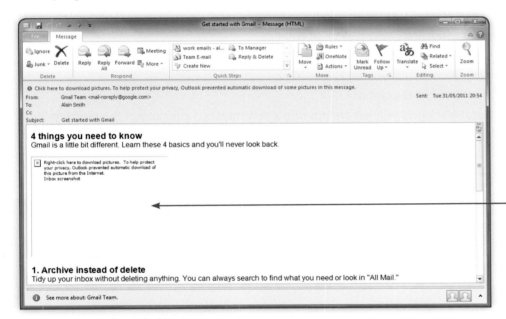

There is an image embedded here but it is hidden unless it is clicked on and you download it

Figure 6.18: Email with hidden images

If you are sure that the email is from a safe source, you can right click on one of the images and choose **Download images** to see the images.

From time to time you will get emails from people you do not know. It is best to delete these messages. Remember:

- Never follow a link in a suspect email, even if it appears to offer something attractive or tempting.
- Never open an attachment from an unknown sender.

Performing either of these actions could allow a virus to infect your computer.

Although you might have signed up to receive news or advertisements from certain companies, these may still be annoying. These are generally known as junk emails. Those you have not signed up for and do not want are known as spam emails.

Remember

You should avoid reading chain messages and phishing emails. More importantly, you should not reply to them.

Other messages you should delete without opening include:

- chain mails, which often ask you to forward the message to others
- phishing emails, which try to get you to send your personal details to someone.

So that you do not receive emails from unknown sources, you can block senders. You will need to do this for each different sender. See *Blocking senders* in section *1.4 Stay safe and respect others when using email* earlier in this unit, page 119.

Check your understanding

1 What is a 'Cc' and what is it used for?
2 Explain the rules of netiquette.
3 Explain the difference between replying to an email and forwarding it.
4 What should you consider when attaching files to an email?
5 How can you block a sender of emails?
6 Why do you need to be cautious when you receive an email with an attachment?
7 How can you create folders within your inbox?
8 You receive an email but the images within it are not displayed. How can you correct this problem?
9 What is spam? How can you deal with it?
10 Explain what phishing is.

ASSESSMENT ACTIVITY

Several people you know have asked you about the ITQ course you are studying. Prepare an email to send to these people.

1 Give details about:
  a how the course is structured
  b the different units you are studying
  c how your progress is assessed.

2 Format the email using a suitable range of colours and fonts. This message is a form of advertising, so it should look interesting and attractive. You should also include a bulleted or numbered list.

3 Write 200–300 words and spell check and proofread your work to make sure there are no errors.

4 Attach a copy of the course specification. You can download this from your awarding body's is website or ask your tutor for a copy.

5 Send the email to your tutor and a copy to someone else. Ask your tutor to reply to your message.

6 When your tutor replies, forward the reply to someone else. Take a screenshot to show that you have done this.

IT software fundamentals

This unit is about the general skills you will need for a variety of software applications available to complete tasks in school, college or the workplace. Although you may only need one software application for simple tasks, more complex ones may require several different applications. Here you will learn how to use the right application to create different types of information. You will also learn the important skill of combining them into a single document.

Learning outcomes

After completing this unit you should be able to achieve the following learning outcomes.

» **LO1** Select and use software applications to meet needs and solve problems

» **LO2** Enter, develop and format different types of information to suit its meaning and purpose

» **LO3** Present information in ways that are fit for purpose and audience

» **LO4** Make effective use of IT tools and facilities to present information

1 Select and use software applications to meet needs and solve problems

1.1 Software applications

With so many different software applications available, it can be difficult to select the right one for a particular task. Table 7.1 lists common applications and examples of their use.

There is, of course, some crossover (overlap) between the applications. For example, you could use a **word processing** program and a **desktop publishing** program to produce a poster. Similarly, **spreadsheet** and **database** programs share many features, although there are also some key differences between them.

Application type	Typical use	Example product name
Word processor	Creating and editing documents such as letters and reports, which can include tables, images etc.	Microsoft® Word® OpenOffice.org™ Writer
Spreadsheet	Entering, calculating, analysing and presenting numerical data	Microsoft® Excel® OpenOffice.org™ Calc
Database	Keeping records of information such as customer details, items in stock, students enrolled on a course	Microsoft® Access® OpenOffice.org™ Base
Presentation	Creating slides to support a presentation. Slides can combine text, images, charts, tables etc.	Microsoft® PowerPoint® OpenOffice.org™ Impress
Email	Creating, sending and receiving emails	Microsoft® Outlook® Hotmail®, Gmail™, Yahoo!®, etc.
Internet browser	Viewing and interacting with web pages	Microsoft® Internet Explorer® Google Chrome™
Graphics software	Creating and editing graphic images	Adobe® Photoshop® Corel® PaintShop Photo™
Desktop publishing (DTP)	Creating complex documents combining text and graphics	Microsoft® Publisher® QuarkXpress® InDesign®
Audio and video editing software	Editing and enhancing audio and video files	Microsoft® MovieMaker® Avid® Studio

Table 7.1: Some application types and examples

A database program will be more suitable if you are working with a large and complex **dataset**. In an application such as Microsoft® Access®, you can create your own forms to enter and view the data or create detailed reports to present data in specific ways. A database also allows you to set controls on the type of data that is entered to make sure it is valid.

Database software has much better search and filter abilities than spreadsheet software, and databases also allow you to link data between multiple lists or tables.

If your task is to produce complex information from different sources, you will first need to decide which applications to use and what sources you will need. This unit uses activities to help you create a set of materials with a variety of applications.

Open and close applications

You can open (launch) software applications in many ways.

How to open (launch) software applications

Below are three different ways to do this.

Option 1

1. Locate the **Desktop** icon. **Double click** on the icon.

Option 2

1. Locate the **Start** button. Click the **Start** button.

2. Then choose **All Programs**.

3. Then scroll through the list and click on the application you want to open.

Option 3

1. Type the name of the application (e.g. Word®, Excel®) in the search box at the bottom of the **Start** menu. Then click on the application in the results that appear.

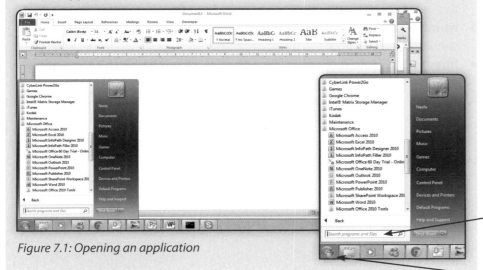

Figure 7.1: Opening an application

Search box

Start menu

How to close an application

1. Click the **Close** icon in the top right of the application window
2. In most applications you can select **Close** or **Exit** from the **File** menu.

Always remember to save your work before you close an application.

Switch between applications

You can run more than one application at a time and swap between them. Icons in the task bar at the bottom of the desktop show which applications are running. Click on the icon of the program you want to switch to. Again, it is a good idea to save your work before switching applications. Although the other application will continue in the background, it may stop responding if too many programs are running at once.

Check your understanding

1 Try the different methods described above to open an application (using the desktop icon, the **All Programs** list and the search box in the **Start** menu).
2 Start up several applications and practise swapping between them using the icons in the **task bar**.
3 Try closing the applications using the different methods described above (**Close** icon and **File** menu).

1.2 Types of information

Before you begin to work on a project, you must identify the types of information needed to complete the task. Make a list of what you will need and where to look for it. For example, if you are asked to advertise a performance by a local band, you might look for the following information.

- **Text**: The name of the band, a brief description of their music, details about the venue, etc. The event organiser will provide this information.
- **Numbers**: The date and time of the gig, the cost of tickets. This information should also come from the event organiser.
- **Images**: You may want to include a photograph of the band. You could get one from the band or take one yourself.
- **Audio**: If you are advertising the performance online, you may wish to include a sample of the band's music, which they should provide.

Alternatively, if you need to create a report on popular products, you could use a program such as Microsoft® Access®.

Remember

It is illegal to reproduce any copyright material without the permission of the copyright holder. Make sure you have permission to use any material you did not create yourself. See section *1.3 Copyright constraints on the use of information* in *Unit 4 IT communication fundamentals*.

Activity: Collecting and presenting information

You have been asked to investigate how satisfied your fellow learners are with various aspects of the course they are on.

● What information will you need?

● How will you collect this information?

● Which software applications could you use to gather and process the information?

● How will you present your results?

Case study: Charity event

Nicky works as a volunteer for a local charity. The charity's director has asked the volunteers to come up with ideas for fundraising events and present them to her.

Nicky's idea is to run a bouncy castle for children at a local funfair. She needs to consider what information to collect and how to prepare her presentation to the director. Nicky has asked for your help in gathering information and preparing for the presentation.

1 Research prices for bouncy castle hire on the Internet. This will be better than using a printed directory (such as Yellow Pages) because you will be able to see what each company has on offer on their website. It will also save you phoning each company for more information.

2 Record all the information you find in a table created in a word processing program. This will make it easier to compare the different companies once you has finished the research. Nicky can then show this information to the charity director.

3 Email the different companies you has researched to check availability and confirm prices for bouncy castle hire. Emails are suitable for this task because Nicky will have the prices in writing if she needs to refer to them later.

Did you know?

If you use Google™ to search for bouncy castle hire companies, it will find companies all over the world, so try using a local directory instead. For example, www.yell.co.uk is an Internet version of the traditional Yellow Pages. You can use this site to search for results in a particular town or postcode in the UK.

Activity: Internet research

1   Search for bouncy castle hire companies in your area. (Search techniques are covered in section 3.1 of *Unit 5 Using the Internet*, page 100.)

2   Use a word processing program to create a table with the following headings:

   a   name of company

   b   telephone number

   c   email address

   d   cost of hire.

   (See section *2.1 Create and modify tables* in *Unit 13 Word processing software*, page 287.)

3   Enter the details of the companies you found for question 1. Once you have filled in the details of four or five companies, save the table. Make sure you give your document a meaningful name and save it where you will be able to find it again.

4   Write an email to someone on your course, telling them that you have done some research about bouncy castle hire companies in the area.

5   Attach your table to the email and send it to your friend.

2 Enter, develop and format different types of information to suit its meaning and purpose

When completing a task – whether at work, in school or college or at home – you must first collect the information you need. Then, in order to prepare it for the purpose, you may need to:

- organise it so you can find it easily and keep it safe
- format and edit it
- combine different types of information in a single document
- adjust the page layout of the final document.

The next section looks at these steps in more detail.

2.1 Organise and format information

You should organise your information so that it is safe and you can find it easily. Searching through lots of folders every time you need a file will waste a lot of time. It is wise to save your documents in separate folders. For example, you could create a folder for each unit of this course to keep all your assignments together.

Here are some tips for organising information.

- Keep all files related to a current project in one folder.
- Create subfolders within the main folder to store different types of information.
- Give every file and folder a unique, meaningful name – do not use default filenames such as Doc1 or Sheet1.
- Make regular backups of your work.

These topics are covered in detail in *section 2 Organise, store and retrieve information* in *Unit 2 IT user fundamentals*, pages 28–32.

Table 7.2 shows some formatting features and techniques you can use in your work.

Headings	Useful to break up a long document. Each section will normally cover a different topic. Headings are normally formatted to stand out from the rest of the text. They are often in bold and/or larger or a different colour.
Lists	Can provide variety in a long, text-based document. Use bullet points or numbering to make a list easier to read.
Tables	Can present sets of data and help make them easier to understand. For example, Table 7.1 at the beginning of this unit lists different applications and their uses (see page 130).
Sorting	Can vary how data in a spreadsheet or database is presented and make it easier to understand. For example, you could sort information about football teams by number of points or goals scored.
Charts and graphs	Very useful for presenting numerical data, as it can be very difficult to spot patterns or trends in a table full of numbers. A graph or chart should make it easier to see what is happening.
Records	Present data relating to one thing (for example, customer records may contain name, address, telephone number, etc.). Records are mainly used in databases, but are also found in spreadsheets and tables.
Calculations	Such as totals, percentages and averages – allow you to interpret numerical data in different ways.

Table 7.2: Formatting features and techniques

Text-based information

With text-based information, you should consider formatting features such as bullets, numbering, alignment, tabs, tables and line spacing. You can also change the appearance of the text by using different colours or font styles and sizes. You will find more information about formatting techniques in section *3 Use word processing tools to format and present documents* in *Unit 13 Word processing software*, pages 290–296.

Numerical information

You can also format numerical information in many ways. Spreadsheet and database applications allow you to set how many digits are displayed after the decimal point (for example, 1.1 shows one decimal place, 1.12 shows two decimal places). This would be useful in scientific and financial applications.

You can also apply specific numerical formats, including:

- **Currency**: In a spreadsheet, if you apply the currency format to a cell, the program will automatically place a currency symbol (e.g. £ or $) before the number, and two digits after the decimal point (e.g. £2.99).
- **Percentage**: This format will add a percentage symbol (%) after the number.

Images

You can adjust the size or position of images, or change features such as brightness and contrast. Formatting images is covered in more detail in *Unit 9 Imaging software*.

Activity: Charity event flyer

You work for a small charity. To raise money for the charity, you have decided to run a bouncy castle at a local funfair. You need to create a flyer to promote the charity and the event you are organising.

Your flyer must include:

- some text explaining what the charity does
- some details of your fundraising event, including a photograph of the bouncy castle
- updates on some of the other projects the charity is working on.

Write some text to cover these points. (You may base your text on information about a real charity.) Organise and format the information using your word processing and image formatting skills.

2.2 Editing techniques

You will probably need to edit your information to make it suitable for the purpose you have in mind. Table 7.3 outlines some useful techniques, but these are covered in more detail in *Unit 9 Imaging software* and *Unit 13 Word processing software*.

Select	You must first select any text or image before you can edit or format it.
Copy	This makes a copy of the selected text or image and stores it on the clipboard. The original text or image is left in place. You can then paste the copy elsewhere.
Cut	This also moves the selected text or image to the clipboard, but deletes it from the original location. As with **Copy**, you can then paste the selection in a new location.
Paste	Use this with **Cut** or **Copy** to move the contents of the clipboard to a chosen place in a document. You can usually **Paste** the same piece of information more than once.
Undo and Redo	**Undo** reverses an editing action and is very useful if you do something by mistake. **Redo** repeats the last editing action.
Drag and drop	This is useful for moving text or images without using Cut/Copy and Paste. Select the text or image, click and hold down the left mouse button and drag the selection to a new place. To copy the selection, hold down **Ctrl** as you drag it.
Find	Use this to search for specific words or phrases in a document.
Replace	This is used with the **Find** function and allows you to replace a specific word or phrase. This is useful if you need to change text often in the same document (for example, '&' to 'and').
Insert	This allows you to add content in the middle of existing material – for example, a new row or column to an existing table or spreadsheet.
Delete	Used to remove text, images or other parts of a document.
Size, crop and position	These are used to edit images. **Size** makes the image larger or smaller and **Crop** removes unwanted parts of the image. **Position** controls the image's place and how text fits around it.

Table 7.3: Editing tools and techniques

2.3 Combine information

Once you have collected all the information you need and edited it as necessary, your next step is to combine the information from different sources into one product. This might be, for example, a report, web page, blog or presentation.

If you have used different software applications to edit images and text, you should bring the information together with an application that best suits the final presentation of the product. For example, if you are aiming to produce a web page, you could use web page development software such as Dreamweaver®.

Annual product numbers per region

Over the course of a year, product numbers varied dramatically. There was also a sharp contrast between the regions.

	Jan-Mar	Apr-Jun	Jul-Sep	Oct-Dec
East	5683	3456	9903	3467
West	5673	2345	6748	3468
North	12345	9056	7899	4567
South	9056	5436	3456	7843

Annual sales figures

The sales figures for the year have been broken down by quarter.

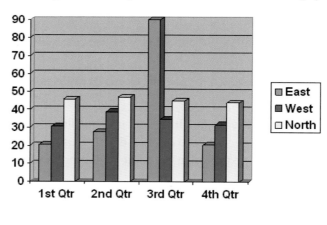

Figure 7.2: A report may combine text, tables and charts

All software applications allow you to combine different types of information.

- A word processed document may contain text and images.
- A spreadsheet program can also be used to produce charts or graphs.
- A presentation program can combine text, images, videos, sound effects and more.

2.4 Page layout

If your document is clear and neat, it will be much easier to read and understand.
If not, it may confuse the reader. It could also draw their attention to its faults
rather than the information in it. Table 7.4 lists layout options to help you present
your work effectively.

Size	You can choose from several paper sizes. A4 paper is generally used for everyday purposes. A5 (half the size of A4) is good for flyers, while A3 (twice the size of A4) may be better for posters.
Orientation	Portrait orientation has the paper with the short edge along the top and the long edge down the side, while landscape has the long edge along the top. Portrait is most commonly used for letters, reports and textbooks. Landscape is often useful for tables or spreadsheets where there are more columns than rows.
Alignment	Paragraphs of text can be aligned to the left, centre or right. In books, newspapers/magazines, reports etc, text is usually justified. This means it is spread evenly across the page so that it aligns at the left and right.
Margins	Margins are the gaps around the edge of a page. If the margins are narrow you can fit more text on the page; however, this may make your document look overcrowded.
Page breaks	Word processing software adds a new page to your document as each page fills up. Spreadsheet software will also split a large document into several pages for printing. If the automatic page breaks do not fall in a suitable place, you can adjust them.
Page numbers	These are important in large documents, as they help readers find their way around. You should add page numbers and dates to all your assignment work. They can be added automatically as part of a header or footer, but are usually placed at the bottom of the page.
Headers and footers	These are word and/or numbers printed at the top and bottom of every page. They are most commonly page numbers but can also provide information such as the document title or author, or the date and time the document was created or printed. It is a good idea to add your name to the header or footer for all assignment work.

Table 7.4: Layout options

Activity: Page layout

1 In Microsoft® Word®, open a new page.
2 Check the page size and, if necessary, change it to A4.
3 Change the orientation to landscape and the margins to 1.8 cm all round.
4 Add page numbers in the centre of the footer.
5 Add a header, with your name on the left-hand side.
6 Add the date and time on the right-hand side of the header.
7 Add some of your favourite photos to the document, each with a text caption describing the photo.
8 Size and position the photographs neatly and consistently.
9 Save the document as 'MyPhotoAlbum' and print out a copy.

3 Present information in ways that are fit for purpose and audience

3.1 Work accurately and proofread

It is important to check the end product for accuracy and correctness. An inaccurate or incorrect document may be misleading and will not be effective. For example, if a leaflet advertising a new company is full of mistakes, potential customers will assume the business is disorganised and poor. The leaflet will not be effective and may put people off.

Making sure a document is accurate involves several things.

Ensure meaning is clear

Read the document to check it makes sense. It is easy to make mistakes when typing, and the spell checker only highlights wrongly spelled words. If you type 'not' when you mean 'now', the spell checker will not highlight it.

Ask for feedback from other people

It is hard to spot errors in your own work because you tend to read what you meant to write rather that what you actually did write. Therefore, it is a good idea to ask someone else to read through it and point out any mistakes you may have missed. They may also be able to suggest improvements.

Consistent layout and format

A document with different fonts and inconsistent formatting will look very poor. Documents such as reports and presentations should be consistent. For example, you should use the same font and size for titles, headings and subheadings. All the main text should also be in the same font and size.

Spell check and proofread

A badly spelled document or one with grammatical errors may be hard to understand and distracts from the purpose of the document. Microsoft® Office® underlines words it thinks are spelling mistakes in red and grammar errors in green. However, not all applications have a spell checker.

Check for accuracy

Your data must be accurate. This is especially important if, for example, you are entering telephone numbers or email addresses into a database or spreadsheet. A telephone number with one digit wrong is no good to anyone.

Check calculations

It is particularly important with spreadsheets that you check the formulas are doing the calculations correctly. It is easy to enter a formula which appears to produce the correct results but is actually not doing the calculation it should be doing. You should therefore check some sample calculations with a calculator to make sure they are correct.

Remember

When sending work-related emails, you must use appropriate language and formatting. Text-style abbreviations (such as 'gr8' for 'great') and emoticons (such as ☺) are fine for messages to your friends, but you should not use them in **formal** messages.

Key term

Formal – according to official or recognised, rules, standards or structure.

Did you know?

In the workplace, the materials you produce reflect your own personality and attitude to work. Messy, inaccurate work with poor spelling and grammar will reflect badly on you.

Use print preview

This is a handy tool found in most Microsoft® Office® applications. It is a good way of saving paper as you can see how your work looks and make sure you are happy with the layout before you print it.

> **Activity: Quality issues**
>
> Working with another learner, look through some of the work you have produced recently. Try to identify any quality issues or inconsistencies in the work. For example, you might find that graphics or images are of poor quality or need to be cropped or resized; or you might find some headings are in a different font from others.

3.2 Produce information that is fit for purpose

Whatever type of document you are using, you need to consider the intended audience and make sure it meets their needs. You need to get your message across clearly. Here are some points you should think about.

Age

A document aimed at young children should look different from one aimed at an older age group. For example, older people may struggle to read information in a small font or with too many bright colours.

Level of IT knowledge

When producing documents on technical subjects – such as how to use email or create a database – you should consider how much expert knowledge your audience might have. Users with IT knowledge and experience will not need as much detail as new users.

Understanding of English

If your audience has a limited understanding of English, you will need to use fairly simple language – or explain difficult words.

You also need to consider the purpose of a document in relation to its overall tone. This is called being fit for purpose. For example, a poster reminding people about health and safety rules on a building site must be clear and to the point, while a poster advertising a music gig can be less formal.

Formal documents that provide important information (such as invoices or stock lists) must be formatted so that the information is clear and easy to understand. For example:

- You could use tables and currency formatting to make numbers easier to read and understand.
- You should include clear headings so that it is easy to work out what each set of numbers is showing.
- Charts and graphs will make it easier to understand financial or numerical information (for example, in a budget report).

Activity: Fit for purpose

If a document is fit for purpose, the information it contains and how you have presented it is appropriate for the audience and the task in question. Complete the following tasks, making sure that the documents you produce are fit for purpose.

1 Write a letter aimed at children (8–10 years old) inviting them to an after-school club. Then write a letter aimed at people over 65 inviting them to a lunch club. Make sure the language and style you use in each letter are appropriate to the audience.

2 Write a set of instructions for someone with very little knowledge of IT, explaining how to scan a USB memory stick for viruses.

3 Modify the instructions you wrote for question 2 so that they are suitable for someone with English as a second language.

4 Make effective use of IT tools and facilities to present information

4.1 Review the effectiveness of the IT tools selected

As well as reviewing and improving your work you should also consider how effective the applications were that you used to complete the task. Here are some things you might consider.

Did I use the right applications?	For example, would a database have been a better choice than a spreadsheet? Or would a desktop publishing program have been better than a word processing program?
Did I have the knowledge and skills needed to use the application effectively?	There may have been editing or formatting tasks you struggled with.
How long did it take to complete the task?	If it took a long time, why? Would you be able to do it quicker next time (as your skills increased)? Was it just a slow and fiddly process to get the result you wanted? (Remember, the higher the quality of the result you want, the longer the task is likely to take.)
Did I have any problems with the software?	Were there any features you could not make work? Did the program crash or mess up your work?
What were the costs involved?	Did you need to buy any new software? Did the document need to be printed in colour? (Colour ink costs much more than black ink.) Were there any other costs involved? For example, did you need to buy extra equipment or consumables such as special paper, memory sticks, CDs, DVDs, etc.?

4.2 Review and modify work

When producing high-quality material it is unlikely that you will get everything right first time. You will need to refine and improve your work before you arrive at a final version.

You should review the quality of the information you used. This is covered in detail in section *2.3 Evaluate information* in *Unit 4 IT communication fundamentals*, pages 79–80.

You will also need to review the work you produce using this information. It can be difficult to review your own work properly, so it is often better to ask someone else to review it and suggest improvements.

You should produce draft versions of your work. Start with a simple sketch of your document (which can be hand drawn). Check this against the requirements you identified at first to see if it meets them. You should also show your draft to the intended audience to check they are happy with it.

Stop and review your progress from time to time. Again, check back against the initial requirements, as it is very easy to lose track. A particular aspect or part of the project may grab your interest. In this case you could end up spending a lot of time on that aspect (which may not be required), while forgetting other important aspects.

ASSESSMENT ACTIVITY

Some students from the Netherlands are visiting. You have been asked to prepare a presentation to give to them about your school, college or workplace and the course you are doing.

1   Make a list of the information you will need and where you will get it from. For example, you might need to look on the school, college or company website for background information. You will also need photographs, maybe of outside and inside the buildings and of your classmates/colleagues. You could even make a short video.

2   Collect the information you need and format and edit it as required. Organise the data by creating a folder to store all the text and photos you will be using.

3   Select suitable software for creating your presentation and combine all the information. Make sure you choose an appropriate page layout so that the information is clear and effective.

4   Check your completed presentation carefully for spelling, grammar and layout errors and correct it as required. You should also think carefully about the learners you have prepared the presentation for. For example:

   a   Is the level of English suitable? The Dutch visitors speak English quite well but it is not their first language. Make sure your language is clear and not too complex.

   b   Does it provide a good overview of your school, college or workplace that will interest young people?

   c   Have you chosen the most appropriate layout? What would you change if your presentation was aimed at older people?

5   Ask a friend to check the presentation for mistakes or anything that could be improved. Make any improvements or corrections suggested.

6   Discuss your presentation with your tutor/supervisor and explain your choices in terms of the information you included, the formatting you used, the page layout you chose etc. Explain how effective the IT tools you chose were in meeting the needs of your presentation.

Database software

Database software is at the centre of most organisations' IT activities and is the reason why many IT systems exist. Organisations need a lot of information about their customers, products and staff. Databases store that information. More importantly, they provide exactly the right amount of detail to everyone who is authorised to receive it.

In this unit you will learn the basic skills and knowledge to set up and use database software. You will also practise using tools and techniques needed to input basic information.

You will retrieve information by creating and running queries, and produce reports to show this information. The database you set up will be single in a flat file database, which looks rather like a spreadsheet (which are covered in *Unit 11 Spreadsheet software*).

Your table will only hold a few records so you can see how it works. This is of course much smaller than the databases used by organisations, which often hold millions of records.

Learning outcomes

After completing this unit you should be able to achieve the following learning outcomes.

» **LO1** Enter, edit and organise structured information in a database

» **LO2** Use database software tools to extract information and produce reports

1 Enter, edit and organise structured information in a database

1.1 Database components

You should be able to identify the main components of a database.

- Tables hold all the information in the database (the **dataset**). A table looks similar to a spreadsheet, but without the calculations. Tables are very useful for making sure data is correct because there are many ways to for mistakes.
- Queries are used to prepare data in the tables for forms and reports. Queries can perform calculations, join tables together in a **relational database** and/ or sort the data into whatever order is needed.
- Forms show information on the screen, allow you to enter data easily and allow you to move around the database using buttons.
- Reports are for printing. Most databases allow you to produce several different types of report, each showing the data in a different way.

Key terms

Dataset – a database store of information in tables. This information or data can be made into a dataset in many ways, for example by running a query, joining tables together or reducing the number of fields. The original data in the tables will not be changed and the dataset can then be used by forms or in reports.

Relational database – uses more than one table to hold different types of information and uses queries to combine this data and produce reports.

```
Table  ➡  Query  ➡  Dataset
 ⬇                      ⬇
Form  ⬅  Navigation  ➡  Report
          form
```

Figure 8.1: Database components

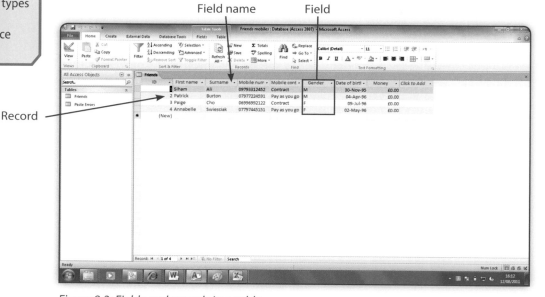

Figure 8.2: Fields and records in a table

1.2 Enter structured data

Before you can enter any data, you will need to create a new database.

How to create a new database

1. Open Microsoft® Access®.

2. Select **Blank database** from the options on screen.

3. Type a name for your database in the **File Name** box on the right-hand side of the screen.

4. Click the **Create** button to start the database.

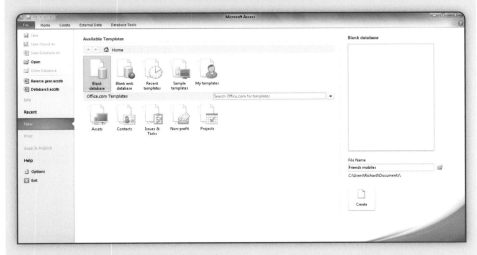

Figure 8.3: Creating a new blank database

Before you can populate (fill) your new database, you need to create a table to store the information that the database will use. IT professionals prefer to use the **Design View** to create their tables.

How to open the Design View

1. Press the **View** button.

2. Select **Design View**.

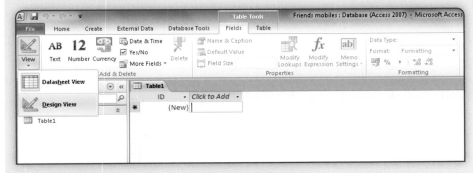

Figure 8.4: Creating a new table using the Design View

continued

3. When you select **Design View**, a **Save As** dialog box will appear. Type the name of your table into this box.

Figure 8.5: Naming a new table

4. Once you have named and saved your table, you will see the **Design View** of the new table you have created.

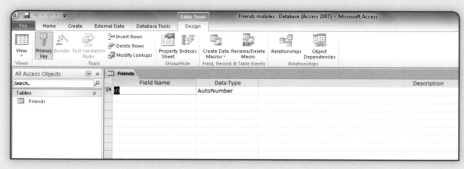

Figure 8.6: The Design View of a new table

Your table will store a lot of records, and each record will include many **fields**. For example, in a database of customer data, each record will hold data about an individual customer. Within these records, each field will hold one piece of data about that customer – for example, their name, address, telephone number and so on.

Add new fields to your table

The first field is called ID and is created automatically whenever a new table is created as the **primary key**. The data type of this field is **AutoNumber**, which means that a new number appears in this field whenever you enter a new record.

Other fields need to be defined (named) for this table. As you add each new field, you can define the data type to be used so that Access® can check the accuracy of the data entered. For example, if you set the data type to **Date/Time** for the date of birth field, the program will check that you have entered a valid (proper) date. Figure 8.7 shows the drop-down list of data types that you can choose from.

Key term

Primary key – a database table usually has a primary key which is used to make sure every record is different. The primary key can also automatically sort the table into order. Microsoft® Access® sets a default primary key ID to every new table which has an autonumber data type. This automatically enters a number for each new record.

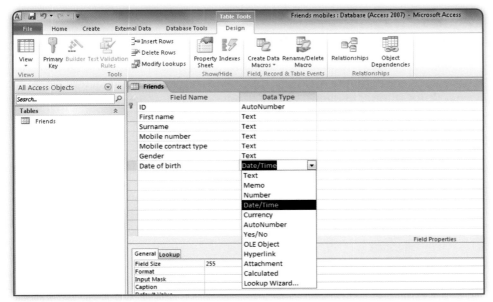

Figure 8.7: Setting the data type for a new field

Activity: Creating a database table

As you work through this section, try creating a database for yourself.

1 Create a new blank database.
2 Open **Design View** and, when the **Save As** box appears, call your table 'Mobile numbers'.
3 Add the following fields to your table:
   a First name
   b Surname
   c Mobile number
   d Mobile contract type
   e Gender
   f Date of birth.

For these fields, you can use the default setting, which is a text data type.

4 Add two more fields to your table:
   a Date of birth – set the data type to date/time
   b Money – set the data type to currency.

Set field length/size

Once you have created all the fields you can set the **Field Size** if necessary. This controls how many characters you can fit into a given field.

- The field length for the mobile number field should be 11 characters, since this is the number of digits in a mobile phone number (see Figure 8.8).
- The field length for gender should be one character, since you will only enter M (male) or F (female) in this field.

Figure 8.8: Setting the Field Size

Create a list box

You can set up your database so that you have a choice of entries for any given field. For example, in the **Mobile contract type** field, you might want **Pay as you go** or **Contract** options.

How to create a list box

1. Select the **Mobile contract type** field.

2. Select the **Lookup** tab.

3. Choose **List Box** (see Figure 8.9).

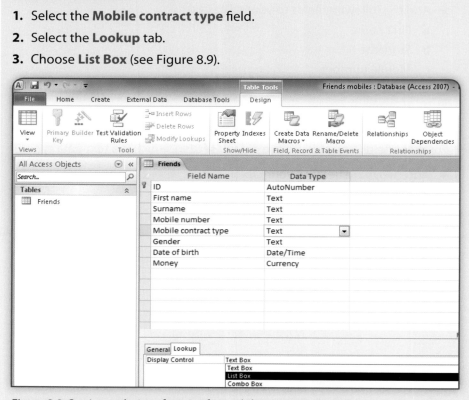

Figure 8.9: Setting a choice of entries for mobile contract type (1)

4. Select **Value List** as the **Row Source Type**.

5. Click '**…**' at the right-hand side of the **Row Source Type** box (see Figure 8.10).

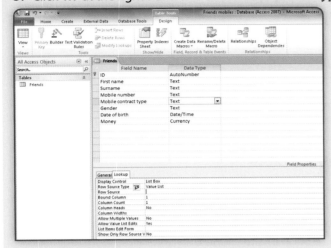

Figure 8.10: Setting a choice of entries for mobile contract type field (2)

6. Select **Value List** as the **Row Source Type**.

7. A dialog box will appear, called **Edit List Items**.

8. Enter your choices for the mobile contract type field and click **OK** to complete.

Figure 8.11: Setting a choice of entries for mobile contract type field (3)

9. Once you have finished setting up your fields, click on **View** to switch to the **Datasheet View**. You must save your data before you can change view (see Figure 8.12).

Figure 8.12: Saving changes to a table

continued

10. Datasheet View looks like a spreadsheet. Here, you can enter your data (see Figure 8.13).

Figure 8.13: Datasheet View of an empty table

Populate your database table

Now that you have created a table in your database, you can populate it by entering some **structured data**. The example in this section is structured so that each record has content for First name, Surname, Mobile number, Mobile contract type, Gender, Date of birth and Money.

Activity: Customising your database table

Open the table you created for the previous activity. You should have called it 'Mobile numbers'.

1 Set the size for the following fields:

   a Mobile number – set to 11

   b Gender – set to 1.

3 Create a list box for the Mobile contract type field so that you can choose between 'Pay as you go' and 'Contract'.

4 Add the following data to your table, so that it looks like Figure 8.14.

First name	Surname	Mobile number	Mobile contract type	Gender	Date of birth	Money
Siham	Ali	09793312452	Contract	M	30-Nov-95	£0.00
Patrick	Burton	07977224591	Pay as you go	M	04-Apr-96	£0.00
Paige	Cho	06996992122	Contract	F	09-Jul-96	£0.00
Annabelle	Swiesciak	07797445151	Pay as you go	F	02-May-96	£0.00

5 Add the details of six friends, so that you have ten records in total.

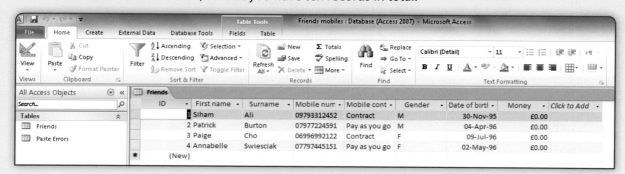

Figure 8.14: Datasheet View of a table with records

1.3 Locate and amend records

You will need to locate (find) some records in your table and make changes. It is easy to find records in a small database such as this. Just use the arrow keys on the keyboard or the mouse to move around the table and look for the records that need changing.

Once found, you can amend data in a similar way to a spreadsheet. You can highlight and type over data to replace it. To change part of a field, click on it with the mouse or use the **F2** key to enter edit mode.

In a larger database, you can search and replace in tables in the same way as in other Office® applications. See section *1.1 Software applications* in *Unit 7 IT user fundamentals*, page 130. You can also use sorting and queries to order your data so that you only see records with specific characteristics. Sorting and queries are covered in more detail in section *2 Use database software tools to extract infomation and produce reports*.

1.4 Data entry errors

Databases are make sure that the data entered into a table is accurate. IT professionals spend a lot of time setting up their tables to check that the data is valid. Your 'Mobile numbers' database has **data validation**, so any errors may be due to:

- **field size** – if too many characters are typed in the Mobile number or Gender field
- **data type** – if an invalid date (e.g. 35th April) is typed into the Date of birth field
- **validation** – if you try to type something other than 'Pay as you go' or 'Contract' in the Contract type field.

If you come across any other errors, or if you are not sure how to correct an error, you can use the Help function. Click on the question mark in the top right-hand corner of the Access® window. You can then search for help on a specific problem or browse through the answers to frequently asked questions (FAQs).

1.5 Check data

Your database must be well structured, error-free and consistent in order to communicate information effectively. If your database is inaccurate, it will not be much use. For instance, a phone number with one digit wrong is no good to anyone.

- Use the Access® spell check tool to make sure there are no spelling mistakes in your database.
- Print your data and read it again carefully. It is a good idea to ask someone else to help you check your database: they may spot errors you have missed.
- As long as each field has been set to the correct data type, it will be difficult to make formatting errors. However, text fields are fairly flexible, which means they can be changed easily. Check the data in these fields particularly carefully.

> **Key term**
>
> **Data validation** – when a table checks that data is valid using techniques such as the size of a data entry. For example, a mobile phone number can be validated to ensure it has 11 characters.

- Check your data for consistency. For instance, make sure you have given numbers the same number of decimal places or used uppercase and lowercase letters in the same way in certain fields. If several different people are entering data into a database, inconsistencies can appear. For example, one person might type surnames as 'Smith' or 'Jones', while another person might put each name in capital letters (as 'SMITH' or 'JONES'). This is inconsistent and will make your database look less professional. It may also make your data more difficult to read when printed.

If you do notice any errors during proofreading and checking, you must correct them.

Check your understanding

1   Explain the terms 'field', 'record' and 'table' and give examples of how these parts of a database are used.
2   How is a database table different from a spreadsheet?
3   Identify four data types. For each one, give an example of data that would be stored using that type.

2 Use database software tools to extract information and produce reports

2.1 Database queries

A query can do almost anything to the information (data) held in a table. The queries you create for this unit will not change the data in your database table. They will just show it in different ways on screen or in print.

Run simple database queries

Database queries rearrange data from a table ready for a report.

How to create a new query

1.   Click on the **Query Design** button in the **Create** toolbar to start a new query (see Figure 8.15).

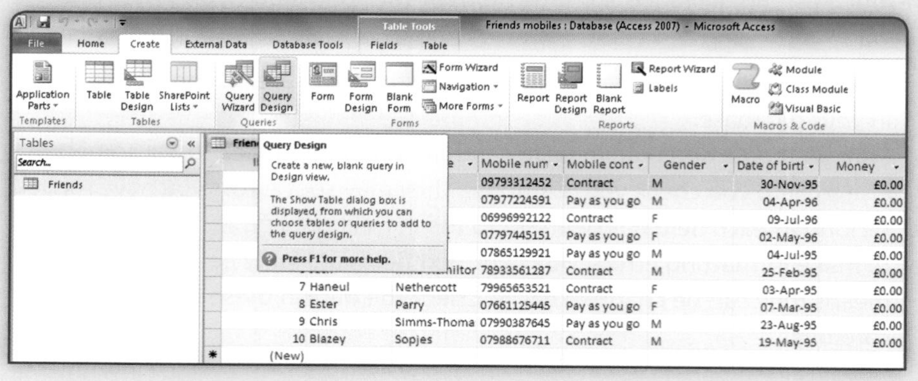

Figure 8.15: Starting a new query

continued

2. Right click the **Query** tab and choose **Save** in the drop-down menu (see Figure 8.16) or save when you close the query.

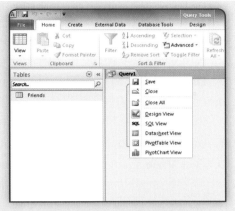

Figure 8.16: Saving a query

When you have saved and closed the query, you may no longer see it in the navigation pane to the left of the screen. To show your query again, click on the navigation pane and then choose **All Access Objects** from the menu (see Figure 8.17). This will show everything in your database.

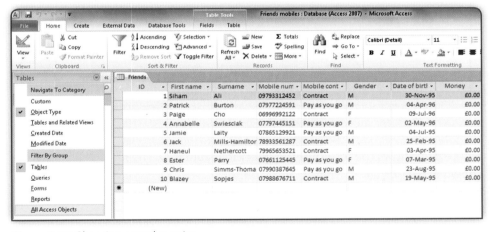

Figure 8.17: Showing saved queries

Alphanumeric sort

An **alphanumeric sort** will put records in order:

- alphabetically (e.g. by surname)
- numerically (e.g. by the number of products in stock)
- by date.

You can choose to sort records in ascending (e.g. A–Z, 0–10) or descending (e.g. Z–A, 10–0) order. To apply an alphanumeric sort, you need to choose which table(s) will be in the query (see Figure 8.18).

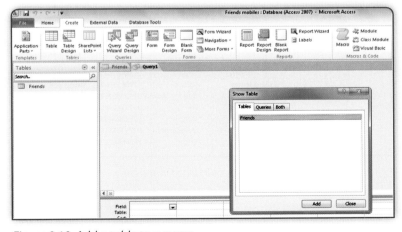

Figure 8.18: Add a table to a query

How to create a new query

1. Click **Query Design** in the **Create** toolbar.

2. Add your table to the query (see Figure 8.18).

3. **Double click** on each field you would like in the query.

4. Click in the **Sort** row below each field to choose how you would like to sort the data in that field – e.g. **Ascending** or **Descending** (see Figure 8.19).

5. Use the **View** button to see the **Datasheet View** of the query.

6. Click **View** again to return to the **Design View**.

Figure 8.19: Query with a date sort in Design View

Figure 8.20 shows the results of the query in Figure 8.19. The records are now shown in date order.

Figure 8.20: Query with a date sort in Datasheet View

Filters

You can use a filter to show only the data you want (e.g. Pay as you go phone numbers). To start a new filter, select the field you wish to filter (such as **Mobile contract**) and click the **Filter** button in the top toolbar.

In the drop-down menu that appears, you can choose to sort alphabetically (A–Z or Z–A) or you can apply a different text filter. If you want to see which of your friends has a mobile phone contract, select only the check box beside **Contract** (see Figure 8.21).

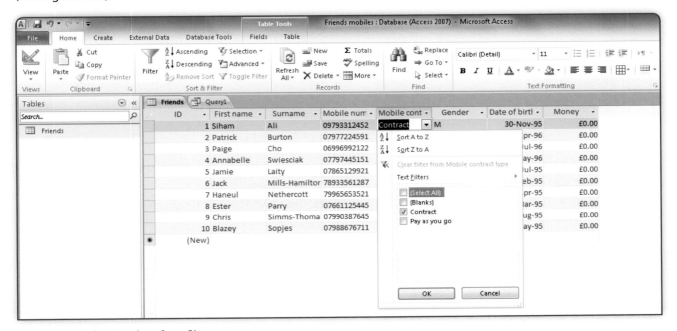

Figure 8.21: Selecting data for a filter

Once you have chosen the filter(s) you would like, click **OK**. Only records containing the values you have selected will be shown (see Figure 8.22).

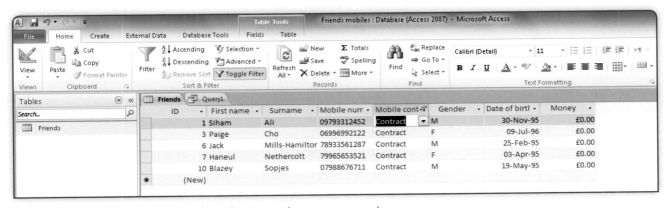

Figure 8.22: Datasheet View with a filter showing only contract records

To switch between the filtered and unfiltered view, click on the **Filtered** button at the bottom of the screen. This will change to **Unfiltered** and all records will be shown. To see only the filtered records again, click on this button a second time.

Activity: Reverse gear

A new television show about motoring has a feature slot where guests drive around a track in reverse gear. Each guest's name and time is put on a board so that the audience can see who completed the lap in the fastest time.

A database is brought in to computerise the board. It can now sort the results to show the best times in dry or wet conditions, or simply list the drivers in order – fastest to slowest or slowest to fastest.

1 Create a new database called 'Reverse Gear' and a table named 'Track Times'. The fields in your table will be:
  a First name
  b Surname
  c Lap time
  d Wet/Dry (create a List Box for this field so that you can only enter 'Wet' or 'Dry').
2 You can also include an ID field.
3 Populate your table with the details of ten celebrities. Guess what lap times you think they might have achieved.
4 Display the table sorted to show:
  a best times in dry conditions
  b best times in wet conditions
  c order of fastest to slowest
  d order of slowest to fastest.

Single criterion queries

Single criterion is a query that looks at one field only to find the information wanted (e.g. everyone who was born before a specific date). To find records where the data in a field starts with a certain letter, you will need to use a wildcard (*).

How to find all records

1. Click the **Query Design** button in the **Create** toolbar.
2. Add your table to the query.
3. **Double click** on every field you would like in your query.

4. Type 'S*' in the query field of the **Surname** column (see Figure 8.23).

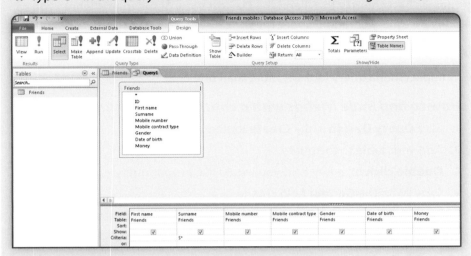

Figure 8.23: Single criterion query for surnames beginning with 'S'

5. Access® will replace 'S*' with 'Like S*' when you move away from the field (see Figure 8.24).

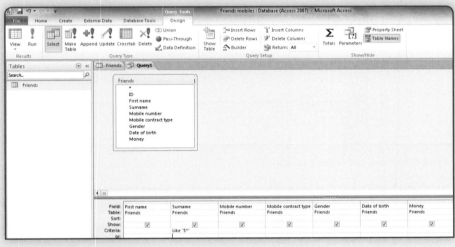

Figure 8.24: Access® replaces 'S*' with 'Like S*'

6. The query will retrieve every record where the data in the chosen field begins with the letter 'S' (see Figure 8.25).

Figure 8.25: Datasheet View of the single criterion query

Use the **View** button to switch between the **Datasheet View** (showing only surnames beginning with 'S') and the **Design View** of the query (where you can modify the query criterion if necessary).

Multiple criteria queries

A multiple criteria query looks at more than one field.

How to find male friends with a contract phone number

1. Click **Query Design** in the **Create** toolbar.

2. Add your table to the query.

3. **Double click** on every field you would like in your query.

4. Type 'M' in the **Gender** field criteria.

5. Type 'Contract' in the **Mobile contract type** field criteria (see Figure 8.26).

Figure 8.26: Multiple criteria query

Once you have typed in your query criteria, click **View** to see the datasheet of your query with results data (see Figure 8.27). If you wish to make any changes to your query, click **View** again to return to the **Design View**.

continued

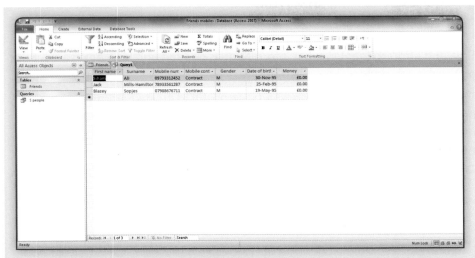

Figure 8.27: Multiple criteria query Datasheet View

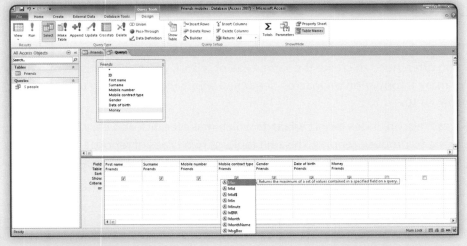

Figure 8.28: Suggested functions

2.2 Database reports

Producing professional database reports is highly skilled work. It takes a lot of time and effort to identify what information is needed and how best to lay it out on the printed page.

Toolbar buttons or keyboard shortcuts are useful to create and run reports. Press and hold the **Alt** key to show shortcuts. To use a shortcut, press **Ctrl** and the letter shown (see Figure 8.29). For example, to create a new record, press **Ctrl+R+N**.

Figure 8.29: Press and hold the Alt key to see keyboard shortcuts which will display as letters in grey boxes

If you often need to create the same type of report, you can also use a **macro**. For more information on macros, see *Unit 1 Improving productivity using IT*, pages 9–10.

Access® also includes report **wizards** which make it quick and easy for almost anyone to produce reports. This unit looks at two types of report:

- **tabular**: the records are printed in a list, one after another (see Figure 8.30)
- **stacked**: each record is laid out separately, often one per page (see Figure 8.31).

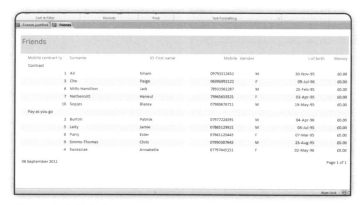

Figure 8.30: Tabular report

Figure 8.31: Stacked report

List reports

You can use the wizards to create a tabular (list) report grouped on the mobile contract type and then ordered by surname.

How to create a list report

1. Click on **Report Wizard** in the **Create** toolbar.

2. Choose the fields you want to include in the report and click the double arrow to copy them to the **Selected Fields** box (Figure 8.32), where they will show up (Figure 8.33).

Figure 8.32: Report Wizard – choosing fields

3. Now click **Next** to move to the next dialog box (Figure 8.33).

4. Choose a field to group the data in your report, such as Mobile contract group (see Figure 8.34).

Figure 8.33: Report Wizard – confirming choice of fields

Figure 8.34: Report Wizard – choose a field for grouping

5. If you choose to add any grouping levels, these will be shown in the box on the right-hand side of the screen. For example, in Figure 8.35 **Mobile contract type** has been selected from grouping.

continued

6. Click **Next** to move to the next dialog box in the wizard.

Figure 8.35: Grouping levels added in the Report Wizard

7. In the next dialog box, you can choose how to sort the records within your report. In Figure 8.36 **Surname** has been selected.

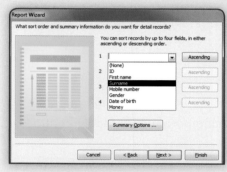

Figure 8.36: Choosing the sequence of records within groups

8. Click **Next** to move to the next dialog box.

9. You can now choose different layout options for your report (see Figure 8.37).

10. Finally, give your report a title. Select **Preview the report** and click **Finish** (see Figure 8.38).

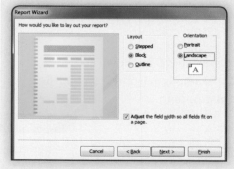

Figure 8.37: Choosing the layout style and orientation for your report

Figure 8.38: Finishing the Report Wizard

There may be problems with the report the wizard produces. For example, in Figure 8.39 you can see that the mobile phone numbers and dates of birth are not showing correctly.

Figure 8.39: Report preview

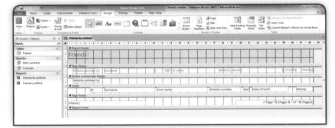

Figure 8.40: Design View of a report

If there are any problems, close the print preview and use the **View** button to enter **Design View** to adjust the report (see Figure 8.40).

Justified reports

To create a justified report using the wizard, use the same basic techniques as when creating a list report but do not choose any grouping levels (see Figure 8.41).

Under **Layout**, select **Justified**. Leave the **Orientation** as **Portrait** (see Figure 8.42), then click **Finish** to view your finished report (see Figure 8.43).

> **Remember**
>
> You can use the **View** button to check how your report looks and then switch back to the **Design View** if more changes are needed. (For example, if you need to adjust the sizes and positions of different fields).

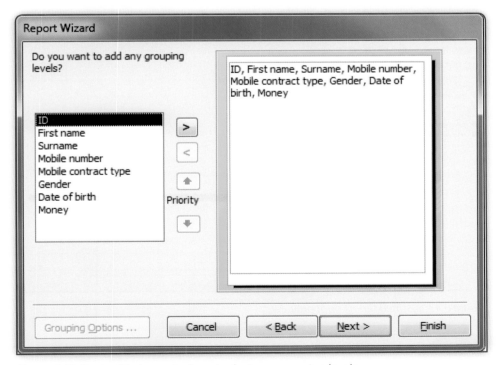

Figure 8.41: For justified reports do not select any grouping levels

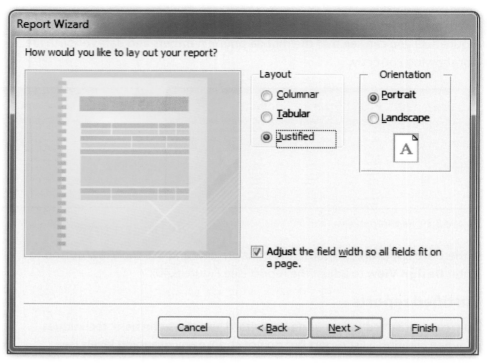

Figure 8.42: Choose a layout for your report

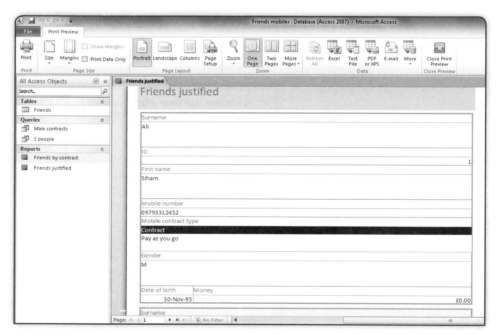

Figure 8.43: Justified report print preview

Check your understanding

1 What is a filter? Give an example of when you might use a filter.
2 Explain how you could use two different queries to rearrange data.
3 Identify two different reports that you could use to prepare printed data.

ASSESSMENT ACTIVITY

You have a part-time job at a leisure centre where regular exercise classes take place. The organiser of the aerobics class asks you to produce a database for him and explain how to operate it. The database is to store member information. The organiser would like you to create one simple table that is easy for him to understand and build upon.

Task 1

1 Create a new database, containing the following fields.

Field	Data type
Name	Text
Home telephone number	Text
Mobile number	Text
Date of birth	Date
Address	Text
Town	Text
Postcode	Text
Paid	Yes/No

2 Add some data to the table. You can use your friends' details if they are happy for you to do so, or make the information up.

3 Once you have added at least ten records, print your database table and proofread it carefully. Mark any errors on the printout, correct them in the database and provide a second printout to show you have done this.

4 Once you are sure your database is accurate, run the following queries.
   a Show all members who have not paid for their classes.
   b Show all members who have paid for their classes.

5 Finally, create the following reports:
   a a list of all members
   b a letter to all members inviting them to a meeting.

Task 2

Create a user guide explaining how to use the database you have created.

1   Write an introduction to your user guide. This should explain what databases are and describe the different components of a database.

2   Provide two annotated screenshots of the database table you created in Task 1. One screenshot should show the blank table and the other should show the table once you have added ten new records.

3   Explain how you can find and amend records in your database, for example:
    a   change a member's address when they move house
    b   update a mobile phone number
    c   change the 'Paid' field from 'No' to 'Yes' once a member has paid for their classes.

Provide annotated screenshots to support your explanations.

4   Create a problem-solving guide explaining what the class organiser should do if he comes across any problems (for example, if a 'bad' date is added to the database).

5   Create a 'How it works' section for your user guide. For each of the queries you ran in Task 1 question 4:
    a   explain how it works
    b   describe how to run it
    c   provide a screenshot showing the results of the query.

6   Explain why reports are needed and how they are to be laid out.

7   Include screenshots or printouts of the two reports you produced for Task 1 question 5. Make sure each report has your name in the footer.

Imaging software

This unit is about creating and editing digital images. Digital images are all around us – on websites, posters, magazines, books and even t-shirts. Digital images are normally based on a digital photograph which is edited in some way to make it suitable for its intended purpose. Alternatively, they are drawn entirely on the computer. Of course some images can be a combination of both of these.

In this unit you will learn how to obtain images from different sources and how to edit them. You will also look at how to choose suitable file formats for different applications and how to be aware of copyright issues.

Learning outcomes

After completing this unit you should be able to achieve the following learning outcomes.

» **LO1** Obtain, insert and combine information for images

» **LO2** Use imaging software tools to create, manipulate and edit images

1 Obtain, insert and combine information for images

There are many different programs you can use to create and edit images. In Microsoft® Word® you can create simple diagrams and make some adjustments to **imported** images. There are also **dedicated** image editing programs. These range from the simple Paint program in Windows® to more complex programs such as CorelDRAW®, Adobe® Illustrator ®, Serif DrawPlus and Microsoft® Visio®.

In this unit you will be using a program called Adobe® Photoshop® CS5. This is the most widely used professional image editing software. Photoshop® has a vast range of features, but you will only be looking at the basic editing tools. When you first open Photoshop® you will see a screen similar to that shown in Figure 9.1.

Figure 9.1: Photoshop® initial screen

As with most applications, to open a file go to the **File** menu, choose **Open**, then the image file you want from the dialog box (see Figure 9.2). Photoshop® can open a wide range of graphics format files. See section *1.6 Identify file formats for saving and exchanging images* later in the unit, pages 185–185.

File menu

Example image you've chosen to open

Figure 9.2: File open in Photoshop®

1.1 Identify what images are needed

Before you start creating or editing an image you need to consider what it will be used for.

- Is it to be used on a web page or a printed document?
- What is the purpose of the image? It might be to advertise a product or to attract people's attention.
- Who is the intended audience?

When designing printed and online documents, many people produce a sketch or mock-up of the layout. This would include the place and type of images.

Suppose you need to provide images for two different documents: one is an instruction manual for a games console and the other is a poster for a children's arts festival. The images for the instruction manual will need to be close-up, clear, detailed photographs showing how to connect the controllers and other cables to the console.

Figure 9.3: A graphics tablet

The images for the poster, on the other hand, could feature some of the children's artwork and might include **scans** of drawings or paintings they have done. A collage of the different pieces of artwork might be a good idea.

Images used on web pages are often quite small. Images used in printed documents, especially something like a poster, may be much larger. As you will see later, it is very important to think about size when sourcing and preparing images. With a printed document you may also have to consider whether the document will be printed in colour or monochrome. Not all colour images look good in monochrome.

Photographs can come from a number of sources.

- They may be downloaded from a digital camera or from your mobile phone.
- They may be scanned images or artwork.

Images also include illustrations, drawings or **clip art**.

1.2 Prepare images

Images that you are not going to create entirely on the computer will need to be sourced, for example from a digital camera or **scanner**. Scanning images and downloading them from a camera is covered later in this unit. Alternatively, you could use a **graphics tablet** to draw images. You can also use clip art and images obtained from websites. However, you need to be aware of copyright restrictions on images from these sources. See section *1.3 Copyright constraints on the use of information* in *Unit 4 IT communication fundamentals*, pages 74–76.

Images downloaded from a camera or scanned are unlikely to be exactly what is required, so you may need to use other preparation techniques.

Size

You will need to consider:

- image dimensions – the physical size at which the image will be displayed
- image file size – how much space the image file takes up.

File size is especially important if the image is to be used on a website, because large files take longer to download. File size is closely related to **resolution**.

Pixels and resolution

A digital image is made up of a grid of individual picture elements or dots called pixels. The number of pixels in an image is referred to as its resolution. This is often quoted as the number of horizontal and vertical pixels that make up the picture. So, for example, a resolution of 640×480 means that the image contains 640 horizontal pixels and 480 vertical ones. This gives a total of 307,200 pixels.

A high-resolution image contains more pixels than a low-resolution image, so its file size will be larger.

Megabytes and kilobytes

File sizes are generally measured in kilobytes (KB) or megabytes (MB). See *Table 2.1: The relationship between bits and terabytes* in *Unit 2 IT user fundamentals*, page 31.

Size and quality

Think about how large the final version of the image will be compared to the original. Although you can resize an image, if you make it too big, it will lose quality.

Let us look at an example. The digital photo in Figure 9.4 has been opened using Photoshop®. It is a low-resolution image taken with a mobile phone and is shown actual size. To see the exact dimensions and resolution of the image, go to the **Image** menu and choose **Image size** (see Figure 9.4).

This image is about 8 cm × 11 cm and has a resolution of 72 pixels per inch (2.5 cm). If you wanted to print this image on a t-shirt, you would need to enlarge it quite a lot. Figure 9.5 shows what happens if you zoom in at 400% (this would make the image about 32 cm × 44 cm). Notice how the image has become **pixelated**.

Key term

Pixelated – pixelation happens when some images are made too large. The pixels become visible and the picture looks blocky and unclear (see also *Unit 12 Website software*).

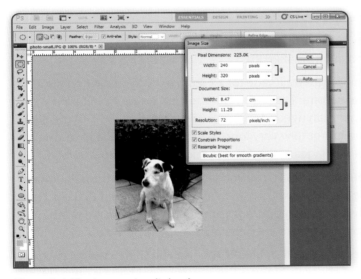

Figure 9.4: The Image size dialog box

Figure 9.5: Image at 400%

However, the image shown earlier (Figure 9.2) has been taken with a high-resolution digital camera. If you look at the **Image Size** dialog box for this image (Figure 9.6), you can see that it is approximately 20 cm × 15 cm and has 480 pixels per inch. Therefore, you would not need to resize this image to print it on a t-shirt.

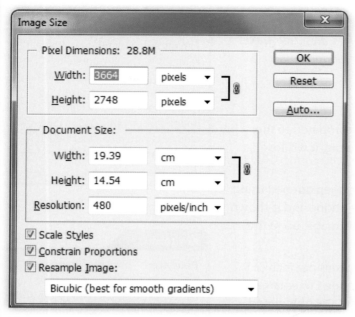

Figure 9.6: High-resolution image size – is 28.8MP

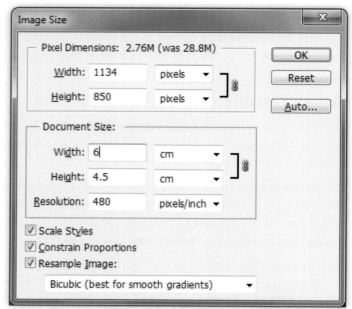

Figure 9.7: Resizing an image – the number of pixels has been reduced, so the images is now 2.76MP

In terms of file size, the two images are very different:

- The low-resolution image is only 41 KB.
- The high-resolution image is 1800 KB.

While you might need a large size image for a t-shirt, a much smaller image might be suitable for a website. The high-resolution image we have been looking at is much larger than needed (20 cm × 15 cm), and at 1800 KB the file is quite large. While it might not take very long to download this image to a web page, a page with lots of images of this file size might be quite slow to load.

In this case it would be wise to resize the image: you can do this from the **Image Size** dialog box. As Figure 9.7 shows, the width has been changed to 6 cm. Here the link symbol is shown between the width and the height. This means the height will automatically change to keep the picture in proportion.

The image will now become much smaller. If you use **File** then **Save As** to create a copy of this image and check its file size, the new smaller image is only 213 KB. This will download quicker on a web page. However, as the resolution is unchanged at 480 pixels per inch, this will not affect the quality of the image.

Crop and position

Cropping an image means cutting part of it off, and is used to remove unwanted parts of a picture. For example, the image in Figure 9.2 has some unwanted background.

How to use the Crop tool

1. Click the **Crop** tool on the left side of the screen.
2. Drag out a marquee (dotted line box) over the area of the image you want to keep (see Figure 9.8).

Figure 9.8: Crop box

3. Now **right click** the image and choose **Crop**. Only the parts of the image that were inside the crop marquee will be kept (see Figure 9.9).
4. If you make a mistake and want to go back to the original image, choose **Edit** from the menu, then **Undo crop**.

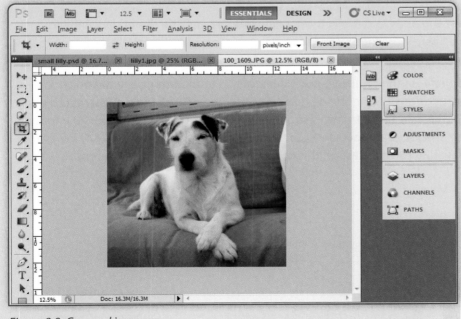

Figure 9.9: Cropped image

An alternative to using the **Crop** tool is to cut and paste. A benefit of this is that it keeps the original image.

How to use cut and paste

1. Select the rectangular **Marquee** tool in the toolbar and drag a marquee over the area of the image you want to keep.
2. From the **Edit** menu choose **Copy**.
3. Now go to the **File** menu and choose **New**.
4. Click **OK** on the new dialog box and you will get an empty image the size of the image you copied.
5. Go to the **Edit** menu and choose **Paste**. The part of the image you copied from the original will appear in the new image.

If you are using more than one image in a file (for example, to create a montage/collage) you may want to position the images relative to each other.

How to position images relative to each other

1. Click the rectangular **Marquee** tool in the toolbar on the left of the screen.
2. Drag a marquee over the image (or part of the image) you want to reposition.
3. Click the **Move** tool in the toolbar at the top of the screen.
4. Click and drag the selected area to move it to a new position.

You can also move a section of an image in the same way.

Adjusting colour, brightness and contrast

An original digital photograph or scan may not have the **colour balance** you are looking for, and may be better with some adjustment.

Some images, especially those taken indoors, may be rather dark and lack contrast. Photoshop® provides many tools for correcting these problems. Let us look at some examples. The image of an apple shown in Figure 9.10 is rather dark.

To increase the brightness of the image, go to the **Image** menu and choose **Adjustments**. From the next submenu, choose **Brightness/Contrast** to bring up the dialog box. In this case, increasing the brightness to about 70 improves the image quite a lot (see Figure 9.10) and Figure 9.11 on page 177. However, adjusting the contrast on this particular image makes little difference.

Key term

Colour balance – the colours in digital images are made up of combinations of red, green and blue (RGB); by adjusting the levels of these colours you can change the overall look of the image.

Figure 9.10: Image before brightness levels are adjusted

Figure 9.11: Image with brightness increased to about 70

The image of a camera shown in Figure 9.12 has rather too much green in it and looks unnatural. To change the colour balance and reduce the amount of green, open the Image menu, select Adjustments and then choose **Color Balance**. The dialog box shown in Figure 9.12 will appear.

Remember

IT tools and applications generally use American spelling, so you will see 'color' rather than 'colour'.

Figure 9.12: Poor colour balance

You can use the sliders on the Color Balance dialog box to adjust the amount of cyan or red, magenta or green and yellow or blue in the image. In Figure 9.12 there is too much green, so move the magenta/green slider towards magenta to reduce the green. Moving the slider to -65 makes the colours look more natural, as shown in Figure 9.13.

Colour level set to –65

Figure 9.13: Colour balance adjusted

1.3 Copyright constraints

You need to check whether the images you use are copyright. If you did not take the photograph or draw the picture yourself and it does not clearly say it is 'copyright free', you should assume you need permission to use it. In this case you will need to ask the creator or owner of the image for their permission. There is more information about copyright, permissions and acknowledgements in section *1.3 Copyright constraints on the use of information* in *Unit 4 IT communication fundamentals*, pages 74–76.

Activity: Find and prepare an image

You have been asked to provide an image to be used for a school fete (or some other event of your choice). The image will be displayed on the school website at a size of about 10 cm × 8 cm.

- Find a suitable image, preferably a photograph you have taken yourself (if not, be aware of copyright).
- Crop and resize the image so it is suitable for use on the website.
- Make adjustments to the brightness and colour balance of the image to improve its appearance.
- Take screenshots of the process you go through to prepare the image and annotate them, explaining what you have done.
- Print the screenshots along with copies of your original and final images and add these documents to your portfolio of evidence for this unit.

1.4 Combine information of different types or from different sources

To create a piece of artwork such as a company logo, poster or t-shirt you may need to combine images from different sources. Let us look at an example.

How to create a logo

You need to create a logo for a local company called North Town Kennels. It runs kennels which look after people's dogs while they are on holiday. In this example you will combine a clip art image of a kennel, a photo of a dog and some text. You will need to assemble the **composite** image in the right order:

a. the kennel as a background
b. the photo of the dog on top of the kennel, as if it were inside the kennel
c. the text last of all.

1. Create an empty image: go to the **File** menu and choose **New**. This will display the **New** dialog box (see Figure 9.14).

Key term

Composite – made up of several parts or elements.

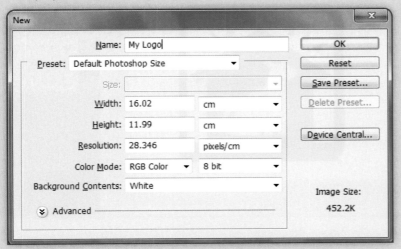

Figure 9.14: New dialog box

continued

2. Enter a name for your new artwork and select **Default Photoshop® size** from the **Preset** drop-down box. Then click **OK**. You will then see a blank image, as shown in Figure 9.15.

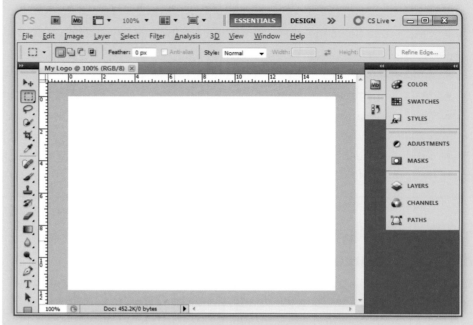

Figure 9.15: Blank image

3. Next, copy and paste the ClipArt image of a kennel from Microsoft® Word® into Photoshop® (see Figure 9.16).

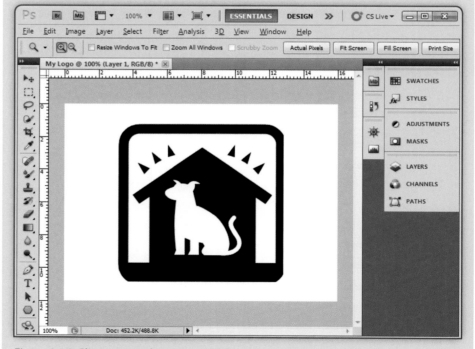

Figure 9.16: ClipArt pasted into image

continued

4. The next step is to insert the photo of the dog into the kennel. Open the photo of the dog in Photoshop®. You will probably have to crop and resize the image as described above. The difficult part is to resize the photo so that it fits inside the kennel, covering the outline of the dog in the ClipArt. You might find it helpful to display both images side by side at the same level of zoom. To do this, go to the **Window** menu and choose **Arrange** then **Tile**. Figure 9.17 shows them both at 100%. As you can see, the dog needs to be resized to make it much smaller.

Figure 9.17: Images side by side

5. After you have resized the photo of the dog, you need to copy and paste it into the kennel. Using the rectangular **Marquee** tool, select the photo, then go to the **Edit** menu, choose **Copy** and click in the window showing the ClipArt. With the same tool, drag out a marquee that fills the kennel, covering the outline of the dog (see Figure 9.17).

continued

181

Figure 9.18: Drawing a marquee

6. Go to the **Edit** menu, choose **Paste Special** and then **Paste into**. This will paste the photo of the dog into the marquee you have drawn (see Figure 9.19).

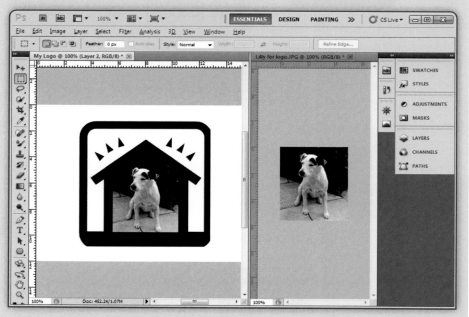

Figure 9.19: Pasting the photo

7. The final step is to add the text. You might find it easier to fill the Photoshop® window with the image of the logo: select that window, then from the **View** menu choose **Fit on screen**. To add text to the logo, click the **Text** tool on the toolbar and choose a suitable colour and text size (see Figure 9.20). Click on the image and then type the text. Do not worry about its position – you can adjust it later.

continued

Figure 9.20: Adding text

8. If you move the mouse pointer under the text, the pointer will change to a four-headed arrow. Use this to drag the text with the mouse to align it with the kennel. You can also add text effects using the **Text Warp** button on the **Text Options** bar. Figure 9.21 shows the completed logo.

9. To save the completed logo, click **File** and then **Save As**. Make sure you save your file in a sensible place and give it a meaningful name so that you can find it again easily.

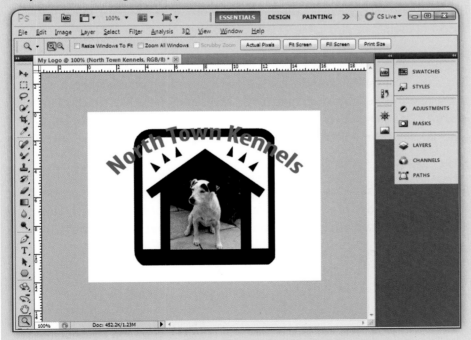

Figure 9.21: Completed logo

continued

You have been asked to design a logo for your local community centre. The logo should combine an image, clip art and some text.

1 What is the purpose of a logo?
2 Who will be the audience for your logo?
3 How can you consider the audience and purpose when creating the logo?
4 Create a suitable logo for your local community centre.

1.5 Identify the context in which the images will be used

As you have seen earlier in the unit, it is important to be aware of how your image will be used. In particular you need to know at what size the image will be displayed. If it is for use on the Internet, the file size may also be important. There are a number of common uses for digital images:

- printed in documents, leaflets, posters, etc.
- for display on a monitor or projector, such as in a PowerPoint® presentation
- for display on a web page.

When you save the file you need to consider how the image will be used so that you can select the most appropriate format to save it in.

1.6 Identify file formats for saving and exchanging images

Photoshop® can open and save many file formats, so which one do you choose? The following section covers the most common formats and the reasons for choosing them. See also Table 12.2 in *Unit 12 Website software*, pages 262–263.

Photoshop® format (.PSD)

This is the best format to choose while you are working on an image. It will keep all the features in Photoshop® and it also saves and opens files quickly. However, it is not a good choice for the final version of your image as it cannot be used by other applications. For example, you cannot import a .PSD file into a web page.

JPEG (JPG)

JPEG is a **compressed** format and is best suited to photographs. This is a good choice if you need to use your image in other applications as it is widely supported. JPEG is also the standard format for photographic images in web pages.

Key term

Compression – reducing the size of the file needed to store an image. Compression can reduce the quality of the image as well, but in most cases this is not very noticeable.

GIF

GIF is also a compressed format and is good for non-photographic images. These could include cartoons or other drawings with areas of the same colour rather than the continuous variations in colour usually seen in a photograph. This is format is also supported by many applications. It is commonly used in web pages.

BMP

BMP (or bitmap) is a grid of coloured pixels that form an image. It stores the colour for each pixel in the image. A BMP is usually a large file. The image is saved at the quality it was made.

1.7 Store and retrieve files

Digital cameras and phones give filenames to your images automatically (such as IMG0358). However, these names give no clue as to the content of the image. Therefore, you should create subfolders within your **Pictures** folder to help organise your work. This is especially important if you are working on several different projects.

It is also often a good idea to give your edited version of an image a different filename from the original. This will leave the original unchanged. If you then decide your edits are not suitable, you can always return to the original file. Also remember to back up your work. See the section *Backups* in *Unit 2 IT user fundamentals*, page 38.

Activity: Saving images

1 Create a new file in Photoshop® and make a simple image.
2 Save the file as a PSD file and then use **Save As** to save it as a JPEG image.
3 Close the file and then open it again. You can use the **Open Recent** option under the **File** menu.
4 Print a copy of the file by going to the **File** menu and choosing **Print**.

Check your understanding

1 What is a graphics tablet?
2 Roughly, how many pixels are there in an image taken on a 4 MP digital camera?
3 What happens if you resize a low-resolution image to three or four times its original size?
4 Explain what colour balance is.
5 How does copyright affect how you may use images you did not create yourself?
6 Which file format should you use to save a Photoshop® image if you want to use it in another application?

2 Use imaging software tools to create, manipulate and edit images

Once you have gathered your images, you may need to edit or adapt them to make sure they are fit for purpose. For example, you may wish to rotate an image (turn it round) or save it in a specific format so that it can be used on a website.

If you cannot find a suitable image, you may need to create one yourself. Photoshop® has various tools which allow you to draw shapes. These are described in more detail in section *2.2 Use suitable tools and techniques to create images*, page 187.

2.1 Check images meet needs

Your images must be fit for purpose. When deciding whether an image is suitable for a specific use, you should think about size, alignment, **orientation** and file format.

Size, alignment and orientation

When you are creating a bitmap image, think about where it will be used (on a poster or a website). Make sure the file you create is similar (or larger) than the size the image will be used at. This is because bitmap images lose quality if you enlarge them.

If you are taking a digital photograph to use in a document, think about the orientation of the image. All digital cameras take rectangular images. If you hold the camera normally, the photographs you take will usually be in landscape orientation. If you turn the camera on its side, you can take images in portrait. Once you have downloaded your photographs into Photoshop®, you can crop them to change their orientation. However, it is better to take the photograph in the correct orientation, if possible.

Suitability of format

Check your images to make sure they are of suitable quality and fit for their purpose and audience. Although you can correct minor quality problems with Photoshop®, you cannot correct problems such as the image being out of focus, dark or of too low a resolution. You must therefore make sure the original image is suitable before you begin to edit it.

Also check that any edits you made to the original meet the requirements and are done in a way that enhances (improves) the original. Remember that there is no spell check function in Photoshop®. You might find it helpful to type any text you need in an application such as Microsoft® Word® and then copy and paste it into Photoshop®.

You must also make sure you save your files in an appropriate format. See section *1.6 Identify file formats for saving and exchanging images*, pages 184–185.

2.2 Use suitable tools and techniques to create images

Photoshop® includes a range of tools that you can use to create specific shapes, draw freehand and change or add to existing images.

Draw basic shapes

To create a drawing, you must first create an empty file of a suitable size. To do this click on **File**, select **New** and choose the size you want. Alternatively, you can add a drawing (or drawings) to an existing file. To do this, simply open the image you want to change and then follow the steps below.

Before you draw the shape you should choose a colour to fill it.

How to select colours and and colour in shapes

1. Click the **Set Foreground color** tool on the left and the **Color Picker** dialog box will appear (see Figure 9.22).

Figure 9.22: The Color Picker dialog box

2. Use the slide in the middle to select the general colour and then click in the panel on the left to choose the exact colour you require.

3. Select the **Shape** tool on the left of the window to open its options bar across the top. You can now choose shape, colour and other settings.

4. To create bitmap rather than a **vector shape**, select the **Fill pixels** option before creating your shape. (Using vector shapes is covered at Level 2.)

continued

Key term

Vector shape – a mathematical description of a form that includes features such as line thickness and type (e.g. dotted) and fill colour, shading, etc.

5. You can then create a shape by dragging with your mouse. Figure 9.23 shows an example of a rectangle.

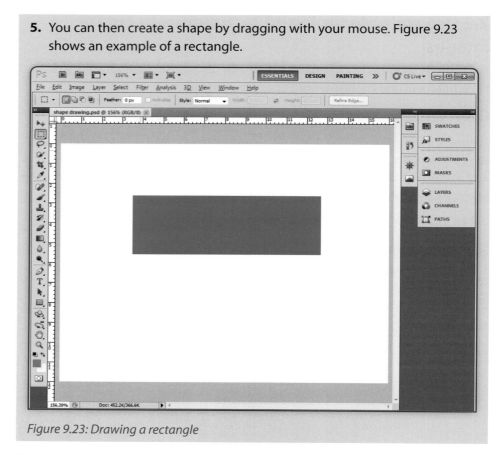

Figure 9.23: Drawing a rectangle

You can also use the **Shape** tool to add rounded rectangles, ellipses, polygons and various lines. Click on the **Shape** tool and select the shape you would like from the options that appear. If you need to add arrow heads at the ends of lines, click the drop-down icon next to the **Polygon** icon and make your choice.

Freehand drawing

You can also draw shapes, words or images freehand. The quality of the images you can draw, and the range of tools, will depend on which software program you're using.

It's a good idea to practise drawing shapes or letters first, before you do it for real.

How to draw freehand

1. Use the **Set Foreground Color** tool to choose the colour you want to draw with and then choose the **Brush** tool on the left.

2. A toolbar will appear across the top with different brush options. Select one and then drag the mouse over the drawing area (see Figure 9.24).

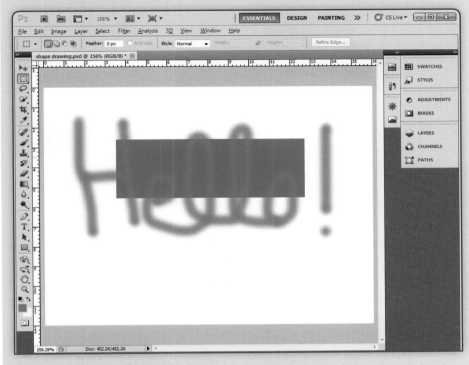

Figure 9.24: Drawing freehand

Bitmap shapes are quite limited because you cannot edit them easily after you have created them. You will be able to work with bitmap shapes more easily if you use layers (which are covered in more detail in Level 2).

How to use layers

1. Before you draw a shape, click **Shape Layers** in the **Shape** toolbar. This puts each vector shape you draw on a new layer.

2. To edit a shape on a certain layer, you must first click on that layer in the menu on the right-hand side of the screen (see Figure 9.25).

continued

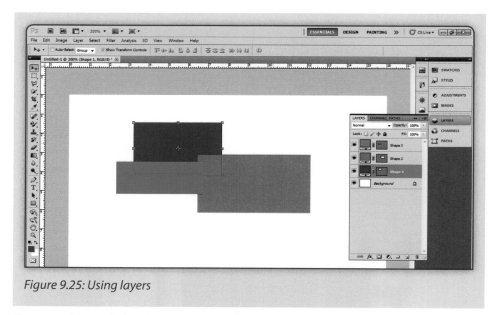

Figure 9.25: Using layers

Once you have all the shapes you need, you can do various things. For example:

- **Align shapes** on different layers. To do this, select both layers (select the first layer, then press the **Ctrl** key and click on the other layer). Then use the **Align** icons on the **Shape** toolbar to align the shapes as you like. Experiment with the different alignment options to see what each button does.
- **Distribute shapes** on different layers. Select the layers containing the shapes you would like to distribute. Then use the **Distribute** icons in the **Shape** toolbar.
- **Group layers together** so that they are treated as a single layer. This is particularly useful if you are drawing a complicated image which is made up of many different shapes. Select the layers you would like to group (use the **Ctrl** key to select several layers at once), open the **Layer** menu and select **Group**.

Activity: Freehand drawing

Freehand drawing with a mouse takes some practise to achieve good results. Use Photoshop®, Paint® or another bitmap painting program to create a freehand image that you can used as a background to the logo you created in the activity for the local community centre (see page 184).

Change properties

You can change the properties of an image.

> ### *How to change the fill colour of a vector shape*
> 1. Select the layer the shape is on.
> 2. **Double click** the existing colour in the **Layer** menu and a colour palette will pop up.
> 3. Select a new colour for the shape.

To change the width of the line used to draw a shape, change the **Weight** in the **Shape** toolbar. A higher number will give a thicker line.

Downloading digital photographs

Most digital cameras connect to your computer via a **USB** port/cable. When you attach the camera, the computer will recognise it and display a window similar to that shown in Figure 9.26. From here you can browse through all the photos on the camera or import them to your **Pictures** folder.

Key term

USB – universal serial bus (USB) is a common standard for connecting external devices to a computer. You can connect all sorts of devices to a USB port: mouse, keyboard, printer, memory stick, digital camera, etc.

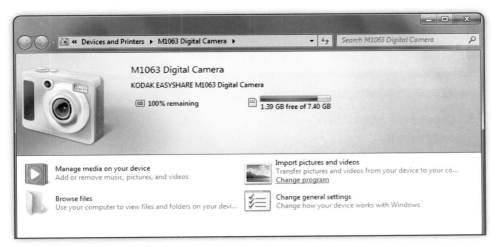

Figure 9.26: Camera window

Most mobile phones will show up in the **My Computer** window as any other USB storage device. You can then go to the folder where the photos are stored (usually a folder called 'DCIM') and copy them to your **Pictures** folder.

Scan images

Scanning an existing artwork, photograph or other item is another way of obtaining an image (but be aware of copyright restrictions).

> ### *How to scan an item*
> 1. Place it in the scanner, following the instructions on the scanner itself or in the user manual.
> 2. Open Photoshop®, open the **File** menu and choose **Import**.

continued

3. From the menu that appears, choose WIA-*scanner name* (*scanner name* will depend on the type and make of scanner you are using).

4. You should see the **Scan** dialog box shown in Figure 9.27.

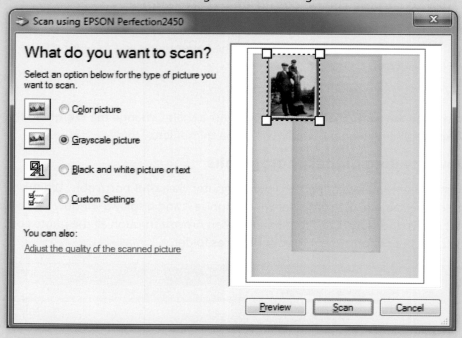

Figure 9.27: Scan dialog box

5. Choose the type of item you want to scan by clicking one of the buttons on the right.

6. Click **Preview** to see a preview of the item to be scanned.

7. Use the selection handles in the preview window to select the area you want to scan.

8. Click the **Scan** button.

The scanner will scan the item and, after a few seconds, the scanned image will appear in Photoshop®. You can now edit the image as required.

Activity: Scanning images

1 Find some hand-drawn artwork that you (or a friend) have created. It could be a drawing, diagram, painting or traditional photographic print. Try to find an image that is smaller than A4 because most scanners cannot cope with documents larger than A4. (However, it is possible to scan a larger piece of artwork in A4 sections and then put the sections back together in Photoshop®.)

2 Scan the artwork into Photoshop® and save it as a digital file.

Add text and other elements

Earlier in this unit you learned how to add a line of text to an image. You can also add a paragraph text box, within which text will wrap. This means that when the text reaches the right-hand side of the box it moves down to a new line.

How to create a paragraph text box

1. Choose the **Text tool** and then drag out a box on the image window.

2. Choose fonts, sizes and colours from the options bar and type your text into the box. You can edit this text as you would in a word processor. Figure 9.28 shows an example.

Figure 9.28: Paragraph text

3. Note that text added to an image is put on a separate layer to the image. Once you have added text, if you try to add more shapes or freehand drawing you will see the message shown in Figure 9.29.

4. Before you click '**OK**' make sure your text is correct because after you do so you will not be able to edit it.

5. Once you click '**OK**' you can add more shapes/drawings.

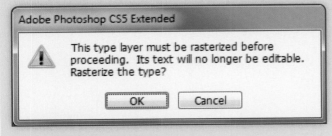

Figure 9.29: Rasterize text message

2.2 Manipulate and edit images

There is a wide range of tools you can use to manipulate (control) and edit your images. This section looks at a few simple examples.

You can **rotate** a whole image or part of an image.

How to rotate the whole image

1. Go to the **Image** menu and choose **Image Rotation**.

2. From the pop-out menu choose the option you want: **CW** stands for clockwise (i.e. rotate to the right); **CCW** stands for counter-clockwise (rotate to the left). The **Arbitrary** option lets you choose any angle of rotation. You can also flip the whole drawing canvas vertically or horizontally.

How to rotate just part of the image

1. Use the rectangular **Marquee** tool to select the part you want to rotate.

2. Go to the **Edit** menu and select **Transform**.

3. From the pop-out menu choose **Rotate**. Handles will then appear around the selection marquee and you can use the mouse to rotate the selection to any angle (see Figure 9.30).

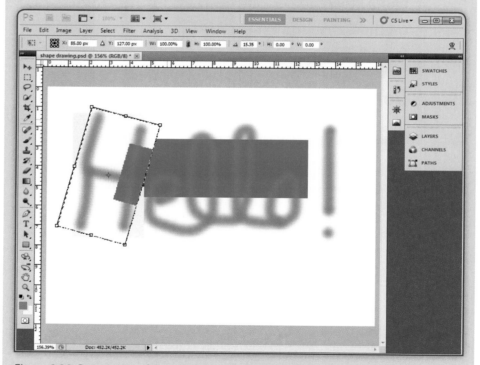

Figure 9.30: Rotating a selection

Transforming images

As you may have noticed, the **Transform** pop-out menu has many other options for transforming a selection, including resize, skew, distort and warp. **Warp** is a particularly interesting transformation as it puts a grid over the selection with lines that you can drag with the mouse to **distort** the image as shown in Figure 9.31.

You can experiment with the other transform functions to see what they do.

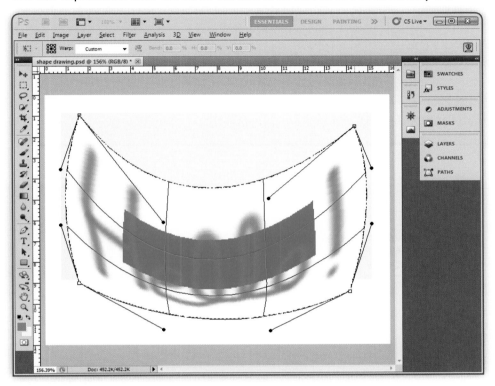

Figure 9.31: Using Warp transform

Cutting and pasting images

How to cut and paste images or parts of images

1. Use the **Marquee** tool to select the image (or part) that you would like to cut or copy.

2. Open the **Edit** menu, select **Cut** or **Copy** and then **Paste**.

The image you have cut or copied will be pasted into a new layer. You can then use the **Move** tool to drag this image (or section) to a new position.

If you want to cut or copy an irregularly (oddly) shaped area of an image (not a rectangular area), use the **Polygonal Lasso** tool. This is under the **Marquee** tool in the toolbar on the left. (You may need to click and hold the lasso button until the submenu appears so that you can choose the **Polygonal Lasso** tool.)

To use the **Polygonal Lasso**, click on several points around the area you want to select. Photoshop® will automatically draw straight lines between the points where you click, selecting an area which you can then copy or cut. You can use this tool to create effects such as copying one person's head onto another person's body.

Activity: Editing an image

Take the image you scanned in the previous activity or the freehand drawing your created earlier. Practise using image rotation and other options in the **Transform** menu to manipulate the image.

Check your understanding

1 Which toolbar tool would you use to create a rectangle?
2 Which toolbar tool would you use to draw freehand?
3 What name is usually given to the folder on a digital camera that stores images?
4 Which menu option is used to obtain images from a scanner?
5 What is the difference between a line of text and a paragraph of text?

ASSESSMENT ACTIVITY

You have been asked to help develop an A4 size leaflet advertising a local business or club. You need to complete the following tasks:

1 Decide what images you need. This must include a logo for the leaflet and at least two photographs.

2 Identify the copyright status of the images you intend to use. If you create them yourself, then you need to state this.

3 Obtain the photographs and prepare them for the document by cropping, sizing and adjusting them as necessary. The images used in the leaflet will need to be around 10 cm × 8 cm. Save them in a format which will allow them to be imported easily into a word processing program.

4 Draw a mock-up of the leaflet. This can be a basic hand-drawn sketch, but it needs to show where the photographs and logo will go in the leaflet.

5 Create a logo for the organisation which combines a freehand drawn image, a photograph and some text.

6 Print final copies of your photographs and logo and check carefully that they are suitable, highlighting anything you could improve. It might be helpful to ask someone else to look at them and suggest improvements. Make any improvements you or whoever reviewed your work suggest.

Presentation software

An electronic presentation is a set of slides designed to be displayed through a projector onto a screen or perhaps on a large monitor.

This unit deals with the use of a software application to produce effective presentations that suit particular needs and audiences. Presentations are now commonly used as a resource to support someone who is talking the audience through the content. However, they can also be set up to run automatically. Presentations can use a combination of media and have various roles in education, training, business and entertainment.

In this unit you will become familiar with common software tools and gain an understanding of their structures and functions. You will also learn about the importance of checking presentations carefully and preparing them for viewing.

Learning outcomes

After completing this unit you should be able to achieve the following learning outcomes.

» **LO1** Input and combine text and other information within presentation slides

» **LO2** Use presentation software tools to structure, edit and format slides

» **LO3** Prepare slides for presentation to meet needs

1 Input and combine text and other information within presentation slides

In this section you will learn how to input and combine different types of information within presentation slides. You will also learn about constraints (limits) that you need to consider when using information in presentations.

1.1 Types of information

When preparing a presentation, you will use various types of information such as:

- text, numbers and images
- sounds, animations and videos.

The ability to use so many different data types will allow you to create interesting and powerful presentations. However, you may run into some problems.

If you use high-resolution graphics, animations or videos, your presentation file may become very large (See the section *Pixels and resolution* in *Unit 9 Imaging software*, page 172.). This might make it difficult to send to other people by email or transfer quickly to a **USB memory stick**.

If you use too many different types of information in the same presentation, you may distract the viewer from the message you are trying to communicate. Your presentation may also seem confusing and too complex to some viewers.

Did you know?

In normal use, the word 'animation' relates to cartoons. However in presentation software, animation refers to the way that slides are presented. For example, the way one slide disappears and the next one appears is a type of presentation animation. You can use animation to make each slide, or parts of it, dissolve (melt away) or bounce in and out, for example. You can also use animation to control the timing of the presentation and emphasise (stress) certain slides or pieces of information.

Activity: Choosing content

For each of the following situations, decide which types of information you might want to use in a presentation. Be prepared to explain your answers.

- A National Trust (NT) property on the coast is famous because it attracts many different seabirds. The director wants to develop a presentation to show to visitors. It should tell them about the birds they might see and give them some information to help them identify the different birds.
- One of the exhibits at the Science Museum in London is a steam engine. The curator needs a presentation that will explain how the steam engine works and give some information about its history.

Enter information into presentation slides

Presentation software may share many features with other programs. In this unit you will be working with Microsoft® PowerPoint®, which is the most commonly used presentation software, PowerPoint® has many of the same features as Microsoft® Word® and Excel®. Through using Microsoft® Office® applications in this course you will already be familiar with many of the techniques in this unit.

Entering text information

If you already have a box to enter information into, just move the cursor into the box (or into the correct position within any existing text) and click the left mouse button. You should see the **flashing I-bar** which shows where your text will be inserted (the insertion point). Type normally and your text will appear in the box.

To add text to a blank area of the slide, you must first insert a text box.

How to insert a text box

1. Open the **Insert** menu.
2. Click on the **Text Box** button (see Figure 10.1).
3. Click on the slide where you would like your text box to be, then hold down the left mouse button and drag the mouse to draw your text box.

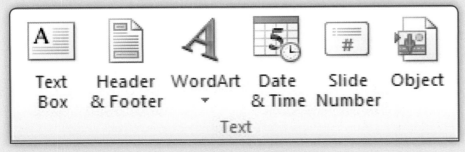

Figure 10.1: Part of the Insert menu showing the Text Box option

You can resize a text box by clicking on one of the **sizing handles** (see Figure 10.2) and holding down the left mouse button while you drag the mouse.

Entering other types of information

Other types of information such as images, charts or tables can be placed from the **Insert** menu (see Figure 10.3).

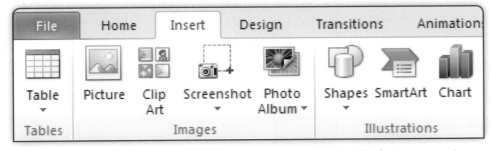

Figure 10.3: Part of the Insert menu showing the Picture option and other image options

How to insert an image

1. Position the cursor where you want to insert the image and click the left mouse button.
2. Open the **Insert** tab and click **Picture**.
3. In the dialog box that opens, find the picture you would like to insert and **double click** on it.

Handles: these can be used to resize or change the shape of the text box. The green handle can be used to rotate the box.

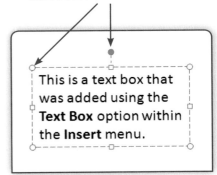

Figure 10.2: Changing the size or shape of a text box

When you resize an image, you may find that it becomes stretched or squashed. If you want to keep the image in proportion, hold down the **Shift** key while you resize the image. If you wish to keep the centre of the image in the same place, hold down the **Ctrl** key while you resize the image.

To keep the image in proportion and keep its centre in the same position, hold down **Ctrl+Shift** while resizing the image.

clip art – ready-made pictures and symbols used to illustrate a range of subjects. They often appear as small cartoons.

How to resize an image

1. Click on the image to select it.
2. Click and drag the **sizing handles** to make the image the size you want it to be.

How to move an image

1. Click on the image to select it.
2. Hold down the left-hand mouse button while you drag the image to the right position.

You can move and resize any object in this way (for example, **clip art**, screenshots or tables).

Activity: Adding and editing slides

In this activity you will create a new presentation and practise adding slides and entering different types of information.

1 Open PowerPoint®. A new blank presentation will be created automatically, which should look like Figure 10.4. At first the presentation will only contain one slide (shown in the window on the left of the screen), with the **Title Slide** layout.

2 Click in the box that says **Click to add title** and type 'Common weeds'. Add your name to the subtitle box.

3 Open the **Home** menu and click **New Slide**.

4 Now select **Layout** from the Home menu and choose **Content with Caption** from the drop-down menu that appears.

5 On your slide, add the information about chickweed provided in the table on page 201. Your tutor should be able to help you find a suitable picture.

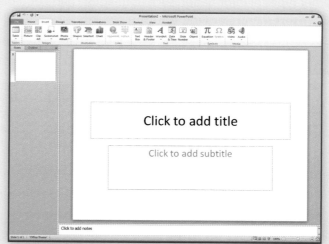

Figure 10.4: Starting a new presentation

continued

Title box	Second text box	Graphic box on right-hand side
Chickweed	One of the commonest weeds, with fragile-looking green stems and leaves and tiny white flowers. This is an annual weed, so easily dealt with – you can feed it to your pet rabbit.	Add graphic from library
Convolvulus or Great Bindweed	A notorious perennial weed, it is almost impossible to get rid of. It forms strings of heart-shaped leaves on twining stems, which can work their way up into trees or over hedges. Large, white trumpet-shaped flowers in summer. Any tiny bit left in the soil will grow into a new plant in no time.	Add graphic from library
Groundsel	An annual, related to Ragwort, without any 'petals', usually borne in small clusters. Rubbery-looking, small, serrated-edged leaves. Anything from an inch to a foot high. It has fluffy seed heads that will spread the seeds all over your garden.	Add graphic from library
Dandelion	Dandelions are easily identified by their bright yellow flowers and deep taproots. They are perennial plants and very difficult to get rid of.	Add graphic from library

6 Insert three more slides and add the information about one of the weeds to each slide.

7 Create another slide, using the **Title with Content** layout. Add some text explaining how to get rid of weeds. The information below is given as a short paragraph – pick out the key points and then present the information as a bulleted list. Click in the **Click to add text** box and enter your points one at a time.

Getting rid of weeds

It is important in most cases to uproot all of a weed otherwise it will re-grow. Use a hand fork to loosen the roots of larger garden weeds.

For perennial garden weeds, a systemic weedkiller such as glyphosate should be used. Use a fork when digging weeds, as it will tease the roots loose; a spade will chop them up, multiplying the problem. Garden weeds invading from adjoining ground can be deterred with a barrier of thick plastic buried in the ground.

1.2 Constraints

You need to be aware of any constraints which may affect your presentation.

Copyright laws

When you are finding information to use in your presentation, you must be very careful that you do not break copyright laws. Any text you use – for example, a poem or an extract from a book – may be copyright. This means that you have to ask the copyright holder for permission before you use their work.

- You must also be very careful before reproducing images or music in a presentation. You may be able to download music or images from the Internet free of charge, but often you will be breaking the law.
- Even if you buy the music or images legally from a retailer such as iTunes, unless you have permission from the copyright holder to reproduce their music in your presentation you will still be breaking the law.
- Your local library may have bought images which you can use freely. However, you should always check whether you need permission to use a piece of information.
- If you are reproducing any type of information for purely educational purposes you are allowed to do this without permission from the copyright holder.
- Even when using text, images or music for educational purposes, do not upload this work to the Internet and do not claim that you created the content yourself.

Acknowledgement of sources

If you use content created by someone else in your work, even for educational purposes, you must acknowledge the source of the text, image or music etc.

Plagiarism

You must also be careful to avoid committing **plagiarism**, whether intentionally or unintentionally (on purpose or not). For example, other people in your school, college or workplace may have taken photographs or made recordings and left them on the network in an open folder. You should not use this information without asking their permission. Even if you do have permission to use it, you must acknowledge in your work the person who found or created the information.

For more information on copyright laws, acknowledgement of sources and plagiarism, see section *1.3 Copyright constraints on the use of information* in *Unit 4 IT communication fundamentals*, pages 74–76.

Key term

Plagiarism – using someone else's work and pretending it is your own. This is taken very seriously and can lead to poor marks or even exclusion from college courses. You could also be sued (taken to court) by the copyright owner of the work. Not all plagiarism is intentional. Simply forgetting to say what the source of your information or images is could be considered plagiarism and could get you into trouble.

File sizes

A further important constraint may be the file sizes of images, music, videos and other material that you are using in your presentation. The size of your final presentation will include these file sizes, so you must try to keep all file sizes as small as possible. Otherwise, your presentation may be too big to fit onto a USB memory stick or to send via email. It will also be more difficult to use the presentation.

For more information, see *Size* and *Size and quality* in section 1.2 of *Unit 9 Imaging software*, pages 173–174.

Local guidelines and equal opportunities

If you are working for an organisation, make sure you know about any company guidelines you have to follow. These may have rules about equal opportunities. For example, in a slide designed for new employees, you must make sure you treat and represent everyone fairly. A simple example might be to avoid using a font size or particular colours that might be hard for people with poor eyesight to read.

Activity: Using pictures

1   Look on the Internet and find images of the following weeds:
   a   Chickweed
   b   Convolvulus or Great Bindweed
   c   Groundsel
   d   Dandelion.
2   Find out how big the image files are (in kilobytes/KB) and choose a size somewhere in the middle. Estimate what the total size would be if you chose to include 100 pictures of weeds in a presentation.
3   Compare this size to the maximum attachment size for your email.

Check your understanding

1   What type of information can you include in presentations?
2   How do you add new slides to a presentation?
3   What is clip art?
4   How does file size of imags affect you presentation?

1.3 Combine information in presentations

In this section, you will learn how to combine three types of information – text, tables and charts – into one presentation.

Activity: Using text, tables and charts

Create one slide that has text, tables and charts. It should include a table showing the sales figures for a company's four national teams. The slide should also have a chart showing how the company's staff are employed in each country.

1 Launch PowerPoint® to open a new presentation.

2 Add an appropriate title to the first slide, for example 'Sales 2011'. Add your name to the second box.

3 Insert one new slide and choose the **Two Content** layout.

4 In the title box, insert the title 'Group Sales by Country'.

5 In the box on the left of the slide, select the **Table** icon and enter the following details:

Team	Sales
England	2500
Wales	1450
Scotland	3700
Northern Ireland	950

Your slide should now look like Figure 10.5.

6 Now click on the **Chart** icon in the box on the right of the slide. A new window will appear, giving you a number of choices (see Figure 10.6). Choose an appropriate chart type (either **Column** or **Pie**).

7 In the spreadsheet that appears, add the following information:

	Sales	Admin	Managers
England	34	4	2
Wales	12	3	1
Scotland	25	4	1
Northern Ireland	7	2	1

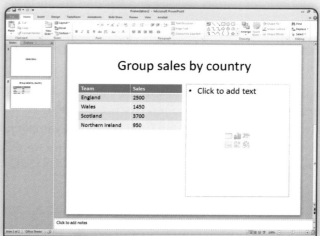

Figure 10.5: Screen after the title and chart have been entered

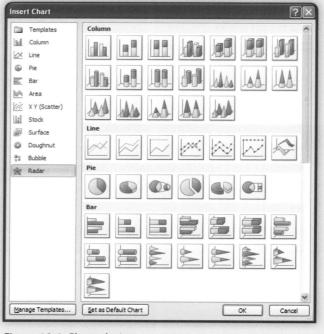

Figure 10.6: Chart choices

continued

8 Close the spreadsheet window and the slide will display both the table and the chart (see Figure 10.7). Change the size and the position of the graph as needed. Also before printing your presentation, add a small text box in a suitable place for your name and the date.

9 **Save** and **Print** the presentation. Follow the steps in section 1.4 (below) if you are not sure how to do this.

10 Think about what the slides are communicating to viewers.

a Imagine you are the senior sales manager for all regions. How would you decide which team was doing the best?

b Why would you choose a pie chart or a bar chart for the graphic and not a line graph?

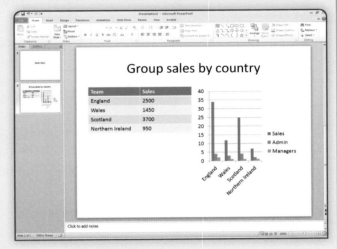

Figure 10.7: Completed team sales slide

1.4 Store and retrieve presentation files effectively

If you have saved, opened files and printed files in other Microsoft® applications, you should find that the process in PowerPoint® is very similar. Before you save your files, ask your teacher, tutor or supervisor where you are expected to store them on the network. You may be given space on a network or asked to use the main hard drive or perhaps an external drive.

Creating a presentation file

Whenever you open PowerPoint® it automatically creates a new blank presentation.

> **How to create a new PowerPoint® presentation**
> 1. Click **File**.
> 2. Select **New** from the options on the left-hand side of the screen.
> 3. Select **Blank presentation**.
> 4. Click **Create** at the right-hand side of the screen.

Any information you add to a new presentation will be stored in the current memory of the computer. This information will be lost if there is a power failure or if your computer develops a fault, so it is important to save your file as soon as possible.

Did you know?

You can use the **Chart Tools**, **Design**, **Layout** and **Format** tabs to introduce styles and make changes. Explore the options on each tab to find out how you can change your chart. Make sure to save your file before you begin to experiment with the options.

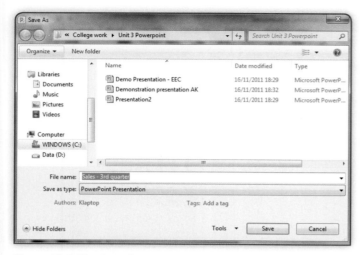

Figure 10.8: The Save As
dialog box

Saving a file for the first time

Click on **File** and select **Save As** from the options on
the left-hand side of the screen. In the dialog box that
appears (Figure 10.8), give your file a meaningful file
name and choose a folder to save it in. If you do not
choose a location, the file will usually be saved in your
own **Documents** folder. However, your teacher, tutor or
supervisor may ask you to save your files somewhere else.
It is wise to create new folders for different parts of your
project.

Saving a named file

You should save your file regularly to make sure you have an up-to-date
version if something goes wrong. Click **File** and select **Save** from the options.
Alternatively, click the **Save** icon in the title bar of the presentation window.

Opening and closing a file

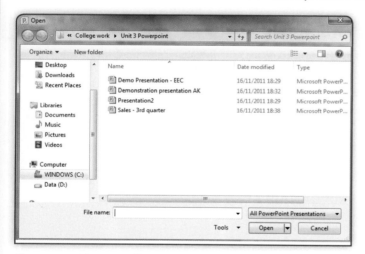

Figure 10.9: The Open file
dialog box

To open a document which is stored on your computer,
click **File** and select **Open** from the options on the left of
the screen. In the **Open** dialog box, find the folder where
your file is stored. Click on the file you need and select
Open (see Figure 10.9).

To close a file, simply click the button in the top right-
hand corner of the open presentation window (the white
cross on a red background). If you have not saved your
most recent changes to the file, a dialog box will prompt
you to do so.

Print a file

To print a presentation file, click **File** and select **Print** from the options on the
left of the screen. The **Print** dialog box has several options you can choose,
including:

- print each slide on a separate sheet of paper
- print multiple slides on one piece of paper with lines for writing notes
- print the presentation showing your notes.

Find a file

If you cannot find a file, you can use the **Search** option. Type the name of the file in the box in the top right-hand corner of the **Open** screen (see Figure 10.10). If you are not sure where your file is saved, search in a higher-level folder (for example, your **Documents** folder rather than one of the subfolders). You can search for all or part of a filename, or you can search for a word or phrase in the file itself.

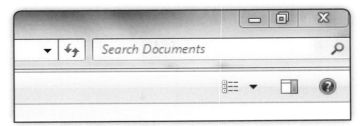

Figure 10.10: Search facility

Key term

Theme – a set of backgrounds, colours, fonts and effects that can be used in a presentation to give a consistent (standard) feel to all the slides; a set of features that are applied to elements in a file.

2 Use presentation software tools to structure, edit and format slides

In this section you will learn how to use software tools to structure, edit and format presentation slides.

2.1 Slide structure to use

It is important to choose an appropriate structure for your presentation. You will need to consider three key areas:

- the layout of your slides
- whether or not you wish to use a template
- any organisation guidelines you have to meet.

Layout

Slide layouts contain formatting, positioning and **placeholders** for different types of information. Placeholders are like containers that you can put information into. There are placeholders for lots of different types of information, including text and bulleted lists, tables, charts, SmartArt™ graphics, movies, sounds, pictures and clip art. Layouts may also use **themes**, which add a specific colour scheme or style to each slide.

Standard layouts

In PowerPoint® you can choose from nine standard slide layouts. You can also modify these layouts if you cannot find one that meets your exact needs. To select a layout click **New Slide** and you will see the menu shown in Figure 10.12.

Did you know?

SmartArt™ graphics provide a library of templates and ready-made shapes that you can quickly add to a presentation.

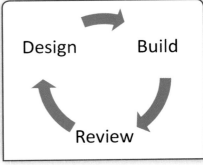

Figure 10.11: Example of a SmartArt™ graphic

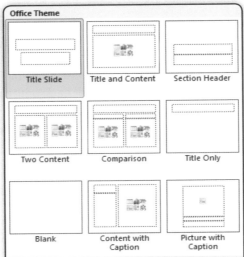

Figure 10.12: Nine standard slide layouts

Choose the layout you would like to use and a new slide will appear with this layout in place (see Figure 10.13).

This box is formatted with bullet points but this can be changed if necessary

This box already has appropriate formatting for a page title. The font and size can be changed.

This box also contains various icons which you can click to add tables, graphs, pictures, videos or SmartArt™ graphics

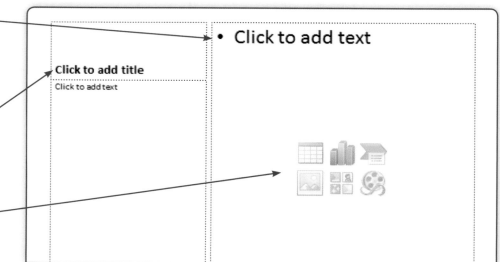

Click to add text

Click to add title
Click to add text

Figure 10.13: Standard layout for 'Content with Caption'

If none of the standard layouts is suitable for a particular slide, you can adapt one of them or create a new layout from scratch. To create a completely new layout, select **Blank** from the drop-down **Layout** menu. Then you can add text boxes and insert objects (images, charts, graphs, etc.) as needed.

Activity: Slide layouts

An estate agency needs to give a presentation about the agency and to show a selection of the properties it has for sale.

The standard slide layout chosen for this example is 'Content with Caption'. You will need to adapt this layout for some of the slides, to show a couple of smaller images as well as the main image of the property.

1 You have been asked to focus on the layout of the slides that will describe the properties. Using the standard layout as a starting point, draw out what you think the new layout should be. Add new boxes as required and change the ones that are already there if necessary. Label each of the boxes to show the content you will add.

2 Explain the advantages of using the same layout for each of the property slides. What possible disadvantages might there be?

When deciding which layout to use, consider the following information about the different standard slide layouts.

Title Slide	This is usually used once only, at the beginning of the presentation. There is very little room for text, although there is a subtitle box where you can add a little more.
Title with Content	This layout is used when the slide is generally about one item or topic. Underneath the title you can add either a bulleted list or a graphic of some sort (for example, an image, table or chart).
Section Header	If your presentation has a number of different parts, you can use this layout to separate them and give the presentation a clear structure.
Two Content	Use this layout if you want to show two or more different aspects of the same topic (for example, a bulleted list and a photograph).
Comparison	This layout is similar to Two Content, but there is space for a heading above each of the content boxes. This means you can choose two different things to compare and provide some information about each one.
Title Only	As the name suggests, this slide only has a title box. You can then choose to add other content as required.
Blank	This is the most flexible layout. No structure is given at all and you can add whatever content you like.
Content with Caption	This is a more complex version of the Title with Content layout, with an extra caption box where you can explain the content in more detail.
Picture with Caption	This allows you to display one large image per slide, with two boxes below it for a title and brief description.

Activity: Designing a presentation

When you have finished a project at school, college or at work, you may need to create a presentation to explain what the project is about and what you have found out. You will need to use different slide layouts in order to display your content as clearly as possible.

1   Which layout would you use for each of the following slides?
    a   Front slide, to give the name of the project and the date
    b   Purpose of the project
    c   Project team members
    d   Project stages
    e   Project outcomes (series of charts and graphs, each with a short explanation)
    f   Summary of lessons learned
    g   List of next steps you need to take.

2   Copy and complete the table below to explain your choices for a) to g).

Question	Layout chosen	Reasons for choice
a		
b		
c		

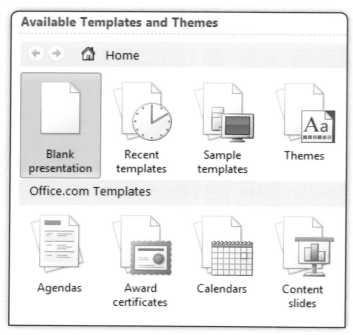

Available Templates and Themes

Home

Blank presentation

Recent templates

Sample templates

Themes

Office.com Templates

Agendas

Award certificates

Calendars

Content slides

Figure 10.14: A fuller set of templates available within the software

Templates, design and styles

Most presentations will use a consistent design and style for all slides. You can control this style by using a **template**, which sets various features (background colour, font style, size and colour, etc.) and applies them to every new slide.

PowerPoint® provides several different templates with pre-set designs and styles for you to use. These appear when you start a new presentation, so you can choose which one you want (see Figure 10.14).

Most organisations provide templates for employees to use. These templates may include the company logo or use the company colours. This will help the organisation present a recognisable and consistent image to its customers. Many company templates recommend slide layouts for different tasks. If your school, college or workplace does this, it is efficient and sensible to use the layouts provided.

Some templates will only be accessible online and may need to be purchased. In this case your teacher, tutor or supervisor may provide a set that you can explore.

Activity: Looking at templates

Create four new presentations, using a different template for each one. As you add content to these presentations:

- describe the particular layouts used
- suggest two possible uses for each layout.

2.2 Techniques for editing slides

Many of the editing tools in presentation software are similar to those found in other types of editing applications such as word processing software. For example, the editing tools in Microsoft® PowerPoint® are basically the same as those in Word®.

Text editing

You can change the text content in slides by using similar techniques to those found in word processing programs. Open the **Home** menu and you will see a range of useful text editing tools.

- To format a section of text, highlight it using the mouse. You can then move the text around, using the mouse to drag and drop it, or by using **Copy** or **Cut** and **Paste**. You can also alter the font, colour, size or alignment of highlighted text as needed.

- You can use **Find** to look for words, phrases or certain kinds of formatting.
- Use **Find and Replace** to find certain formatting or words and replace them with new formatting or words.
- You can also use **Undo** and **Redo** to undo the editing choices you have made. If you then change your mind you can make the change again.

These functions are available at the right-hand side of the Home menu. For more on this, see section *1.5 Use editing tools* in *Unit 13 Word processing software*, pages 283–287.

Cropping

If you **crop** an image, you remove (delete) part of it so that you only have the section you want.

How to use the Crop tool

1. Click on the image and the **Picture Tools Format** menu will open at the top of the screen (see Figure 10.15).

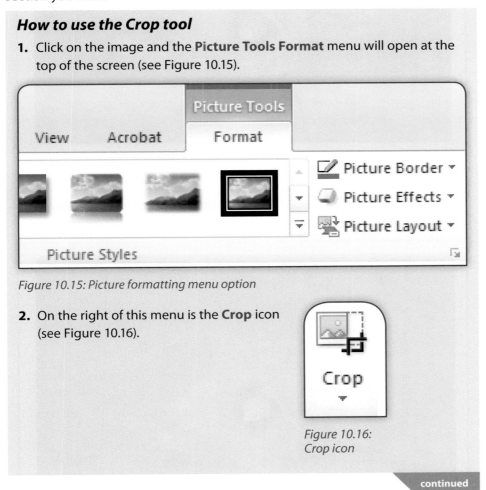

Figure 10.15: Picture formatting menu option

2. On the right of this menu is the **Crop** icon (see Figure 10.16).

Figure 10.16: Crop icon

continued

3. Click on this icon and choose **Crop** from the drop-down menu. The handles around the image look like black lines rather than the squares or circles you usually see when you select an image (see Figure 10.17).

Cropping handles

Figure 10.17: Cropping handles

4. Click and drag on the cropping handles until you have selected the part of the image you wish to keep. (See Figure 10.18.)

Figure 10.18: Cropped image

5. Now click anywhere outside the picture and only the selected section of the image will be shown. The rest has been cropped.

Wrap text

This makes text flow within a set text box or wrap around an image. If you do not use this feature, text will not sit as you want it to within a text box, table or around an image.

Adding additional features

You can add additional features to your presentation, such as extra lines and shapes.

How to add extra lines and shapes to your presentation

1. Open the **Insert** menu and select **Shapes**.

2. Click on the shape you would like to use (see Figure 10.19).

3. Position the cursor on the slide, then click and hold down the left mouse button while you drag the mouse to insert your shape. (This will put the object where you want it on the slide.) You can also change the size of the object by clicking on a corner of the image and dragging the shape while holding down the mouse until the image is the right size.

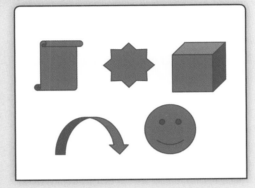

Figure 10.19: Examples of shapes that you can add

Changing the order of slides

Sometimes, you will need to change the order of the slides in your presentation. This is easiest if you open the **Slide Sorter View**.

How to change the order of slides

1. Open the **View** toolbar and select **Slide Sorter** from the options.

2. Click on the **Slide Sorter** icon in the bottom right-hand corner of the screen. The **View** icons are shown in Figure 10.20.

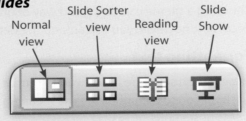

Figure 10:20: View icons

How to move a slide

1. Open the **Slide Sorter view** to display small images of all the slides.

2. Click on the slide you want and hold down the left mouse button while you drag it to a new position.

Activity: Editing a presentation

Open the 'Common weeds' presentation you created earlier in the unit and make these changes.

1   Add the following text as two bullet points on the last slide.

> *Mowing or strimming an area of nettles or ground elder will eventually eradicate these garden weeds. Continually removing as many roots as possible will eventually do the trick.*

2   Create a new slide, choosing the most appropriate place for the slide and the best slide layout for the job, and enter the following information.

> **Types of weeds**
>
> *Weeds can be divided into three types:*
>
> - *Annual weeds: these germinate and mature in one season and then die away, leaving a supply of seed to germinate in the following year.*
> - *Biennial weeds: these take two growing seasons to mature enough to produce seeds, and then die away. In the first season they germinate in early summer and grow. In the second season, they produce an upright stem which flowers and seeds.*
> - *Perennial: these weeds have an energy storage system in their roots and live for many seasons.*

3   In the text about dandelions, replace the word 'eradicate' with the words 'get rid of'.

4   Find out about at least two more weeds and add the information to your presentation. Edit this information so it looks the same as the other text in the presentation.

2.3 Techniques to format slides

You need to select and use appropriate techniques to format slides. This section covers some of these techniques.

Choosing and formatting themes

Themes include different combinations of colours, fonts, backgrounds and effects. A number of standard themes are available in Microsoft® Office®. Choosing a theme can be a good way of giving your slides a clear style. If necessary, however, you can amend the detail of each standard or pre-set theme.

Formatting text

Presentation software allows you to format text in several different ways. This will help you to communicate the meaning of the text and emphasise particular words or sections.

To format a word or a section of text, you must first highlight it with the mouse. You can then click on the appropriate icon in the **Home** toolbar (see Figure 10.21).

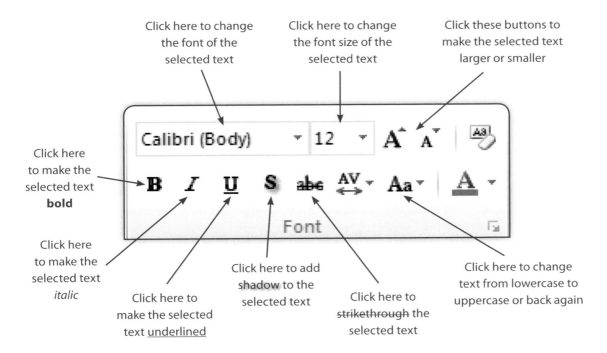

Figure 10.21: The formatting icons

You would usually use formatting to pick out the words you would emphasise if you were speaking. For example, you could make these words or phrases **bold**, use a different font colour, or change the font or size. You can also make sections of text superscript or subscript.

Formatting paragraphs

It is also possible to format whole paragraphs rather than individual words or phrases. You can change:

- paragraph alignment
- the use of bullets and numbered lists
- line spacing.

Paragraph alignment

Usually in English, text is left aligned. This means that the left-hand end of each line is lined up with the left-hand side of the page. Most of the text in this book is left aligned.

Alternatively, text can be right aligned. This means that the right-hand end of each line is lined up with the right-hand side of the page. This paragraph is right aligned.

Headings are often centred, like this sentence.

Text can be justified, like this paragraph. This means that every line is the same length, and both sides of the paragraph are aligned with the sides of the page. This will make your text look neater.

Bullets and numbering

Bullet points are used often in this book, for example to:

- break up paragraphs of text
- present important information in simple lists.

Presentation slides often contain a limited amount of text, showing only the most important information. For this reason, bullet points (or numbered lists) are used a lot.

You may find that the software program automatically indents the text a little when it applies the bullet points. This moves the text away from the edge and is an extra effect to help separate the bullet points from any other text on the slide.

How to apply bullets or numbering to a list

1. Highlight the text.
2. Click on the **Bullets** icon or the **Numbering** icon (see Figure 10.22) and select the style you would like from the drop-down menu that appears.

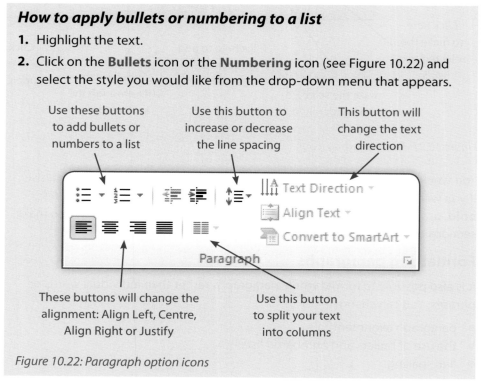

Use these buttons to add bullets or numbers to a list

Use this button to increase or decrease the line spacing

This button will change the text direction

These buttons will change the alignment: Align Left, Centre, Align Right or Justify

Use this button to split your text into columns

Figure 10.22: Paragraph option icons

Line spacing

You will not usually need to think about line spacing because the software you are using will choose a sensible spacing. This paragraph has double line spacing. You probably will not need to change the line spacing in your presentation because there will not be much text on your slides.

How to change line spacing

1. Highlight the paragraph you want to change.
2. Click on the **Line Spacing** icon (see Figure 10.22) and choose an appropriate spacing from the drop-down menu.

Text direction

It is possible to change the direction of text in a text box. For example, you can rotate the text so that it runs vertically along the side of an image. To understand this effect, highlight a section of text, click on the **Text Direction** button in the **Home** toolbar (see Figure 10.22), and experiment with the different options to see what you can do.

3 Prepare slides for presentation to meet needs

In this section you will learn how to present your slides effectively, prepare slides for a presentation and check your presentation.

3.1 Present slides

You need to be able to identify how to present slides to meet different needs and to communicate effectively.

Client and audience

Every piece of work you produce must meet the needs of a client, even if that client is you. In this case, the client is the person who has asked you to create a presentation for a particular purpose (for example, a supervisor at work or your teacher or tutor at school or college).

However, you will also need to consider your audience, since they will have to watch your presentation. They are the people the presentation is for. You must make sure that your presentation is suitable for your audience.

If you are presenting to young children, you may choose to use bright colours, simple text and lots of pictures. On the other hand, if you are talking to adults, you will be able to use more complex language. However, it is still a good idea to break up the text with pictures or diagrams.

In some cases, the people watching your presentation will already be interested in the topic and will want lots of detailed information. However, your client may have asked you to capture the interest of people who are not already interested in the topic. To do this, your presentation will need to be dynamic and eye-catching.

At the beginning of this unit, you looked at the following example:

> *One of the exhibits at the Science Museum in London is a steam engine. The curator needs a presentation that will explain how the steam engine works and give some information about its history.*

In this case the curator is the client who has asked you to create the presentation for a specific purpose. However, the curator is not the audience for the presentation.

1 List the types of people who might visit the Science Museum and watch your presentation.

2 Consider your answer to question 1 and make a list of your audience's needs. You must take these needs into account when designing and producing your presentation.

You cannot design your presentation until you understand the purpose of the presentation and the characteristics of your audience.

Slide timing

When planning your presentation, you must also think about the time you have for it. If you are asked to prepare a presentation that is 5 minutes long, you will need to think carefully about what to include. If you include too much information, you will be rushing to get through it all and you are likely to overrun.

Once you have prepared the content for your presentation, you must think about how you are going to move from one slide to the next. There are two ways of doing this.

1. Manually. This means that the person giving the presentation chooses when to show the next slide. To move on to the next slide, you can:
- press the space bar
- click the left mouse button
- use the → or ↓ arrow keys on the keyboard.

2. Using timings. This means that each slide will be shown for a set length of time, before the next slide is shown automatically. Think carefully about how much time to allow between slides. You need to give people enough time to read the information on the slide, but not so long that they get bored and lose interest before the slide changes.

You would use option 1 if you were giving a presentation in person. You can never be sure how much time people will need to look at a slide. If someone stops you to ask a question, you do not want your presentation to carry on without you.

You would use option 2 for a presentation such as the Science Museum example. Visitors (the audience) will be passing the exhibit throughout the day. It would not be possible for a member of staff to stand beside the presentation all day and click through the slides. In this situation, you would probably want to run your presentation on a loop. This means that it will restart automatically each time it finishes.

Setting timings

You can set the timings for your slides using the **Transitions** toolbar.

How to set timings using the Transitions toolbar

1. Open your presentation and run through the slides in order. Write down how long (in seconds) you think it will take someone to read each slide.

2. Open the **Transitions** menu.

3. Select each slide in turn, check the **After** box and set how long that slide should be shown for (see Figure 10.23).

4. If you want to show all your slides for the same length of time, set the timing for the first slide and then click **Apply to All**.

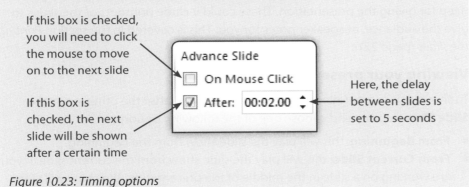

If this box is checked, you will need to click the mouse to move on to the next slide

If this box is checked, the next slide will be shown after a certain time

Here, the delay between slides is set to 5 seconds

Figure 10.23: Timing options

> **Did you know?**
>
> You can select multiple items by holding down the **Ctrl** key as you select them with the mouse.

Transitions

The **Transitions** menu also allows you to control how one slide changes to the next (see Figure 10.24). As with timings, you can have a different transition for every slide or you can set the transition for the first slide and then click **Apply to All**.

Click here to view more transition styles

Click here to view all available transition styles in a drop down menu

Figure 10.24: The Transitions options menu

Experiment with the different settings in the **Transitions** menu to see what each option does. However, remember that complicated transitions can be distracting or even annoying. They may divert the viewer's attention from the purpose of the presentation.

Activity: Setting timings

1   Add timings to your 'Common weeds' presentation and set it to run automatically. Set all slides to display for 4 seconds, except the final slide. Set the final slide to display for 8 seconds.

2   View the presentation and test the timings.

3   Add transitions between the slides if you wish. Experiment with a few different ones before deciding which one to choose.

3.2 Prepare slides

After creating your presentation, you must prepare any materials you might need for giving the presentation. These could include printouts of the slides to give the audience, or speaker notes for you. This is covered in the section *Printing the slides* (page 221).

Viewing your presentation

To show your presentation as a series of slides, one after the other, open the **Slide Show** toolbar and choose one of the following options.

- **From Beginning**: this will play the slide show from the beginning.
- **From Current Slide**: this will play the slide show from the current slide. If you are working on a slide in the middle of the presentation, the show will start from the middle of the presentation.

Once you feel confident, add more slides to your presentation and explore the other options on this menu.

Re-order slides

If you decide that you need to present the information in a different order you can re-order your slides to fit your needs. To learn how to re-order slides, see *Changing the order of slides* in section *2.2 Techniques for editing slides*, earlier in this unit, pages 210–214.

Rehearse timing

You should practise giving your presentation so that you know you will stay within the time you are allowed for it. If you have used timings, check that you have enough time to talk through each slide. You might choose manual timing so that you can decide how long you want to talk about each slide.

Printing the slides

It is unusual to print each presentation slide on a separate page unless the slides include lots of fine detail or background notes. Usually, you should print three or even six slides per page, at a smaller size. If you do this, you must make sure that the text is still large enough to read.

Most presentations use colour images, which may be difficult to see in black and white. For this reason, the software allows you to print coloured slides as **Grayscale** if you do not have a colour printer. This changes each colour to a different shade of grey so you can still see what the image or graph is meant to show.

To print your presentation, open the **File** menu and select **Print** from the column on the left-hand side of the screen to open a new window (see Figure 10.25).

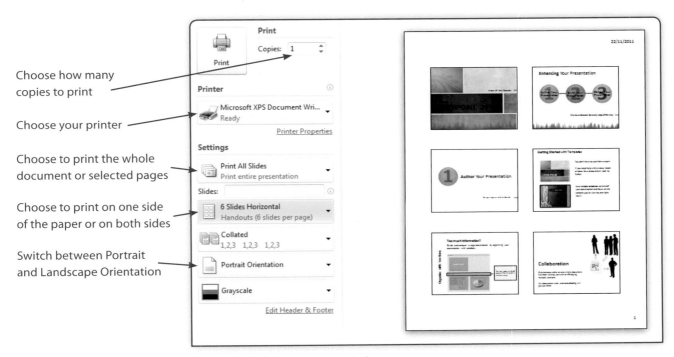

Figure 10.25: Printer options window

Figure 10.25 shows that the following choices have been made:

✓ Print **1** copy of the presentation.
✓ Printer: **Microsoft® XPS Document Writer**.
✓ **Print All Slides** – this will print the whole presentation.
✓ Print **6 slides per page** – the preview on the right-hand side shows how this will look.
✓ Use **Portrait** orientation.
✓ Print in **Grayscale** – because the chosen printer cannot print in colour.

To change any of these options, simply click on the down arrow beside it and choose the option you would like from the drop-down menu that appears. There are also options for printing handouts and speaker notes.

Handouts and speaker notes

It may be useful to print handouts to give to the audience. Handouts can show a number of slides (usually three) on each page. Each slide will have blank writing lines beside it for the audience to make notes during the presentation.

Speaker notes show each slide on a page with the notes you have included in your presentation below. You can use these notes to remind yourself about extra information you want to talk about at that point in your presentation. The audience cannot see the speaker notes of your presentation.

Activity: Printing your presentation

1   Experiment with different printing options until you are familiar with them. Try changing different settings and see how the **Print Preview** changes.
2   Print out one of your presentations, using appropriate print options. Show the printout to your teacher, tutor or supervisor and ask for their feedback.

3.3 Check presentation

As with any project, it is important that you constantly check the materials you are producing. You should ask yourself:

- Does your presentation meet the needs of the client and the audience?
- Are you using the right IT tools?

You should also correct any spelling and grammar mistakes. Although PowerPoint® has a spelling and grammar checker, you must still proofread your work carefully (slide by slide, line by line, word by word) to make sure there are no errors. It is particularly important to check any numerical information because it is easy to make mistakes when you are typing numbers. Remember, your presentation will be much less effective if the information is inaccurate.

Once you have completed your presentation, you must also refer back to your client's original requirements and make sure you have not left anything out or added unnecessary content.

Check the main features, such as slide layouts and the order of the slides. Also consider the 'Dos and Don'ts' in Table 10.1, page 225.

Do	Don't
✓ Organise your ideas on paper first ✓ Divide the content into sections ✓ Always have opening and closing slides ✓ Be brief – usually no more than 6–8 bullet points per slide ✓ Use a large font size – walk to the back of the room where you will give your presentation and check that you can still read the text ✓ Use sensible colour combinations – not too bright ✓ Use consistent style options ✓ Check that you have done what you were asked to do by the client ✓ Rehearse the slide show to check the timings and transitions ✓ Ask for help if you need it	✗ Work on the visual parts of the presentation first (you should focus on the content and structure first) ✗ Put everything on one slide – too much text is hard to read and the audience will get bored if you simply read the text on your slides ✗ Use too many different colours, fonts and animation effects on each slide ✗ Forget your audience and their needs ✗ Rely on the **AutoSave** feature ✗ Forget to check your presentation for accuracy (the information you are giving must be correct) ✗ Forget to check that your text alignment and formatting is correct

Table 10.1: The Dos and Don'ts of slide presentation

Activity: Checking your work

Ask someone else on your course to check one of the presentations you have prepared for this unit, while you check one of theirs. Make sure you explain the purpose of your presentation and describe your target audience. This way, the person checking can decide how well your presentation meets the brief.

Check your understanding

1 Name the two ways you can move through slides?
2 Explain the term 'transition'.
3 How can you use speaker notes?

ASSESSMENT ACTIVITY

You have just started work as an office assistant in a food processing plant. The company has decided to be more open and aware of the range and impact of food additives. The management (client) has asked you to do some research on this topic and then present some background information to the management team.

One of the managers has identified some basic requirements that you need to cover in your presentation:

a Range of additives in common use

b General consumer opinions and concerns

c Specific additives that you feel should be avoided, with the reasons

d Benefits of additives to consumers and the industry

e Next steps.

You are expected to make the presentation interesting with a few graphics and tables. You are advised to ask a number of people to identify possible consumer opinions and concerns as well as research the topic on the Internet.

You are tasked with the following:

1 Research the topic and collect the information needed.

2 Consider the client's requirements and the needs of the audience and write a short report identifying:
- the overall template or theme style and structure that might best communicate the information you have collected
- the types of information you need and how you might best structure it
- the different slide layouts needed for each part.

3 Add the content to the slides. Use appropriate tools and techniques to edit and format the slides to make the whole presentation consistent and interesting. Save the presentation regularly using an appropriate filename in keeping with guidelines provided.

4 Identify any copyright issues with the material you have used. Take advice on how you might need to acknowledge the sources or on whether you need to amend the presentation to remove copyright material for which you do not have permission.

5 Check that the final presentation meets the requirements of the client and the needs of the audience, and adapt it as necessary.

Spreadsheet software

Spreadsheet programs such as Microsoft® Excel® are used by organisations for lots of different reasons.

Calculations come to life in a spreadsheet, giving quick, easy and accurate results. If you change one of the numbers in a spreadsheet calculation the result updates instantly. Many people set up spreadsheets to make predictions using this process and to explore 'what if' scenarios: 'What if I increase the price of this product?', 'What if I sell more?', 'What if I sell less?', 'What if I use better quality components?', 'What if I use cheaper components?', 'What if I take on more staff?'.

Spreadsheets are great for creating forms that you can print for any situation where a paper-based form is needed. Spreadsheets are also excellent at sorting lists in many ways. A spreadsheet can produce charts and graphs quickly and easily from numerical information. This helps people understand the meaning of the data.

In this unit you will gain Excel® skills and knowledge that enable you to create and edit your own spreadsheets to meet IT user needs. You will also learn how to use various tools and techniques to produce and present spreadsheets that look professional.

Learning outcomes

After completing this unit you should be able to achieve the following learning outcomes.

» **LO1** Use a spreadsheet to enter, edit and organise numerical and other data

» **LO2** Use appropriate formulas and tools to summarise and display spreadsheet information

» **LO3** Select and use appropriate tools and techniques to present spreadsheet information effectively

1 Use a spreadsheet to enter, edit and organise numerical and other data

Computers have always been used to carry out calculations. Spreadsheet software will help you to do this more easily. In this section you will learn how to use a spreadsheet to store, organise and edit all sorts of data.

1.1 Identify what numerical and other information is needed

A spreadsheet program such as Microsoft® Excel® is great for displaying and structuring information. Spreadsheets can use many types of information, including:

- **numbers** – for calculations and to produce statistics
- **text** – but not in simple calculations
- **charts** – to show information in different ways, helping people to understand what the information means; charts can be based on numbers or text
- **graphs** – to show information in different ways and help people understand it; graphs are based on numbers, not text
- **images** – to give the information a more professional appearance.

1.2 Spreadsheet structure

A spreadsheet file is known as a **workbook**. Each workbook is made up of **worksheets** (or pages). A spreadsheet can have as many worksheets as it needs. You can use worksheets to keep information separate. For example, if you use a spreadsheet for timetabling, you could save each timetable on a separate worksheet. When you save a spreadsheet file, all the worksheets in that file will be saved together.

Each worksheet is labelled by tabs on its bottom edge. You can move between worksheets by clicking on these tabs.

The term 'spreadsheet' may be used to describe a workbook or a worksheet. However, this unit uses the term to describe a worksheet.

Spreadsheets use **cells** to hold items that can be used in calculations. A calculation could be a simple **formula** to add two numbers together. It could also be a function which can work in other ways, such as to find the smallest item in a list.

Cell references

We think of cells as being in rows (across the page) and columns (up and down). Each column has a different letter to identify it, and each row has a number. This means that you can identify any cell by a reference – for example, B4 for the cell in the B column at row 4 (see Figure 11.1). When you select a cell in a spreadsheet, the cell reference of that cell is shown in the **name box** (see Figure 11.1).

The cell reference of the selected cell is shown here, in the **cell name box**

Each little rectangle in a spreadsheet is called a cell

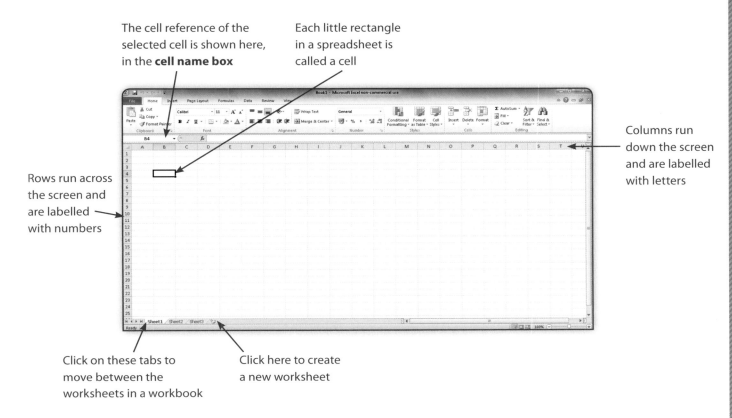

Columns run down the screen and are labelled with letters

Rows run across the screen and are labelled with numbers

Click on these tabs to move between the worksheets in a workbook

Click here to create a new worksheet

Figure 11.1: Cells, rows and columns

Spreadsheet design

You should structure your spreadsheet so that similar information is grouped together. However, you should keep some white space or empty cells around it to separate it from information in the worksheet. You can use different worksheets to store different types of information within the same workbook.

When using calculations, you can create links to other worksheets in your workbook. This will allow the different pages of the spreadsheet to work together.

To begin planning your spreadsheet structure and layout, you need to identify what numerical and other information you need. You should also think about how to structure the spreadsheet to meet the users' needs.

- The most important aspect here is that you can make sense of the spreadsheet you create. If it means something to you, it will certainly mean something to others.
- Read the spreadsheet requirements carefully to find the information that is needed.
- Think about how that information can be laid out in a spreadsheet. How can you structure it to produce the meaning that is wanted?
- Consider using empty cells to separate sets of data to make them easier to read.

You should be able to identify the results that are needed and decide how these can be calculated. Then you will be able to enter the formulas and functions required to do this.

Using charts to display information

If your spreadsheet contains a lot of numbers, it may be very difficult to understand. Graphs and charts help to show numerical information more clearly. Excel® provides a wide range of charts and graphs. These are described in more detail later in this unit, in section *3.3 Format charts and graphs*, pages 247–248.

1.3 Enter and edit data accurately

Excel® creates a new spreadsheet every time you open the program. If the program is already open, you can create a new spreadsheet by clicking **Ctrl+N**.

How to create a new spreadsheet

1. Open the **File** tab.
2. Select **New** from the column at the left-hand side of the screen.
3. Select **Blank Workbook** from the options available.
4. Click **Create** at the right of the screen (see Figure 11.2).

Figure 11.2: Creating a new workbook

When you first open a workbook, the different worksheets are called Sheet1, Sheet2 and so on. However, it is a good idea to change these names to something more meaningful. This is especially important if you are using several different worksheets.

To rename a worksheet, double click on the tab or right click and select **Rename** from the menu that appears. You will then be able to type a new name.

Enter data

How to enter data in a cell

1. Select a cell by clicking on it with the mouse or by using the keyboard. You can move between cells using the **arrow** keys or the **Tab** key.

2. Once a cell is selected, type in your information. Alternatively, you can select a cell and then type into the **formula bar** at the top of the screen (see Figure 11.3).

Cancel by clicking here or pressing the **Esc** key

Click here or press the **Enter** key to complete the data entry

Type your data here

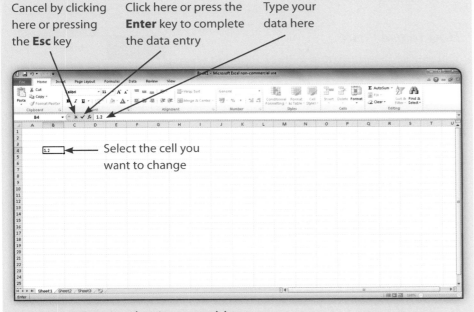

Select the cell you want to change

Figure 11.3: Entering data in a spreadsheet

Edit data

To change the contents of a cell, just select the cell and type in your new information. The original contents will be replaced as you type. Once you have finished entering new information, press the **Enter** key or click on the 'tick' beside the formula bar to accept the changes. To cancel the changes you have made, press **Esc** or click the 'cross' beside the **Formula bar** (see Figure 11.3).

How to delete the contents of a cell

1. Select the cell and use the **Del** key.

2. To clear the contents of multiple cells, select the cells you want to clear, **right click** on one of them and choose **Clear Contents** from the menu that appears.

How to use Copy

You can copy information in three different ways.

1. **Right click** and select **Copy** from the menu that appears.
2. Press **Ctrl+C** on the keyboard.
3. Click **Copy** on the **Home** toolbar (see Figure 11.4).

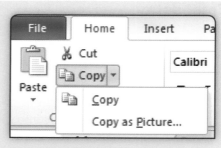

Figure 11.4: The Copy button

How to use Paste

You can paste information in three different ways.

1. **Right click** and select **Paste** from the menu that appears.
2. Press **Ctrl+V** on the keyboard.
3. Click **Paste** on the **Home** toolbar (see Figure 11.5).

Figure 11.5: The Paste button

You can also copy along a row or down a column.

How to copy rows and columns

1. Select the data you would like to copy.
2. Put the mouse pointer over the bottom right-hand corner of the cell. It will change to a small black cross.
3. Click on this cross and hold down the left mouse button while you drag the pointer along the row or down the column (see Figure 11.6).

	C22		f_x	Learner
	A	B	C	D
22	L2 Eng		1 Learner	Button title
23	L2 Eng		1 Learner	Button title
24	L2 Eng	Window	Learner	The name of the product
25	L2 Eng		2 Learner	Button title
26	L2 Eng		2 Learner	Button title
27	L2 Eng		3 Learner	All Tasks - E-scenario sheets
28	L2 Eng		3 Learner	Button title
29	L2 Eng	Content issue	Learner	l2_e_t14_as
30	L2 Eng		2 Learner	File missing
31	L2 Eng	Content issue	Learner	Task 1
32	L2 Eng	Content issue	Learner	Task 14
33	L2 Eng	Content issue	Learner	l2_e_pfa_ep
34	L2 Eng	Troubleshooting	Learner	
35	L2 Eng	Installing to local PC	Learner	
36	L2 Eng	Desktop Icon		
37	L2 Eng	Post installation checks		

Figure 11.6: Copying down a column

The data in the original cell will be copied into all the cells you selected. This function is particularly useful if you want to create a list. For example, if the cell you selected contained the number 1, Excel® will put a number 2 in the next cell, a 3 in the cell after that and so on.

Find and replace

Excel® has a find and replace function that allows you to search for data in your spreadsheet and replace it if necessary.

Figure 11.7: The Find & Select icon

How to use Find and Replace

1. Open the **Home** toolbar and choose **Find** or **Replace**. These options will appear if you click on the **Find & Select** button (see Figure 11.7).

2. A dialog box will appear where you can type the information you wish to find and/or replace.

Insert and delete rows and columns

How to insert a new row

1. Right click on the row number below the point where you would like to add the row. For example, if you want to add a new row between rows 5 and 6, right click on the number 6.

2. Then select **Insert** from the menu that appears.

How to insert a new column

1. Right click on the column letter to the right of the point where you would like a new column. For example, if you would like to add a column between columns B and C, right click on the letter C.

2. Select **Insert** from the menu that appears.

How to delete a column or a row

1. Right click on the row number or the column letter and select **Delete** from the menu that appears.

1.4 Store and retrieve spreadsheet files

There are several ways to save a file:

- Click **Ctrl+S**.
- Click on the **Save** icon in the title bar at the top of the program window.
- Click on **File** and select **Save** from the options at the left of the screen.

When you save a file for the first time, the **Save As** dialog box will appear.

How to save a file using the Save As dialog box

1. Enter a meaningful name for your workbook.
2. Choose a location in which to save your file.
3. Click **Save** or press **Enter**.

If you make changes to a file but want to keep your original spreadsheet, you can save a new version of it. Use **Save As** and give your file a different name and/or save it in a different place.

As always, you should organise your documents in clearly named folders so that you can find them easily. Give each file a meaningful name so that you know what it contains.

Closing files

To close Excel®, click the red 'X' in the top right-hand corner of the application window. This will close any workbooks that are open. As usual, you will be prompted to save any changes you have made.

How to close a single workbook if you have several workbooks open

1. Click on the lower, grey 'X' in the top right-hand corner of the application window.
2. Click on **File** and select **Close** from the column on the left of the screen.

Retrieve and print files

To open a file that you have already saved, press **Ctrl+O** or click **File** and select **Open** from the options. In the **Open** dialog box, find and select the file you want and click **Open** (or press **Enter**).

To print your spreadsheet, click **File** and select **Print** from the column on the left-hand side of the screen. This will show familiar options for changing the way the printed spreadsheet looks (for example, paper size, orientation). A **Print Preview** shows automatically when you click **Print**. The preview will be updated as you change the print options, so you can check that your spreadsheet will print correctly.

How to print part of your spreadsheet

1. Select the section you wish to print.
2. Click **File** and select **Print**.
3. In the first drop-down menu under **Settings**, choose **Print Selection**.

Activity: Booking schedule

Billy Diamond is the leader of a local band called Diamond Nights, He uses Microsoft® Excel® to keep a booking schedule of the band's gigs in pubs and clubs. Billy keeps details of the dates, times, venues and fees in the spreadsheet. He sends this out to the other band members as an email attachment every time a new gig is booked.

Billy does this not only to keep everyone up to date, but also to get early warning of any booking clashes so they can be resolved quickly.

The spreadsheet also provides useful information. For example, Billy has entered figures to show totals and averages for some gigs.

1 Create a spreadsheet for a band you know, to hold similar information to Billy's spreadsheet. Insert functions to calculate:

- the total earnings from all gigs
- the average earnings from each gig
- the smallest fee from all the gigs
- the largest fee from all the gigs.

2 Design and create a chart that will add meaning to your data by showing which venues have provided the most bookings.

Check your understanding

1 In a spreadsheet, what are rows and columns?
2 How would you cancel changes you have made to a cell?
3 What is the difference between a chart and a graph?

2 Use appropriate formulas and tools to summarise and display spreadsheet information

Microsoft® Excel® has a wide range of tools you can use to summarise and display the information in your spreadsheet. For example:

- Formulas will allow you carry out calculations quickly and easily.
- Graphs or charts will help you display information clearly and simply.

2.1 Summarise and interpret information

A spreadsheet can hold a vast amount of information. However, most people will struggle to understand this information unless it is summarised in some way.

Totals and summary information

A subtotal is what you get when you add together a block of numbers. If you add these subtotals together, you will get a total. If you use a separate column for subtotals and totals, it will be much easier to set up calculations in your spreadsheet (see Figure 11.8).

If you are only adding together two or three figures, you can simply type (for example) **=A1+A2+A3.** However, if you are adding together a large number of figures, it will be much quicker to use the **Sum (Σ)** function (see Figure 11.9).

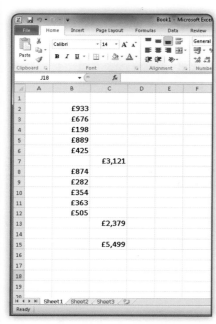

Figure 11.8: Subtotals are used to add together a block of numbers in a spreadsheet

How to use the Sum (Σ) function

1. Select the cell where you want the total to appear.

2. Type **=SUM/** (use the mouse to select the cells you would like to add up, then type).

3. Press **Enter** and the total will appear.

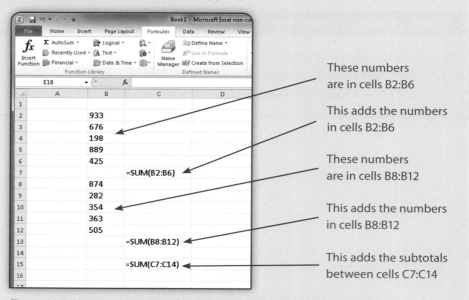

Figure 11.9: You can use a SUM function to calculate subtotals and totals

Sorting and display order

You can often make your spreadsheet easier to read by sorting the data into order. For example:

- If you have a list of names, it will be much easier to find the name you want if they are in alphabetical order.
- If you have a list of sales figures, it will be much easier to see which products are most popular if the figures are in order (highest to lowest or lowest to highest).

How to sort a list of information

1. Select the column containing the information you wish to sort.
2. Open the **Data** toolbar.
3. Click the **A–Z** button to put the list into alphabetical order (or to order figures from smallest to largest).
4. Alternatively, click **Z–A** to put the list in reverse alphabetical order or to order figures from largest to smallest (see Figure 11.10).

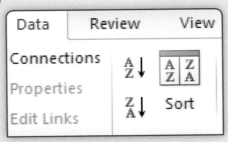

Figure 11.10: The sorting buttons

A sort may have more than one level. The first level could be quite general (such as separating customers according to gender). The second level will order the data within the first-level categories. For example, it could put customers' names in alphabetical order but still keep male and female customers separate (see Figure 11.11).

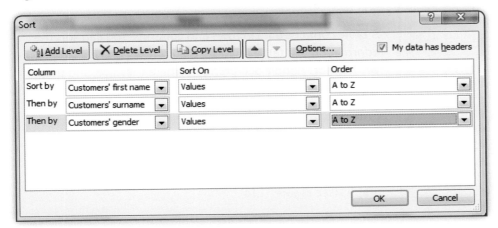

Figure 11.11: The Sort dialog box

Viewing your spreadsheet

You can view your spreadsheet in two ways:

- **Data view** is the default (normal) view. It shows the spreadsheet with the results of calculations and formatting (see Figure 11.12).
- **Formula view** will show you the formulas used in the spreadsheet. To switch to formula view, open the **Formulas** toolbar and click **Show Formulas** (see Figure 11.13). To switch back to data view, click this button again.

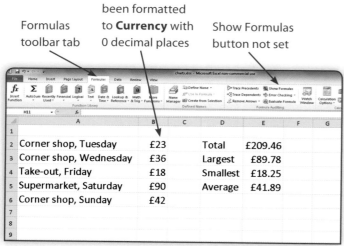

These cells have been formatted to **Currency** with 0 decimal places

Formulas toolbar tab

Show Formulas button not set

Figure 11.12: Data view is the default view for a spreadsheet

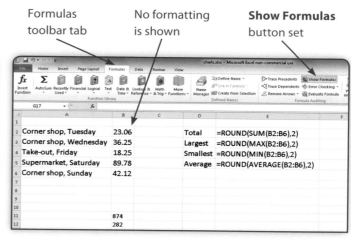

Formulas toolbar tab

No formatting is shown

Show Formulas button set

Figure 11.13: Use the Show formulas button to see the spreadsheet workings

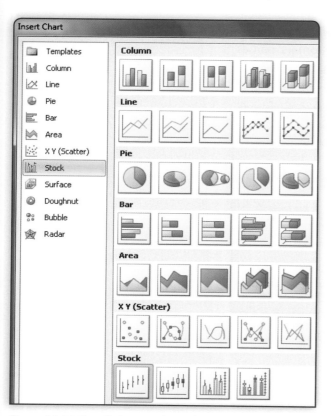

Figure 11.14: Excel® chart and graph types

Lists, tables, charts and graphs

A list is simply a collection of cells containing similar information, such as names. A spreadsheet can sort the list into order to make it easier to find a particular name.

A table contains data in rows and columns. You can sort the information in a table on more than one level. For example, you can sort people according to where they live, and then order those people by name, alphabetically.

Charts

Charts are useful if your spreadsheet contains words and numbers – for example, if you want to show sales figures for different products. Excel® offers a good range of charts and graphs (see Figure 11.14).

- **Pie charts** are useful for showing how separate items of data go to make up a whole. For example, Figure 11.15 shows popcorn sales at a local cinema broken down by size. This allows the cinema manager to see which sizes are the most popular. Pie charts are also useful for showing survey results.

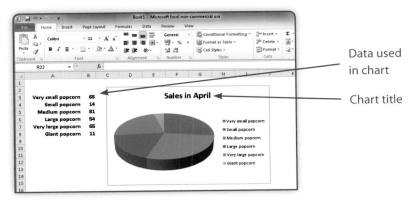

Figure 11.15: A pie chart

- **Bar** and **column charts** are useful for comparing sets of data. For example, a business may use a bar chart to compare sales of different products (see Figure 11.16).

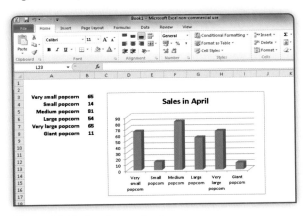

Figure 11.16: A column chart

- **Stacked bar** and **column charts** are useful if you wish to compare sets of data over a period of time – for example, to show the mix of sales each month (see Figure 11.17).

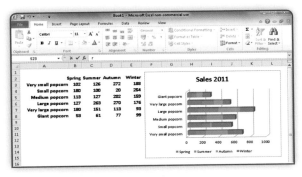

Figure 11.17: A stacked bar chart

- **3D charts** can be used as an alternative to stacked bar or column charts. They allow you to show a mix of items over a period of time. However, you must prepare them carefully to make sure information is not hidden (see Figure 11.18).

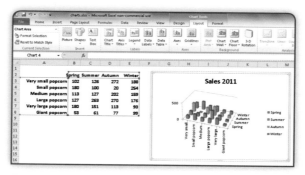

Figure 11.18: A 3D column chart

How to create a chart

1. Highlight the data you would like to use and then click on one of the **Chart** buttons in the **Insert** toolbar.

2. You can change the chart's design, layout and format using the **Chart Tools** toolbar, which appears if you click on the chart.

Graphs

An XY scatter graph is similar to a chart but it uses numerical data for both the **X-axis** and the **Y-axis**. For example, a supermarket might use an XY scatter graph to plot sales of a product against the length of shelf space used to display that product (see Figure 11.19). It is important to label both axes of a graph so that people can work out what it shows.

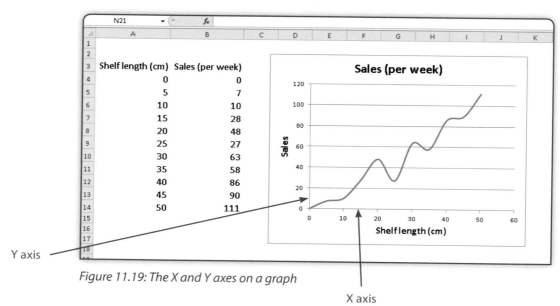

Figure 11.19: The X and Y axes on a graph

An XY scatter graph can be used to predict or estimate new figures. It does this by extending the existing (known) data with a trendline. You can estimate a new value by drawing a line from one axis to the data trendline and then drawing a line from the trendline to the other axis to see the predicted value. For example, a supermarket could use an XY scatter graph to predict how much shelf space it would need to sell a target amount of a product (see Figure 11.20).

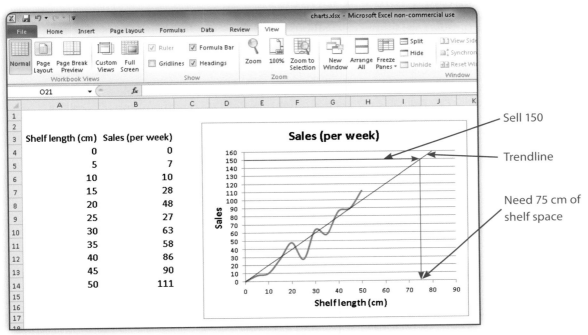

Figure 11.20: A graph to estimate how much shelf space is needed to sell a target amount of product

Decide when and how to use different methods

When deciding which type of chart or graph to use, the most important thing to consider is the type of data you need to show.

- A chart is best if you have a dataset containing words and numbers – for example, a list of products (words) and a sales figure (a number) for each product.
- You should choose a chart which explains your information as clearly as possible.
- If you are not sure which chart to use, try different ones and see which one you find easiest to read.
- An XY scatter graph is best if you have two sets of figures and one set depends on the other – for example, weight and height of children. If you add a trendline to your scatter graph, you can then use it to make predictions (as described above).

2.2 Use functions and formulas

Spreadsheets are very flexible and can be used for many different tasks. However, they are most commonly used to store and analyse numerical data. This is because spreadsheet software uses functions and formulas to perform calculations quickly, easily and accurately.

Simple arithmetic formulas

Formulas are simple calculations using +, –, / or * (used instead of ×) to add, subtract (take away), divide or multiply. Every formula must start with an equals sign (=), followed by the sum to be worked out. For example:

- **=C4+D4** will add together the numbers in cells C4 and D4
- **=C4–D4** will subtract the number in cell D4 from the number in cell C4
- **=C4*D4** will multiply the numbers in cells C4 and D4 together
- **=C4/D4** will divide the number in cell C4 by the number in cell D4.

When you type a formula into Excel®, you can use actual numbers (for example, =14+24) or cell references (=A1+B1). Using cell references in the calculations is very useful if you might need to update the figures in your spreadsheet. If you change the number in one of the cells in the calculation, the answer will update automatically.

If you type **=A4+B4** into cell C4, the program will add together the numbers in A4 and B4 and show the answer in cell C4. To perform this calculation, you can either type =A4+B4 or use the mouse to select the cells to be used.

How to use the =A4+B4 **formula**

1. Select the cell where the answer to the calculation will go (**C4**).
2. Type =
3. Click on cell **A4**.
4. Type +
5. Click on cell **B4**.
6. Press **Enter** or click the tick to the left of the formula bar to show the result (see Figure 11.21).

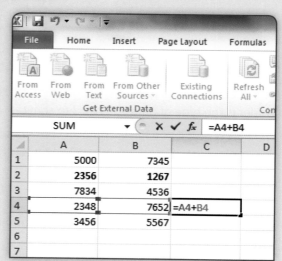

Figure 11.21: Entering a formula

Common functions

A function is a named calculation which you can select and use. As with formulas, every function must start with an equals sign. Some common functions as listed below.

- **=SUM()**
  This is used to add up the numbers in a range of cells. For example, =SUM(A4:D4) will add up the numbers in cells A4, B4, C4 and D4.

- **=AVERAGE()**
  This is used to find the average of numbers in a range of cells. For example, =AVERAGE(A4:D4) will find the average of the numbers in cells A4, B4, C4 and D4. It does this by adding them together and then dividing the result by how many numbers there are (as in a normal sum). If A4=5, B4=6, C4=8 and D4=9, the average will be 5+6+8+9 (= 28)/4 = 7.

- **=ROUND()**
  This controls how a number is rounded up or down. For example, if cell A4 contains the number 5.25, you could round this number up to 5.3 (one decimal place) using =ROUND(A4,1). Alternatively, you could round it down to 5 (0 decimal places) using =ROUND(A4,0).

  Using the ROUND function is not the same as using cell formatting to control the number of decimal places. Cell formatting only changes the way the number is shown. On the other hand, the ROUND function changes the actual value of the cell. For example, if cell A4 contains the number 5.25:

  - You can use the ROUND function to round the number up to 5.3. If you then type =A4*2 in another cell, the answer will be 10.6.
  - You can format the cell so that only one decimal place is shown (5.3). Now if you type =A4*2 in another cell, the answer will be 10.5 because the new calculation still uses 5.25 as the value in cell A4.

- **=MIN()**
  This will show the smallest number in the range of cells identified in brackets.

- **=MAX()**
  This will show the largest number in the range of cells identified in brackets.

There is more information about cell formatting in section *3.1 Format cells*, pages 243–244.

Designing formulas

You should be able to design formulas so that you can find the answers you want. To do this, you must understand:

- what you want from the formula
- how the calculation will work
- where the values used in the calculation will come from.

Values may be numbers or words typed into the calculation, or they could be cell references. Look at Figure 11.22 and imagine you want to use your spreadsheet to show the 15 times table. To do this you would take the following steps:

1. Type the numbers **1** to **12** in cells A3 to A14.

2. Type the letter '**x**' in each cell between B3 and B14.

3. Type the number **15** in each cell between C3 and C14.

4. Type an equals sign (=) in each cell between D3 and D14.

5. Type your formulas in cells E3 to E14.

Each formula will multiply the numbers in columns A and C, so:

● in cell E3, type =A3*C3
● in cell E4, type =A4*C4 and so on.

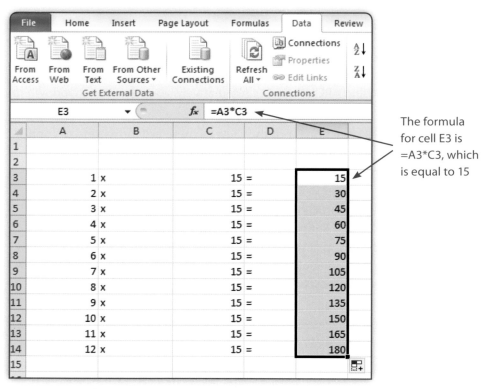

The formula for cell E3 is =A3*C3, which is equal to 15

Figure 11.22: Calculating the 15 times table using formula designs

To save time, you can copy the formula down column E.

How to copy formula

1. Type **=A3*C3** into cell E3 and press **Enter**.

2. Click on cell **E3** and move the cursor over the bottom right-hand corner of the cell. The cursor should change to look like a small black cross.

3. Click and hold down the left mouse button while you drag the cursor down column E. The formula will automatically update so that cell E4 reads =A4*C4, cell E5 reads =A5*C5 and so on.

Activity: Growth rate

Your next door neighbour has a 5-year-old daughter called Natalie. Every year on her birthday, Natalie is measured against a growth chart in her bedroom. Natalie went to a theme park as a treat for her last birthday, but was disappointed because the best rides had height restrictions of 1.4 metres. Her mother wants to know how old Natalie will be before she is expected to grow to 1.4 metres. She has asked for your help in estimating this using a spreadsheet.

Natalie's height so far has been 45 cm at birth; 70 cm at year 1; 79 cm at year 2; 89 cm at year 3; 94 cm at year 4 and 99 cm at year 5.

1 Create a spreadsheet with an XY scatter graph to plot Natalie's growth.
2 Draw an extension on the trendline to predict when Natalie will be 140 cm (1.4 m) tall.

Check your understanding

1 Describe two uses for a two-level sort.
2 Use the Internet to find and describe three spreadsheet functions.

3 Select and use appropriate tools and techniques to present spreadsheet information effectively

If every cell in your spreadsheet looks the same, it will be difficult to find and understand the information you want. In Microsoft® Excel® (as in other programs), you can change the look of your spreadsheet in various ways. For example, you can:

- change the colour of certain cells or the text inside them
- change the font style or size
- add borders to certain cells.

This will allow you to draw attention to important pieces of information and make your spreadsheet easier to read and understand.

3.1 Format cells

In order to format a cell or cells to change their look, you must first select (highlight) them. You can then change the formatting by using the following buttons in the **Home** toolbar (see Figure 11.23).

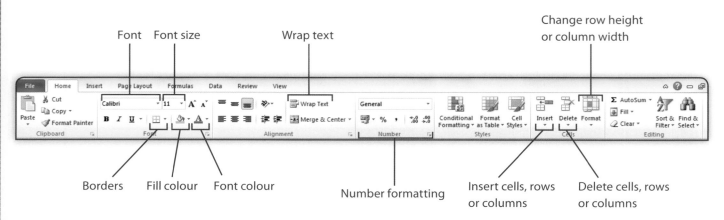

Figure 11.23: Using the formatting toolbar

Font	To change the appearance of the words or numbers in the spreadsheet
Font size	To change the size of the words or numbers
Font colour	To change the colour of the words or numbers
Fill colour	To change the background colour of a cell, row or column
Alignment	To change the position of data in a cell. If you do not change this setting, Excel® will automatically align words to the left of the cell and numbers to the right.
Text wrap	If you type a lot of text in a cell, it will spill over the edges and you will not be able to read all the text. If you use text wrapping, the cell will grow to fit in all the text you type.
Borders	To add borders to the cells. Borders are useful if you need to separate data into different sections or highlight important information.
Number formatting	To control how numbers, dates and times are shown.
Row height	To make rows taller or shorter.
Column width	To make columns wider or narrower.

Table 11.1: Formatting options

Number formatting

Excel® allows you to display numbers in several ways. For example, you can:

- change the number of decimal places shown
- add a symbol, such as £ or $, to figures relating to money (currency)
- change whether or not the spreadsheet uses a comma in long numbers (such as 1,234,567)
- adjust the format of dates (e.g. 31/12/11, 31/12/2011, 31-Dec-2011, etc.).

Some of these settings will use a specific formatting style, such as:

Currency

This adds a symbol before the number (e.g. £ or $) and shows 0 or two decimal places (see Figure 11.24). It is best to choose 0 decimal places (e.g. £3) if you are working with large figures such as thousands or millions. However, for smaller figures, you should probably choose two decimal places, so that figures are shown in pounds and pence (e.g. £2.95).

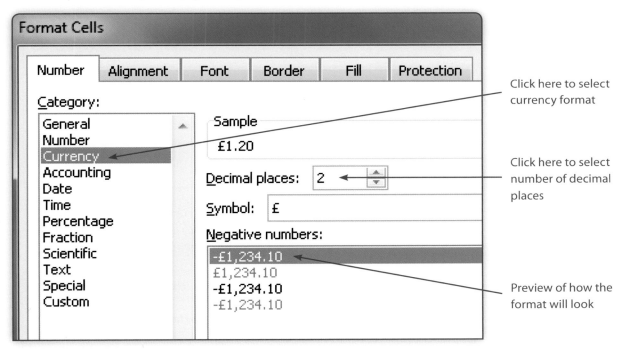

Figure 11.24: Currency format dialog box

Percentage

If you type a number such as 20% into a cell, Excel® will automatically set the format for that cell to percentage. This is useful for calculations using percentages. For example, suppose cell A4=20% and cell B4=100. If you type =A4*B4 in cell C4, the program will multiply 100 by 0.2 to work out 20% of 100 (i.e. 20).

Number

This removes other formatting (such as currency or percentage) so that figures are displayed exactly as you type them in.

3.2 Format rows and columns

As mentioned, you can adjust the height of a row or the width of a column. You can do this in several ways. However, remember you must first highlight the row(s) or column(s) you want to change.

Use the Format menu

You can use the **Format** menu to change the row height and column width.

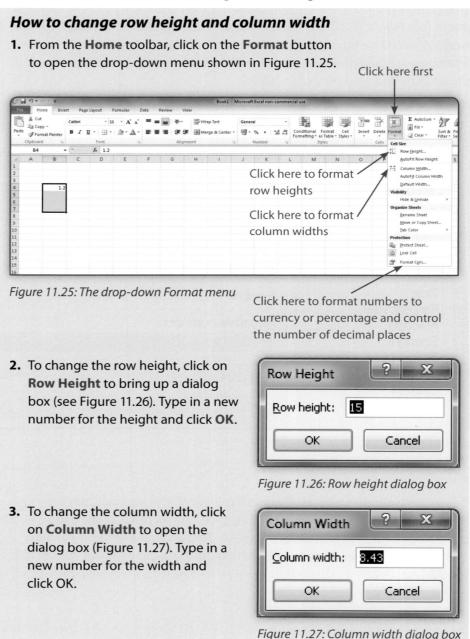

How to change row height and column width

1. From the **Home** toolbar, click on the **Format** button to open the drop-down menu shown in Figure 11.25.

Click here first

Click here to format row heights

Click here to format column widths

Figure 11.25: The drop-down Format menu

Click here to format numbers to currency or percentage and control the number of decimal places

2. To change the row height, click on **Row Height** to bring up a dialog box (see Figure 11.26). Type in a new number for the height and click **OK**.

Row Height

Row height: 15

OK   Cancel

Figure 11.26: Row height dialog box

3. To change the column width, click on **Column Width** to open the dialog box (Figure 11.27). Type in a new number for the width and click OK.

Column Width

Column width: 3.43

OK   Cancel

Figure 11.27: Column width dialog box

Use the mouse

You can also use your mouse to directly make changes. To change the height of a row, position the mouse pointer in the column showing the row numbers, over the line at the bottom of the row you want to change. The mouse cursor will change to a black cross with arrows (see Figure 11.28). Hold down the left-hand mouse button and drag the pointer up or down to change the height of the row.

To change the height of several rows at once – so that they are all the same height – select the relevant rows and then drag the line between any two selected rows (see Figure 11.29).

To change the width of a column, use the same method described above, but put the cursor between the letters of the columns you want to change.

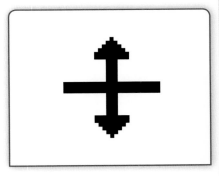

Figure 11.28: The cursor when you use the mouse to change row height

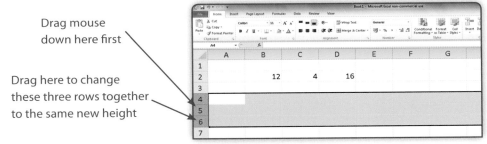

Drag mouse down here first

Drag here to change these three rows together to the same new height

Figure 11.29: Changing row height using the mouse

Use AutoFit

The third way to make formatting changes is to use **AutoFit**. The **AutoFit Row Height** or **AutoFit Column Width** options are in the drop-down **Format** menu. You can use these to set row height or column width so that the contents of the selected row or column fit exactly.

3.3 Generating charts and graphs

You have seen how to use Excel® to produce a range of charts and graphs. However, the charts and graphs you create will be difficult to understand unless you provide the following information.

A title

This states (briefly) what the chart or graph is showing. To add a title: open the **Layout** tab in the **Chart Tools** (see Figure 11.30) and choose **Chart Title**.

Axis titles

These explain what the figures on each axis represent – for example, 'Shelf length (cm)'. Excel® will usually add axis titles when the chart or graph is created. If it does not, open the **Chart Tools** menu as above and select **Axis Titles**.

A legend

This explains the data shown in the chart. For example, if you have a bar chart comparing two sets of data, the legend will tell you which colour is used for each dataset. Excel® will usually create a legend automatically when you create a chart or graph. To add a legend later (or edit the existing legend), open **Chart Tools** and choose **Legend**.

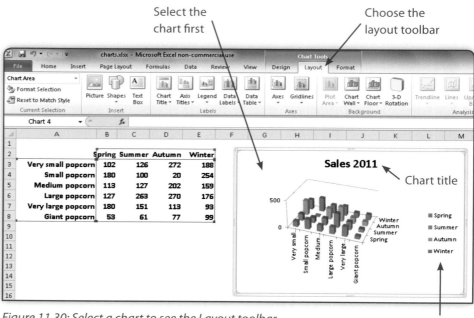

Select the chart first

Choose the layout toolbar

Chart title

Legend

Figure 11.30: Select a chart to see the Layout toolbar

3.4 Use appropriate page layouts

There are some very good print options in the dialog box that opens when you click on **Page Setup** (see Figure 11.31). From here you can set a header or footer which will print at the top or bottom of every page. You can also include page numbers or the date and time the spreadsheet was printed.

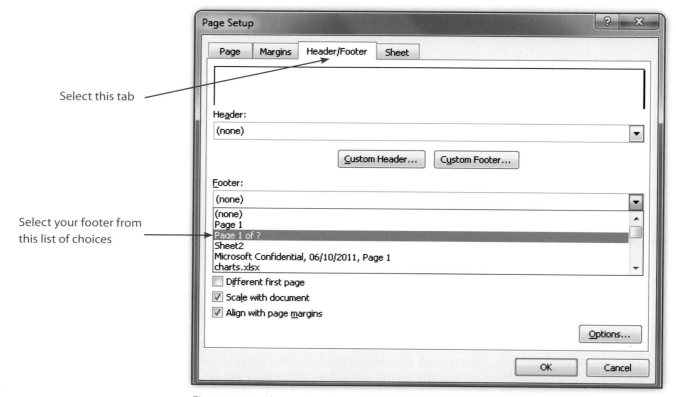

Select this tab

Select your footer from this list of choices

Figure 11.31: Change headers and footers in the Page Setup dialog box

You can also change the print area by opening the **Page Layout** toolbar and clicking on **Print Area**. If you click on **Set Print Area**, the area to be printed will be highlighted (see Figure 11.33). Click and drag the margins of the printed area to change it.

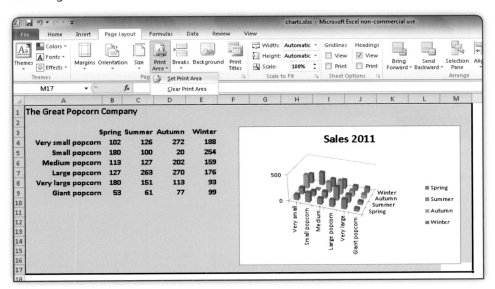

Figure 11.32: Set the print area from the Page Layout toolbar

If you just want to print a chart, select it before printing. If you wish to print a mixture of spreadsheets and charts, make sure that no chart is selected before printing.

If you select **Print** from the **File** menu, a print preview will show how the printout will look (see Figure 11.33).

There is very good control from the print preview.

- You can set the **orientation** to landscape or portrait.
- **Scaling** gives good size control. You can set it to fit the whole spreadsheet on one page or to make it print bigger (e.g. 200%) or smaller (e.g. 50%).
- The **margins** button allows you to set how much white space is between the edge of the paper and the printed spreadsheet.

Figure 11.33: The Print menu shows a print preview

3.5 Check spreadsheet information

In order to communicate information effectively, digital products and documents must be well structured, appropriately styled and error free. As always, you should check your work carefully. This is especially important with the type of data used in spreadsheets.

- Use spelling and grammar checkers. Excel® has a spell checker in the **Review** toolbar, to help you with proofreading (see Figure 11.34).
- Proofread text and numbers.
- Make use of feedback from others to help ensure good quality.
- Re-read the tasks you were set to make sure your spreadsheet meets the original needs.
- Check that your formulas are correct.
- If you identify any problems, you should make any corrections that are needed.

Click here to perform
a spell check

Select the
Review toolbar

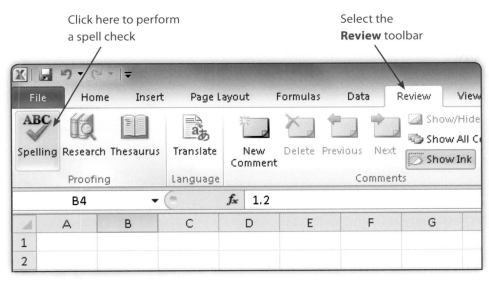

Figure 11.34: Excel® spell checker

Remember

A spell checker program will not pick up every mistake, so make sure you check your work carefully. Better still, ask someone else to check it for you.

Accuracy

Accuracy is very important, especially if your spreadsheet contains lots of calculations. One incorrect entry may affect the calculations and produce the wrong results.

You can check a calculation by selecting the cell it is in. Excel® will colour-code different parts of the calculation. It uses the same colour to highlight cells used in each part of the calculation (see Figure 11.35).

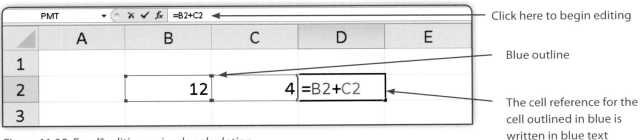

Click here to begin editing

Blue outline

The cell reference for the cell outlined in blue is written in blue text

Figure 11.35: Excel® editing a simple calculation

Activity: Expenses sheet

Your friend Sam works part-time making wooden toys for a craft shop run by Mr Ali. The job pays an hourly rate and a bonus for each toy made.

Mr Ali has been using pencil and paper to work out how much to pay his staff every week. This is slow and sometimes he makes mistakes, so he wants to do these calculations using a computer spreadsheet program instead.

As you are studying for an IT qualification, Mr Ali has offered to pay you to set up a simple spreadsheet he can use to do this work.

Staff pay is worked out as the number of hours, times the hourly rate, plus a bonus based on how many toys were made that week.

The hourly rate is £6 and the bonus is 50p per toy made. So, for a week where 20 hours were taken to make 30 toys, Sam was paid £135.

All the workers are on the same hourly rate and bonus scheme.

1 Create a spreadsheet for Mr Ali to use to calculate the pay for Sam and the other workers. The spreadsheet needs separate cells for the hourly rate and the bonus paid per toy so that it will be very easy to change these, if needed.

Check your understanding

1 If a cell holds 0.03, what would it show if it is set to percentage format?
2 Can you find three examples of charts from the Internet?
3 What are the legend and title used for in a chart?
4 What is a trendline?

ASSESSMENT ACTIVITY

You and some friends have been helping a local charity shop by donating unwanted items for the shop to sell on. The manager of the shop has asked you to prepare a spreadsheet that clearly shows the contributions you and your friends have made. The table shows how many items your group has donated during the year.

	Jan	Feb	Mar	Apr	May	Jun	Jul	Aug	Sep	Oct	Nov	Dec
Mo	14	12	13	15	10	12	11	11	12	14	15	11
Mary	12	12	15	16	16	10	14	17	13	17	15	11
Sally	12	13	12	12	10	14	11	11	10	11	12	11
Simon	11	12	10	12	11	11	10	11	11	12	12	11
Brae	10	12	11	12	11	12	13	13	12	11	15	13

The manager would also like to be able to print an information sheet from your spreadsheet. This needs to show clearly how much each of your friends has contributed throughout the year, and also during three-month (quarterly) periods (i.e. Jan–Mar, Apr–Jun, Jul–Sep, Oct–Dec).

1 Create a word processed document and save it as 'Your name Charity notes' (e.g. Richard Charity Notes). In this document explain how you will choose the information to include in your spreadsheet. Include a sketch to show how you will lay out your spreadsheet.

2 Create a spreadsheet, following your plan. Check that you have entered all relevant information correctly. Print your spreadsheet and label it SS#1.

3 Save your spreadsheet as 'Your name Charity' (e.g. Richard Charity) in a folder called 'Unit 11 Spreadsheet software'. In the Notes document that you started in question 1, include a screenshot showing that you have saved your spreadsheet correctly.

4 Add to your Notes document, explaining what you will do to summarise and display the required information. Make sure you explain which functions and calculations you will use to work out each person's quarterly and year-end performance. Also identify any graphs or charts you will use. Explain why you think these graphs and/or charts will be appropriate to display the information.

5 In your spreadsheet, add the functions and formulas you identified in question 4. Print a formula view of your spreadsheet and label it SS#2.

6 In your spreadsheet, create the charts and/or graphs you identified in question 4. Print and label them SS#3.

7 As well as being clear and easy to read, your spreadsheet should also look professional. Format your spreadsheet using any techniques you think are appropriate (e.g. make headings bold, change the colour of key cells etc.). Take a screenshot of your formatted spreadsheet and paste it into your Notes document. Use callouts to explain the formatting you have used.

8 Add to your Notes document to explain the tools and techniques you used to format and improve your charts and/or graphs.

9 Use the Print Preview menu to adjust the page layout so that your spreadsheet looks right for printing. Take a screenshot of this screen and paste it into your Notes document. Add callouts to explain what you changed and why.

10 Print your spreadsheet again and label this version SS#4.

11 Proofread your printed spreadsheet, correct any errors and print a final version. Label this printout SS#5.

Website software

The Internet is one of the most exciting developments in IT. It has fundamentally changed not only the business world, but also the way we all now live our lives. It allows us to communicate, to access information and be entertained. It even makes learning easier and more fun.

The Internet is made up of billions of web pages and in this unit you will learn how to make a website of your own. You will design and create a site of at least three pages with at least two different types of content. You will also learn how to add hyperlinks so that users can navigate around your pages. You will then upload your website so it can be viewed on the Internet or an intranet.

Learning outcomes

After completing this unit you should be able to achieve the following learning outcomes.

» **LO1** Plan and create web pages

» **LO2** Use website software tools to structure and format web pages

» **LO3** Publish web pages to the Internet or an intranet

1 Plan and create web pages

Websites can be used for many different purposes. For example, they may provide information, sell products or services, or allow people to interact with each other. In this section, you will learn about:

- the types of content you may find in web pages
- the file types you may need to use
- the importance of careful planning.

1.1 Content and layout

Web pages are a form of multimedia. This means they can use all types of content. This could include text, images, animation, video, sound and even games. A web page is like a container which holds all these items. When designing a web page, you should also think about the background – you could choose a particular colour or image.

The content on web pages can be broken into five general categories. Table 12.1 outlines these categories.

Text	The words on a web page might be headings (title), body text (the main text on the page) or captions (small sections of text, separate from the body text, used to describe images or other elements). A web page designer will need to think about how the text looks (e.g. font, size, colour) and the content of the text (e.g. whether it has been proofread, whether it gives the correct information).
Images	The images used on a website may be photographs, diagrams or drawings. You must consider their size and quality, as any that are too large or of very high quality may slow the website down.
Numbers	Numbers can be presented in many ways – for example, a table listing the prices of different products, or a pie chart showing the results of a survey. You should always present numbers so that they are easy to understand. Graphs also help to display information more clearly.
Background	There are several options for a background, including solid colour, gradients, patterns, textures or images. You should think about what content will be put over the background to make sure that it is still clear and that the text on the page is readable. It is also important to make sure that the background does not distract you from the main content.
Interactive elements	Interactive elements may include video, buttons, **hyperlinks** or menus. These elements must be intuitive – in other words, you must be able to work out how to use them without being told.

Table 12.1: Types of web page content

Storyboard

A storyboard is a design which shows what a product will look like (see Figure 12.1). Sometimes it also shows how it will function. For a website, you should sketch each page and draw lines between the sketches to show how the pages will link together.

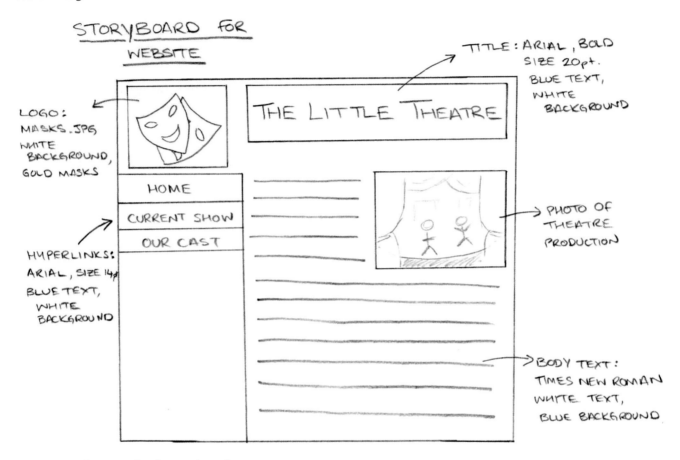

Figure 12.1: An example of a storyboard

The sketches should be quite rough. For example, instead of writing out text or drawing a picture, you could just draw a box with 'text' or 'image' written in it. However, the sketches should show the layout of each page and describe what you will be including. You can then use your storyboard to list everything you will need to collect for your web pages.

Make sure you annotate your storyboard carefully. This means you should draw a line to each item and describe what it will look like. For example, for text, you might describe the font, size, colour and alignment you will use. For an image, you might say what the picture will show and whether it will be a photograph or a drawing.

When drawing lines to show how the pages link, also include arrows to show the direction of the links. Ideally, in a well designed website, every page will be connected to every other page. In other words, on every page there will be links to all the other pages.

Activity: Website design

The owner of the Paws for Thought pet shop in your town has decided to create a website to attract customers. The site needs to give details of the pets for sale. It may also offer information and advice about how to care for different animals.

The owner has asked you to produce the website for Paws for Thought. Before you can create the site, you need to produce a detailed design.

Picture in your mind how the website will look. You will probably need a heading, information about the shop, an image of one of the pets for sale and perhaps a logo.

1 Describe your website in words, stating at least three important things it must have (think about how it looks).

2 Create a design for your web pages. Consider all parts of the design, including background, text and images you will use.

3 Label your design to explain it in detail. For example, label each section of text and describe the font, size, colour etc.

4 In a separate document, write the content for your web pages. Make sure you proofread it.

Remember to save all your files and give them meaningful names.

Purpose

What is the purpose of your website? The answer to that question should help you decide what it will look like, the style you are going to use and what contents you should include.

- **Entertainment**: For a website that is meant to entertain, bright colours, bold lines and a simple layout may be best.
- **Sales/advertising**: If your website is designed to sell products or services, it must look professional, with high-quality images. It must also be easy to navigate.
- **Information**: If your website is providing information, it must have clear text which is divided into sections to make it easy to understand.

Audience

Who is the website for? Who are you trying to attract to it? This will also affect how each page looks. A website for children will probably use bright, primary colours, but a website for adults might use more complex colours. You should also consider the fonts you choose: will a website using Comic Sans look professional?

Paws for Thought specialises in domestic pets such as cats, dogs, guinea pigs, hamsters and rabbits. Although the shop is not planning to sell pets through their website at this stage, they would like it to:

- promote the business
- give details of how customers can find the shop
- allow contact through email
- show pictures of some of their pets for sale.

1 Describe the purpose of the Paws for Thought website. You may wish to write the main purpose in sentences and use bullet points for specific aims.

2 Describe the target audience for the website. Think about age group, gender, background, etc. Is there more than one target audience? Is one audience likely to be more important than another?

1.2 Website templates

Website templates are ready-made layouts which you simply add content to. For example, the template might have text boxes with the font and colours already set, so that all you need to do is type in your text. A template might also have boxes for you to add images or other items. You can use the same template over and over again to make sure every page in your website looks the same.

When selecting a template, you must consider the following questions.

- Does the template match your design? If not, you will not be able to create the website you want.
- How much can you change in the template, and how much is locked by the person who created it? For example, can you adapt the layout if you need to?
- Can you add extra pages or delete ones you do not need?
- Can you upload the template to the Internet where you need to?
- How much technical knowledge will you need to use the template? Do you have the skills you will need to create your web pages?
- Does the template come with tools to help you edit it (as sites such as WordPress™ and Blogger™ do)? If not, can you put the template into a web page editor (such as Adobe® Dreamweaver®) or edit it in a different way?

Once you have selected your template, you must save it in an appropriate place. Then you can start adding your own content and adjusting the layout. Your content will include text, images, numbers and background (see section *1.6 Store and retrieve files*, page 264).

1.3 Combine information needed for web pages

Websites can include many different types of information, including text, images, sounds and video. Although you may not use all these items on every web page, you should know how to combine different types of information effectively.

Hamsters are available in a range of colours and cost £7.50

Figure 12.2: Using a photograph with a caption on your website

Combine images with text (use photo captions)

When designing a web page, you should not consider the text or the images alone. Think about the page as a whole and decide how the images and text will work together.

If you are using both images and text, you need to think about how to place them. For example, you could keep the images separate or use word wrap. This is where the text flows around the images.

You may use captions to explain what your images show. For example, on the Paws for Thought website you could add a caption to a picture of a hamster so that the viewer knows it is a hamster and not a gerbil or a guinea pig. You could also use the caption to give more information such as the breed or the price.

Activity: Picture this

Research on the Internet and find three websites which have used images in different ways. Answer the following questions for each website.

1 How have the images been placed on the page?
2 Are there captions?
3 What are the good points and bad points of each website, in terms of the images used?

Add audio and/or video

Key term

Embedded – part of a document or file itself.

Besides text and images, web pages can also include audio and/or video. The audio could be background music which plays when the user enters the website. Alternatively, it could be **embedded** in the page so that you have to click a play button to hear music or speech.

You can use audio to describe some of the content on the page. This is particularly useful for very young children or people with disabilities.

Video can be used to entertain or inform. Usually, videos are embedded so that you have to click a play button to watch them. This is because if a video plays automatically when the web page is opened, users with slower Internet connections will find that the page takes a long time to load. It can also be very annoying if a video starts playing every time you return to the page. Video can be very effective, but must not be overused.

Present numbers in charts or graphs

Numbers can be shown, for example, in bar charts, pie charts or scatter graphs. These may help people understand the information you are giving them. For example, if you have done a customer survey, you could present your results in a table or you could produce a pie chart (see Figure 12.3). Users may find it difficult to understand the table. However, with a pie chart they can easily see which answer has the most votes.

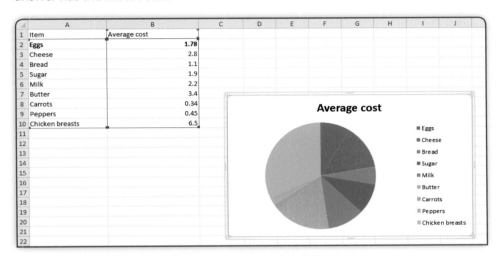

Figure 12.3: A pie chart

1.4 Copyright constraints

Copyright law protects someone's work and stops other people from copying it or using it without permission. In the UK, copyright is covered by the Copyright Designs and Patents Act 1988. There is more information about acknowledging sources under section *1.3 Copyright constraints on the use of information* in *Unit 4 IT communication fundamentals*, pages 74–76.

Education is exempt from copyright law, as it only applies when the item being copied is used to make money. For example, if you make a website for selling products and you use someone else's content without permission you will be breaking the law. However, the website you produce for this unit is purely for educational purposes, so you will not be breaking copyright law.

Plagiarism is another word for copying: this is NEVER allowed. To learn more about plagiarism, see *Unit 4 IT communication fundamentals*, pages 75–76.

1.5 File types

Table 12.2 shows some of the many different file types you might come across while making your website.

Extension	Full Name	Description
Web pages		
.htm **.html**	Hypertext Markup Language	HTML is the basic language in which web pages are written. Web pages made in Dreamweaver® usually use these **extensions**.
.xml	eXtensible Markup Language	XML is an updated version of HTML. If you are using templates, you may come across this file type.
.css	Cascading Style Sheets	If you are using templates, you might see CSS files. These hold the formatting of a web page separately to the actual page.
Text		
.rtf	Rich Text Format	A format used to allow other word processing software to open Microsoft® Word® documents.
.doc	Microsoft® Word® Document	A document made in Word®.
.txt	Textfile	A very basic text file, often made in Notepad.
.pdf	Portable Document Format	A document file which can be opened in all systems and is locked, meaning it cannot be edited. You will need a PDF viewer before you can open a PDF. The most common program of this type is Adobe® Reader®, which is free to download from the Adobe® website.
Images		
.bmp	Bitmap	Usually a large file. The image is saved at the quality it was made. Often produced from Microsoft® Paint.
.gif	Graphics Interchange Format	Usually small files, which are good for websites. Can have a transparent background, but often can be lower quality. Can be produced from Adobe® Photoshop® and similar graphics software. Can also be used to save small animations.
.jpg **.jpeg**	Joint Photographic Experts Group	Usually a larger file than GIF but often higher quality. Good for photographs. Can be produced from Photoshop® and similar graphics software.

.png	Portable Network Graphic	Usually a small file (smaller than a GIF), and good for websites. Can have a transparent background, although often is lower quality. Can be produced from Photoshop® and similar graphics software.
.psd	Adobe® Photoshop® Drawing	An image created in Photoshop® which can only be opened in Photoshop®. This file would need to be saved as a different file type before being used on a web page.
.tiff	Tagged Image File Format	May be the raw file type used by a camera to save the images taken. Usually used to save print publishing because the files are large and able to store a lot of detailed information.
Audio		
.wav	Microsoft® WAVE	A sound file suitable for playing on Windows® systems and Microsoft® software such as Windows® Media Player®. Often a large file, as it is uncompressed.
.wma	Windows Media Audio	A sound file suitable for playing on Windows® systems and Microsoft® software such as Windows Media® Player®. Often a small file as it is compressed but can lose quality.
.mp3	MPEG-2 Audio Layer III	A sound file suitable for playing on all systems. Often a very small file, as it is compressed. Lower quality than raw CD-quality audio tracks and often lower quality than other compressed audio tracks.
General		
.swf	Shockwave Flash® Movie	An animation made in Flash®.
.exe	Executable	An executable file, meaning one which will run – such as a game or other program.
.avi, .flv, .mpeg, .mov, .wmv	See description	Movie file types: Audio Video Interleave, Flash® Video, Motion Picture Experts Group, QuickTime® Video, Windows Media Video
.xls	Microsoft® Excel® spreadsheet	A spreadsheet file that can be used for numerical and financial data, including calculations and graphs.

Table 12.2: File types used in making web pages

When you save content from other sources (for example, images from the Internet), you must make sure you use an appropriate file type. If not, you will need to convert the file.

How to convert files

You can do this in two ways.

1. Open the item using the appropriate software (for example, open an image in Photoshop®). Then use **Save As** and select the correct file type.
2. Use a conversion program or conversion website such as **www.convertfiles.com** or **www.zamzar.com**.

1.6 Store and retrieve files

Before you begin to make your website, you must decide how you will save it. You will create lots of different files during this project. Therefore, you must give these files meaningful names and save them in a suitable location. Otherwise, you will waste time looking for them during the project. You will also have problems when you try to upload them to your website.

You should create a folder for all your website files and give it a name such as 'Website software project'. Inside this main folder, you could create subfolders, perhaps for images, text, pages and so on. Whenever you save a part of your website, you must make sure it is saved in the appropriate folder.

When saving web pages and web page content, you should be very careful with filenames. Make sure you follow these rules.

*   Do not include spaces.
*   Do not include any symbols except underscore (_).
*   Keep filenames short (fewer than 20 characters).

Filenames which do not follow these rules may work for a while. However, you will run into problems if you try to upload them to the Internet or make the web page more complicated.

Your home page should always be called **index**. Most web browsers are programmed to recognise the index as the first page and will look for an index file in your website files. If the browser does not find an index file, it may produce an error message or load a different page as the home page.

In business, it is good practice to use clear filenames for the following reasons.

*   If something happens to the designer, or if they leave the company, someone else will need to finish the website. If this happens, the new designer must be able to understand the filenames.
*   Many websites are maintained by someone other than the designer. This person will need to understand the filenames so that they can maintain the website properly.

You now need to start to create the website for Paws for Thought. Create the following materials:

- a selected template which you will use to create the pages in your website
- prepared content ready to be put into the website in Microsoft® Word®
- a list of sources you have used, with dates and identifying any copyright and other constraints
- a list of content created with the file types used, with explanations
- a demonstration of good information management, showing folders and sensible filenames.

Note: You do not need to produce all the content which will go onto your website – you can use content which has been created by other people. However, you MUST state who wrote/produced it, where you got it from (e.g. a website address) and the date on which you found the information. You should also explain what copyright applies to the content you use and make sure you understand any other constraints on its use.

Check your understanding

1. Name five types of content which can be included in a web page.
2. Why is it important to state the purpose and audience of a website when designing it?
3. Why is a web page template useful?
4. What is copyright?
5. What are the differences between a .gif and a .jpg?
6. Why is it useful to create a new folder before starting to make a website?
7. Why are meaningful filenames helpful?

2 Use website software tools to structure and format web pages

2.1 Website features

Your website must be simple to use and to understand. If it is not, visitors to the site will quickly move on. You can use various features to make your website user friendly. For example, hyperlinks will make it easier to move between different areas on the site.

Navigation and hyperlinks

A **hyperlink** is a feature used to connect different web pages, or different parts of the same web page. Hyperlinks help you navigate around or between websites. When you click on a hyperlink, the connected web page will open. You can use several different types of hyperlink in a web page.

Rollover – a type of button which changes when the mouse pointer passes over it. Usually, the image will change to show interaction. Buttons can also change when they are clicked.

Easter Egg – a secret put into a computer product, such as a website or a computer game. Easter Eggs are hidden but designed to be found by users. They usually contain bonus content (often something funny).

Pixelated – pixelation happens when a bitmap image is made too large. The pixels become visible and the picture looks blocky and unclear (see also *Unit 9 Imaging software*, page 172).

- A **text hyperlink** is a word or set of words which have been turned into a hyperlink. The word(s) will often be blue and/or underlined. When clicked, they take you to another web page or a different section of the same page.
- An **image hyperlink** is an image which has been made into a hyperlink. When clicked, it will take you to the linked page or section. Image hyperlinks can also have **rollovers**.
- A **button hyperlink** is a special animation which has been made into a hyperlink. There are some button hyperlinks in Dreamweaver® which have been pre-made in Flash®.
- A **hotspot** is an area which has been made into a hyperlink. This is often on an image but it could also be a section of text or even something hidden, such as an **Easter Egg**. Clicking on any part of the hotspot will take you to the hyperlink destination.

Clarity and accessibility

A website should be clear and understandable. To make sure the text is readable and useful, you should consider the following points.

- Is the text visible against the background? For example, yellow text on a white background is very difficult to read, just as black text will be difficult to read on a dark coloured background.
- Is the text in a suitable font and size? For young children or older people, you could use a large font size that is easier to read.
- Has the text been spell checked and proofread?
- Is the text clear and does it make sense?
- Does the text provide all the information the user will need? If not, are there links to other information sources?

When using images, you must make sure they are not **pixelated**. If an image pixelates when you stretch it to the size you want, you have two choices. You can use the image at a smaller size or you can use a different image. If you created the image, reopen the original file and check which file type you have used. Perhaps a different file type would work better, such as a .jpg instead of a .gif.

Figure 12.4: A pixelated image

2.2 Editing techniques

When creating content for your web page, you may use various editing techniques. Table 12.3 lists some of these.

Select	You can select elements on a web page by highlighting (for text) or clicking and holding with the mouse (for images etc.).
Copy and paste	When you copy and paste, you make a duplicate (another copy) of something, identical to the original. You can then paste this copy somewhere else. You may be able to copy by pressing **Ctrl+C** and paste by pressing **Ctrl+V** on the keyboard.
Cut and paste	When you cut and paste, you remove the original and put it somewhere else. You may be able to cut by pressing **Ctrl+X** and paste by pressing **Ctrl+V**.
Undo	**Undo** will cancel the last action you took. You may be able to undo by pressing **Ctrl+Z** on the keyboard.
Redo	If you have used **Undo**, **Redo** will 'uncancel' the last action you took. If you have not used Undo, Redo may repeat your last action. You may be able to redo by pressing **Ctrl+Y**.
Drag and drop	To drag, 'pick up' an element of a web page by clicking on it with the mouse and holding down the left mouse button. Then drag the mouse so that the element moves with the cursor. To drop the item into a new location, release the left mouse button. This is very useful if you need to move items around on a web page but do not want to cut and paste.
Find	Find will search for a word or phrase on a page. You may be able to find by pressing **Ctrl+F**.
Replace	This will find a word or phrase on a page and replace it with different text. You may be able to replace by pressing **Ctrl+H**.
Size	It is very easy to resize an image or other element on your web page. Click on the image and small squares or circles (called handles) will appear on the edges. Drag the handles in or out to make the picture smaller or larger. Take care to keep the picture in proportion or it may begin to look stretched or squashed as you resize it. Holding down the **Shift** key while you resize an image should keep it in proportion.
Crop	Crop allows you to remove part of an image. See also *Crop* in section *1.2 Prepare images* in *Unit 9 Imaging software*, pages 172–179.

Table 12.3: Editing techniques

Activity: Formatting your website content

Open the document containing the content for your website that you wrote for the earlier activity, 'Creating website content' (page 265).

1 Make sure the content is complete, proofread and spell checked.

2 Copy your content, section by section, into your website template. Be careful to only copy heading text into the heading section, body text into body text and so on.

3 Check your website for any errors and make sure the formatting is correct (font, size, colour, etc.).

Key term

WYSIWYG – 'What You See Is What You Get'. This is where what you have designed on your screen is what the final product will look like. This is good for website creation software as what you see when you are designing will be what the users will see when the site is on the Internet.

2.3 Check web pages

As you are creating your web pages, you should check regularly to make sure they work and look the way you expect. You may be using a **WYSIWYG** editor such as Dreamweaver®. However, you will not know what the website will actually look like on the Internet unless you test it. In Dreamweaver®, do this by pressing **F12** at the top of the keyboard.

There are several IT tools you can use to check your web pages.

● **Spell checker**: Programs such as Dreamweaver® do not have spell checkers, so it is best to copy the text into a word processing program such as Word® and check it there. You could do this while you are writing the text or at the end.

● **Grammar checker**: You might also find this word processing tool useful for checking that your grammar (sentence structure, punctuation etc.) is correct.

● **Word count**: This tool is useful to check how much text you have on a page – numbers of words, paragraphs and sometimes characters (individual letters and numbers). You can then decide whether you have too much or too little text.

It is important to check the image size on web pages. Large images will slow the page down, both when you are working on it and when the end user views it.

Think about the alignment of text and images. You can use left, centre or right to move items to those positions on the web page. You can also use justified for text, which will straighten both edges of the text, as in a book.

Check your web pages in a browser such as Internet Explorer® to see what they will actually look like online. In Dreamweaver®, press **F12** to do this. This will make sure that the text is readable, the images are clear and the right size and the layout of all content is correct.

Suitability of file format

Make sure you have saved all your files using a suitable format.

- Are the files small enough to upload quickly?
- If any are very large, can you make them smaller? For example, if you have saved an image as a .jpg, can you save it as a .gif to make it smaller, or will this reduce the quality too much?

When checking your files, you must also ensure that your website is suitable for the original purpose and audience. Look again at your design notes and make sure you have met the brief.

Activity: Creating your website

1   Create the website you have designed for Paws for Thought. You should:
   a   use a variety of editing and formatting techniques
   b   ensure the text and images on the site are clear
   c   make sure your website has enough pages to cover the content
   d   make sure you have a good navigation structure to allow users to move between the pages easily.
2   When you have completed your website, test it using IT tools. Make sure it is suitable for the purpose and audience you identified and that it matches your designs. Make any corrections necessary and then retest the site.

Check your understanding

1   Name three ways in which you can make text clearer on web pages.
2   What is pixelation and how does it happen?
3   Describe four types of hyperlink.
4   What key would you press to test a website in Dreamweaver®?
5   Why are small file sizes preferred for websites?

3 Publish web pages to the Internet or an intranet

Once you have created your website, checked that all the content is correct and tested the site to make sure it works correctly, you are ready to publish it.

3.1 Upload content to a website

When you upload a website, you copy the site and all related files (text files, images etc.) to a web server so that anyone can see it on the Internet. This web server has the **URL** (Internet address) for your website. When users type in the address, they will be able to access the files on the web server and view your website on their own Internet browser.

The owner of a website must buy a domain name in order to give their website a specific address. For example, the online retailer Amazon owns the domain names amazon.com, amazon.co.uk, amazon.de and so on. The company has purchased these domain names and linked them to their web servers so that their customers can find the websites easily.

In a web address, anything after the extension (such as .com or .co.uk) refers to a specific page on the web server. For example, **www.amazon.co.uk/books** might take the user to the 'books' page on the Amazon website (see Figure 12.3).

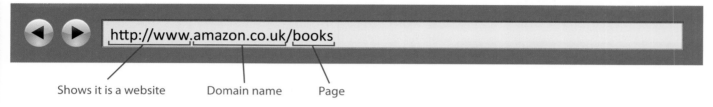

Shows it is a website Domain name Page

Figure 12.5: Parts of a web address

To view a website, you must open your **Internet browser** (such as Internet Explorer® or Firefox®) and type a web address into the address bar (see Figure 12.6). This sends a message to the web server to request the page you want to see. If the page is there, a copy is sent back and downloaded to your computer.

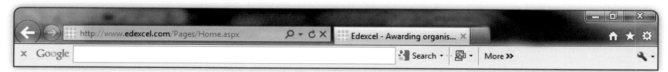

Figure 12.6: The address bar in an Internet browser

You can also publish your website in other ways. One of these is to upload it to your school, college or workplace intranet or virtual learning environment (VLE). An intranet is an online network limited to people within an organisation (such as a college). For example, content on a college intranet can only be seen by members of the college (students and tutors).

The administrators (managers) of the intranet (probably the IT support team) will usually give each user a username and password. Different types of user (tutors, students) will have access to different areas of the intranet. When you upload a website to an intranet or to the Internet, it is important that users can see your website but not make changes to it.

Activity: Accessing your site

1 When you use the computers at your school, college or workplace, do you have to log in? Are there parts of the network which you are not allowed to access?

2 Draw a diagram to show how a user will access your website. Make sure you include the following elements.

    a the web designer (you) uploading the website to a web server

    b a user using an Internet browser and the web address

    c the Internet in the middle (this is often drawn as a cloud).

Test a web page

An Internet browser is a program which understands the code that makes up web pages and displays them visually for the user. Most browsers are fairly similar. However, they may understand the code in different ways. This means that your web page may look slightly different, depending on the browser used.

As mentioned earlier, you can test your web pages in Dreamweaver® by previewing them in your browser. Press the **F12** key to do this.

● Check that the pages look right.
● Compare the preview with the original design to make sure it is accurate.

Problems with websites

Although you will have checked your web pages thoroughly, there may be some problems with your website after it has been uploaded to the Internet. These problems may include:

● layout issues, where content has moved
● content which is missing or not appropriate
● text which is missing or unreadable
● images which are not shown, are the wrong size or are rotated incorrectly.

If any elements are missing, make sure all the files you need have been uploaded to the web server, saved in the right folders with the correct filenames.

ASSESSMENT ACTIVITY

Athletikids is an organisation who provides sports activities for young people on evenings, weekends and during school holidays. They have asked you to create a website to promote them and the activities that they provide, with details of locations, age ranges and prices.

Task 1

1 Describe the purpose of the Athletikids website. You may wish to write the main purpose in sentences and use bullet points for specific aims.

2 Describe the target audience for the website. Think about age group, gender, background, etc. Is there more than one target audience? Is one audience likely to be more important than another?

3 On paper, design each page of the website. Show all parts of the design including background, text and the images you will use. Label your design to explain it in detail, (e.g. each section of text) and describe the font, size, colour, etc.

Task 2

You are now ready to create the website for Athletikids.

1 Find all of the materials you will need for your website including the template, text and images.

2 Create a list of sources you have used, including dates and identifying any copyright and other constraints.

3 List the file types you have used and explain why.

4 Demonstrate that you have used good information management, showing folders and sensible filenames.

5 Add all of the materials to your website, including using your template

6 Use a variety of editing and formatting techniques, and create your navigation structure using hyperlinks

7 Make sure it is complete, proofread and spell checked

Task 3

1 Upload your content/website so it can be viewed on the Internet or an intranet.

2 Test the website to check that it can be viewed correctly.

3 Keep a log of all problems you found and how you dealt with them. You may wish to use this table format.

Problem number	Status	Date found	Problem	Action taken	Date resolved

Word processing software

This unit will provide you with the knowledge and skills that you need to edit, combine, structure, format and present information using a word processing program. It will introduce you to a range of documents that are commonly used by organisations. Using various templates, tables and forms you will then design your own documents to meet a particular purpose or function.

Word processing software is essential to both business and everyday users and in this unit you will learn how to use it effectively. This unit works well alongside *Unit 2 IT user fundamentals*.

Learning outcomes

After completing this unit you should be able to achieve the following learning outcomes.

» **LO1** Enter, edit and combine text and other information accurately within word processing documents

» **LO2** Structure information within word processing documents

» **LO3** Use word processing software tools to format and present documents

1 Enter, edit and combine text and other information accurately within word processing documents

1.1 Types of information

Documents can be made up of different types of information, including:

- text
- numbers and graphics such as tables and charts
- photographs and other images
- simple graphic images such as lines and borders.

Key term

Agenda – list of items or matters to be discussed in a meeting.

The type of information you will need in a document will depend on the purpose of the document and who will be reading it. For example, a letter to a customer will include standard items such as date and name and address of both sender and recipient. A notice about a meeting would give the date, time, location and purpose of the meeting and include an **agenda**. Figure 13.1 shows an example agenda for a meeting between a builder and the clients.

Date: 1st October 2012

Time: 10.00am

Venue: Meeting Room 2

Agenda

1. Apologies
2. Minutes of last meeting
3. Flooring options
4. Type of wood for doors and finish to be used
5. Choice of kitchen cabinets
6. Installation dates
6. AOB (Any Other Business)
7. Date and time of next meeting

Figure 13.1: An example agenda

Information in a poster will be limited and factual. The text will be large and images will be designed to catch people's attention.

Memos are short, formal messages used in businesses. They may vary in style and layout, but tend to use the same structure (see Figure 13.2).

Memo

From: Head of Business

To: All Business teaching staff

Date: 16th November 2012

Re: End of Term

Please note that the end of term this year is on December 18th. Classes will finish early at 2.30pm. Make sure that all of your students know this date and that they hand in all outstanding assignments before they leave for the Christmas holiday.

Figure 13.2: An example memo

Activity: Leaflets

1 Collect some of the leaflets that come through your door at home. Your teacher, tutor or supervisor may also provide some examples.

2 Look at the leaflets you have collected and identify their common features. Are any of them particularly effective? If so, why? Do any of them have important information missing?

1.2 Templates

A template can be seen as a 'fill in the blanks' document. Most of the fixed titles, structures and fonts are already set, so all you have to do is add the specific information you want to record. Templates may be:

- simple word processed documents that can be reused
- special files that have been created using word processing software.

If you need to create a new document and you have already produced a similar one (for example, a letter), you can simply open the old document, delete the original information and use the document as a template. This is particularly useful if you have spent time getting the headings, layout, fonts etc. just right. However, you MUST make sure you save the document with a new filename. If not, you will overwrite the original document and the information in it will be lost.

Activity: Creating templates

1 Type up the agenda shown in Figure 13.1. Save and print it.
2 Find out the meanings of any of the agenda items you are unsure of.
3 Delete some of the text to create a new template document that you can use every time you need to create an agenda. Make sure you save your template with a new filename.
4 Imagine that you work in a newsagent's shop and that you are responsible for the small advertisements in the front window. Design and create a simple document template to give to people who want to place an advertisement. This will make sure that all the advertisements look similar and include the important details.

1.3 Combine information of different types or from different sources

Word processed documents are usually made up of text. However, you can also use images or tables – for example, to add interest or to present information more clearly. In some documents, such as instruction manuals, diagrams are essential to help the reader understand what needs to be done. If your document includes numerical information, you may be able to present it better by using charts or tables.

Inserting images into documents

Microsoft® Office® includes a library of ready-made ClipArt images which you can use freely within your documents. You can also insert pictures that you have downloaded from the Internet or photographs you have taken yourself and saved on your computer. However, before using any image, you must make sure that you have the right to do so. See section 1.3 *Copyright constraints on the use of information* in Unit 4 IT communication fundamentals, pages 74–76.

How to insert a piece of ClipArt

1. Click where you would like the picture to appear in your document.

2. Open the **Insert** menu and click on **ClipArt**. A dialog box will open on the right-hand side of the page.

3. In the **Search** box, type in what you are looking for (e.g. meeting) and click **Go**. A selection of images will appear (see Figure 13.3).

4. Choose an image and click on it to insert it in your document.

Click here to insert a picture you have saved on your computer

Click here to insert a piece of clip art

Type what you are looking for in this box and then click **Go**.

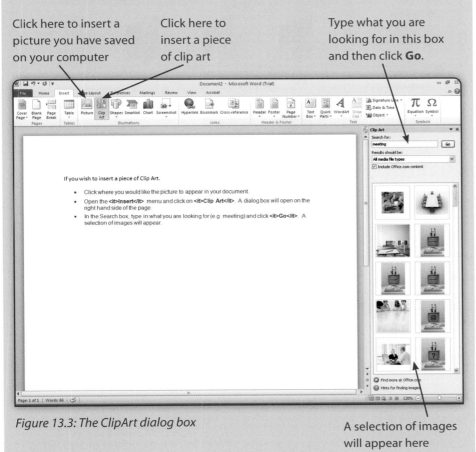

A selection of images will appear here

Figure 13.3: The ClipArt dialog box

How to insert an image that is saved on your computer

1. Click where you would like the picture to appear in your document.

2. Open the **Insert** menu and click on **Picture** (see Figure 13.4).

3. In the dialog box that opens, navigate through the folders to find the picture you would like to insert.

continued

4. Click on your picture and then click **Insert**.

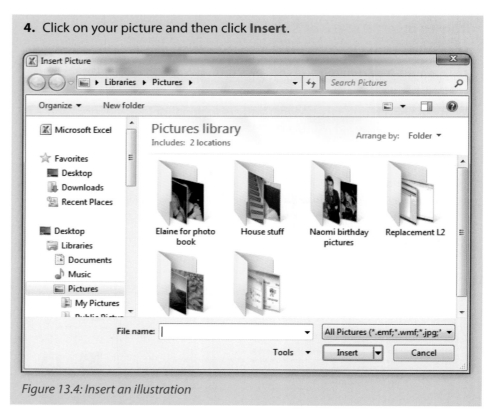

Figure 13.4: Insert an illustration

If the image you have inserted is the wrong size or in the wrong place, you can change it.

How to make changes to an image

1. Click on the image to select it. Small squares or circles (known as sizing handles) will appear around it.

2. To change the size of the image but keep the height and width in proportion: click, hold and drag one of the **corner handles** until the size is right.

3. To change the width of the image: click, hold and drag one of the **side handles** until the size is right. Your image will be stretched or squashed sideways.

4. To change the height of the image: click, hold and drag one of the **top** or **bottom handles** until the size is right. Your image will be stretched or squashed vertically.

5. To move the image: click in the centre of the image, hold down the **left-hand mouse button** and drag the image to a new location.

Remember

You can find hundreds of thousands of pictures on the Internet. However, this does not mean that they are copyright free and available for use. You must be very careful when using images in documents that are going to be published or made public. ALWAYS check whether you have permission to use an image – otherwise, you may be breaking the law.

If you only want to use part of an image, you can **crop** the image to cut off the areas you do not want. You can find out how to crop an image in *Unit 10 Presentation software*, pages 211–212. It is a good idea to save your document before you crop the image, in case you make a mistake.

Activity: Creating a poster

1 Open Microsoft® Word®. A new, blank document will be created automatically.

2 Type in the following text and format it so that it is centred on the page:
   - Shortcroft Allotments Society
   - End of season sale of vegetables
   - Bring your spare vegetables along to the allotment site on
   - Sunday 12th October
   - Sale starts at 2:00pm

3 Save your document as 'Vegetable Sale' with your initials (e.g. Vegetable Sale AK).

4 Check the text carefully and correct any errors.

5 Insert an appropriate image, either clip art or a picture you have taken yourself.

6 Add your name and the date at the bottom of the document and save it again.

7 Print your poster.

Shortcroft Allotments Society

End of season sale of vegetables

Bring your spare vegetables along to the allotment site on

Sunday 12th October

Sale starts at 2.00pm

Figure 13.5: Your finished poster may look something like this

1.4 Inputting information

You can input text to a system in several ways, but the most popular way is to type it using a keyboard. This could be on a desktop computer, a laptop, mobile phone or other portable device. Alternatively, you can use a mouse to point and click or drag and drop.

The other main ways of inputting information are:

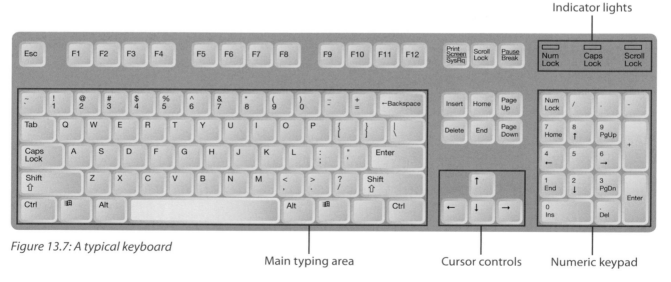

- **Voice recognition** – This is an alternative to typing on a keyboard. If you speak to the computer, software will convert the words you say into text to display on the screen. This can be much quicker than typing. It can also be very useful for people with disabilities who may find typing difficult or painful.
- **Touch screen** – Touch screen technology allows an electronic device (e.g. a mobile phone, tablet computer or games console) to recognise and respond to touch. The user touches the screen itself with a finger or a stylus, rather than using a keyboard or mouse.
- **Stylus** – This is an input tool similar to a pencil and is used with devices such as graphics tablets and hand-held games consoles. Instead of using your finger to press buttons on the touch screen, you use the stylus. This allows you to work more accurately on a small screen. It also avoids getting fingerprints all over the screen.

Figure 13.6: A touch screen device

Using the keyboard

In English-speaking countries, keyboards are laid out so that the keys used most often (such as the letter E) are easy to reach. The keyboard layout shown in Figure 13.7 is typical, although you may find slight differences in the keyboard you use.

Figure 13.7: A typical keyboard

The most commonly used keys are the letters A to Z. The top line of letter keys begins with the letters QWERTY, so this is known as a QWERTY keyboard. This follows the same order as old-fashioned typewriters.

Although Microsoft® Word® provides tools to help you to check your documents, it is important that you try to type accurately at all times. Typing fast may result in **typos** such as 'teh' instead of 'the'. Although the **Spell Check** program would highlight this particular example, other typos may not be spotted or corrected. Therefore, you should keep checking what you have typed to make sure you have not made mistakes.

You should also try to be efficient when creating documents. It is a good idea to learn some keyboard **shortcuts**, as they can save a lot of time. Common shortcuts include copy (**Ctrl+C**), cut (**Ctrl+X**) and paste (**Ctrl+V**). See section *1.5 Use editing tools to amend document content*, page 283.

Other 'special' keys

Caps Lock If you press the **Caps Lock** key once, it will cause all of the alphabetic letters to be capitals. Press it again to return to lowercase letters.

Shift If you press and hold the **Shift** key, you will switch the letter keys from lowercase to uppercase (or uppercase to lowercase if Caps Lock is on). You can also use the Shift key to access the top character on keys. For example, if you press **Shift+ @ 2** , you will get the @ symbol instead of a number 2.

Ctrl The **Ctrl** or Control key is always used with another key to access a shortcut. For example:

1. Press **Ctrl+S** to save a document.

2. Press **Ctrl+P** to open the **Print** window.

Print Screen SysRq The **Print Screen** key is used to send an image of the current screen to the printer. However, it now places the image on the **clipboard** so that you can paste it into a document.

Key terms

Typos – typographical errors (typos) are mistakes made when setting out text.
Clipboard – when you cut or copy an image or a piece of text, it is stored on the clipboard. You can then paste the contents of the clipboard into a different place in the same document or into a different document in any Microsoft® Office® application.

Activity: Explore your keyboard

1 Experiment, use the **Help** function or use other sources of information to find out:
   - how you can move the cursor around with document (e.g. by using the mouse or the arrow keys)
   - the difference between the **Backspace** key and the **Delete** key
   - how you can activate the numeric keypad (at the right-hand side of the keyboard) to allow you to type numbers more quickly.
2 Immediately to the left of the **Q** key and above the **Caps Lock** key is the **Tab** key. Experiment with this if necessary and explain what it does and when you might use it.

Enter information into existing tables, forms and templates

As mentioned on page 276, a template has fixed titles, structures and fonts and you simply add information. Similarly, you may be asked to enter information into pre-set tables or forms. A form is usually a very structured document to which you need to add specific information in certain places. You have probably filled in many forms – for example, to join a course, register an email address, join a library etc.

These days, many forms are online. However, you complete them in much the same way as any other document (see Figure 13.8). Simply make sure the cursor is in the right place and then type in your text as usual.

Join the library

Please complete the registration form below. Fields marked with a * must be completed.

Your details

Title	[▾]
First name*	[ ]
Surmane*	[ ]
Gender*	[ ]
Date of birth*	Day [▾] Month [▾] Year [▾]

Your address

House number*	[ ]
Street	[ ]
Town/City	[ ]
County	[ ]
Postcode*	[ ]

Your contact details

Home phone number	[ ]
Work phone number	[ ]
Mobile phone number	[ ]
Email address	[ ]
Confirm email address	[ ]

Once you have filled in all your details, click **Done** and your request will be processed. **DONE**

Figure 13.8: An example of an online form

1.5 Use editing tools to amend document content

Microsoft® Word® has a number of editing tools that allow you to correct mistakes or make changes to your document.

To amend an existing document, you just need to open it and add or delete text or images. However, when adding text you must make sure you type in the right place.

How to add text

1. When you move the mouse, the cursor moves. This usually looks like a capital letter I. Position the **cursor** where you would like to add your text and click the left mouse button.

2. A blinking vertical line will appear where the cursor was – this is called the **insertion point**. The insertion point will stay where it is when you move the cursor away.

3. Any text you type will be added to the document at the insertion point.

Before you type new text, it is important to make sure your keyboard is in the right 'mode'.

- **Insert**: This means that, as you type new text any text after the insertion point will be pushed to the right to make room for it.
- **Overtype**: As you type new text any text after the insertion point will be 'overwritten' – the original text will be deleted to make room for the new text.

To switch from **Insert** to **Overtype** mode, press the **Insert** key. Press this key again to change back to **Insert** mode. Experiment with these options for yourself to make sure you understand how they work.

How to delete text

1. You can delete characters to the right of the insertion point by pressing the **Delete** key.

2. You can delete characters to the left of the cursor by pressing **Backspace**.

3. To delete larger sections of a document, highlight the text and/or images you want to delete and press either the **Backspace** or the **Insert** key.

Did you know?

You will need to highlight text and objects for many reasons (to delete them, move them or change the colour/font/size, etc.). To highlight, position the cursor at one end of the text you wish to select, hold down the left mouse button and drag the cursor over the text. When it is highlighted, the background colour will change.

Activity: Amending a document

1 Open the blank agenda document you created earlier in this unit and create two new agendas. Use the following details.
   - A meeting planned for 9:00am on 4 December. The meeting will take place in the canteen. The meeting is mainly about the roof to be constructed. The three main items for discussion are the types of tiles to be used, insulation and when the roof will be installed.
   - A follow-up meeting on 11 December at 10:00am in the canteen. The meeting will recheck decisions about the roof and then discuss the damp course and possible flooding risks.

2 Save your documents as 'Agenda 4 December' and 'Agenda 11 December', with your initials at the end of the file name (e.g. 'Agenda 4 December AK').

3 Print both agendas and check them carefully. Correct any errors.

Other useful editing tools

The wide range of editing tools available in Microsoft® Word® was outlined in section *2.2 Editing techniques* in *Unit 7 IT software fundamentals*, page 137. Here we will look again at some of the most useful tools for amending documents.

Copy, cut and paste

The **Copy**, **Cut** and **Paste** functions make recreating text and images very simple.

1. You can use **Copy** to create one or many copies of selected text or images. The original text or image is left in place.

2. The **Cut** tool removes the selected text or image and stores it on the clipboard for pasting to a new location.

3. Use the **Paste** tool to insert the copy in a different document or in a new location in the same document.

How to use Copy, Cut and Paste in different ways

When you have highlighted a section of text or an image, you can copy, cut and paste in three different ways.

1. Use the buttons on the **Home** menu on the toolbar (see Figure 13.8).

2. **Right click** on the selected text/image and choose an option from the menu that appears.

3. Use one of the following keyboard shortcuts: **Ctrl+C** to copy, **Ctrl+X** to cut or **Ctrl+V** to paste.

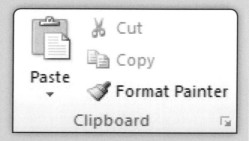

Figure 13.9: The Cut, Copy and Paste buttons in the Format toolbar

Drag and drop

Another way to move items or files is to drag and drop them.

How to use drag and drop

1. Select the text or image

2. Click on it and hold down the left mouse button.

3. Drag the text to a new location.

You could experiment with this technique as you may find it quicker and simpler than using **Cut** and **Paste**.

Undo and redo

Undo cancels the last action you took, which can be very useful if you make a mistake. Click the **Undo** button in the title bar or press **Ctrl+Z** on the keyboard.

If you have used Undo, the **Redo** tool will 'uncancel' the last action you took. If you have not used Undo, Redo may repeat your last action. To redo something, click the Redo button in the title bar or press **Ctrl+Y**.

Find and replace

Use the **Find** tool to find a word or phrase in a document. Hold down **Ctrl** and press **F** to pull up the **Find and Replace** box or go to the **Editing** section and select the button you want to use.

You can use **Replace** to replace every example of a certain word with an alternative (see Figure 13.9). This is useful if you need to change the same thing several times in a document. For example, if a customer's name has been spelled incorrectly throughout a document, you can correct all the mistakes at the same time. This will save you having to read through the letter and change the name each time it appears.

Figure 13.10: The Find and Replace buttons

1.7 Store and retrieve document files effectively

From your work in earlier units, you will know how to save and open documents in other Microsoft® programs such as Excel® or PowerPoint®.

When you open Word®, a new document is created automatically. Any information you add to this document is stored in the current (temporary) memory of the computer. This information will be lost if there is a power cut or if the computer develops a fault, so it is important to save your document as soon as possible.

Saving a file

It's important to save your work – and keep saving it as you create it – otherwise your work will be lost.

> #### How to save a document for the first time
> 1. Open the **File** menu and select **Save As**.
> 2. In the dialog box that appears, give your file a meaningful name and choose a folder to save it in.

If you do not choose a folder, the file will probably be saved in your **Documents** folder. However, you should ask your teacher, tutor or supervisor where you are expected to save your files. You may be asked to create new folders for each aspect of your work.

After you have saved a document for the first time it is important to save it regularly as you work on it. This way you will not lose too much work if there is an IT problem. To save a document, click the **Save** icon in the title bar or select **Save** from the **File** menu.

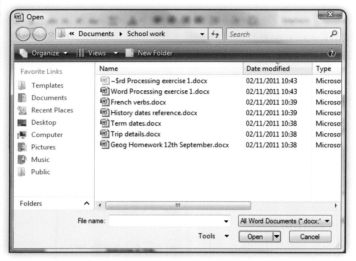

Figure 13.11: The Open dialog box

Opening an existing file

Most of your documents will be already stored on your computer.

How to open a stored document

1. Open the **File** menu and select **Open**. A dialog box will open (see Figure 13.11).
2. Find the folder where your file is saved, click on the file and click **Open**.

If you cannot find the file you are looking for, you may need to ask for help.

Printing a file

To print a document, select **Print** from the **File** menu, choose your print options (see Figure 13.12) and then click **OK**. When you click **Print**, you will see a **Print Preview** view of your document. This changes as you change the print options, so you can check how your printout will look.

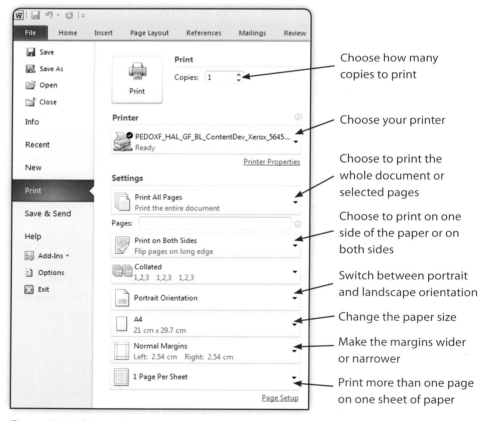

Figure 13.12: Print options

Closing a file

To close Microsoft® Word® completely, click the red 'X' in the top right-hand corner of the application window, or select **Close** from the **File** menu. You will be prompted to save your work if you have not already done so.

Check your understanding

1 Describe why templates are useful.

2 List four different input methods, apart from a keyboard.

3 Give two reasons why it is sensible to use the Find and Replace tool to replace words in a large document.

4 You have been asked to produce a document which shows how many calories there are in different foods. Describe the type(s) of information you would use – for example, unformatted text, text with tabs, a table or a bar chart.

5 A friend has asked you to check a letter he is sending to a library about a part-time Saturday job. What tools will you use to check his letter? How else could you make sure that he has not made any mistakes?

2 Structure information within word processing documents

If your document has a good structure, it will be easier to read and understand. If your document contains a lot of text, you can give each section or paragraph a new heading – this book uses that technique to add structure. In other situations, however, you may need to present your information in tables.

2.1 Create and modify tables

Tables are very useful if you need to display information that is naturally divided into sections. Look at the examples in Table 13.1 and Table 13.2 to see how you might use a table to present information.

Temperature in °C	Temperature in °F
0	32
5	41
10	50
15	59
20	68
25	77
30	89

Table 13.1: Equivalent temperatures in centigrade and Fahrenheit

Task	Date set	Date completed	Comments
Make a template agenda document	1 Nov	8 Nov	Try not to rely on the spell checker program when checking documents
Make a poster for the vegetable sale	8 Nov	15 Nov	Practise using formatting techniques to make the poster more interesting
Create two new agenda documents	15 Nov	22 Nov	Remember to save each document with a new name
Answer *Check your understanding* questions	22 Nov	29 Nov	Keep notes for reference

Table 13.2: Homework tasks for iTQ Unit 13 Word processing software unit

Creating a table

You can create a table in a Word® document or other programs, such as Excel®.

How to create a table in a Word® document

1. Click in your document where you would like to insert the table.

2. Open the **Insert** menu and select **Table**.

3. Draw the cursor over the boxes (cells) to choose how many rows and columns you would like in your table. Click the left mouse button to create the table (see Figure 13.13).

4. To add information to your table, just click in the required cell and type as normal.

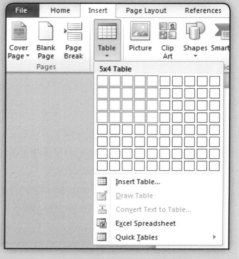

Figure 13.13: Inserting a table

Add and delete rows and columns

It is very easy to add or delete rows and columns to spreadsheets.

How to add a new row

1. Select and **right click** on the row where you would like your new row to go.

2. Select **Insert** from the drop-down menu and choose an option from the new menu that appears – either **Insert Rows Above** or **Insert Rows Below** (see Figure 13.14).

How to add a new column

1. Select and **right click** on the column where you would like your new column to go.

2. Select **Insert** from the drop-down menu and choose an option from the new menu that appears – either **Insert Columns to the Left** or **Insert Columns to the Right**.

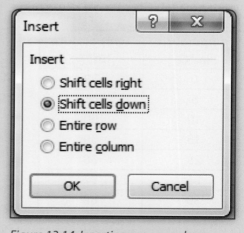

Figure 13.14: Inserting rows or columns

How to delete a row or column

1. Highlight and **right click** on the row(s) or column(s) you would like to delete.
2. Select **Delete Rows** or **Delete Columns** from the drop-down menu.

Activity: Creating a table

1   In a new document, create a table with three columns and at least seven rows.
2   Label the columns 'Destination', 'Airport' and 'Flight time'.
3   Carry out some research on the Internet. Choose at least six holiday destinations and, for each one, find out:
   a   which airports you can fly from to travel to that destination
   b   how long it takes to fly there (just the flight time, not time spent at the airport).
4   Add this information to your table.
5   Give your table a suitable title and type your name and the date at the bottom of the document.
6   Save your document as 'Flight times' with your initials (e.g. 'Flight Times AK') and print it out.
7   Add another column to your table, between the columns for 'Destination' and 'Airport'. Fill in the right country for each destination (e.g. Destination = Paris, Country = France).
8   Add a new row and type in the details of one more destination.
9   Save and print the updated version of your table.

2.2 Select and apply heading styles to text

In many formal documents (such as reports), information will be divided into chapters or sections. You should make sure that all headings of the same level are given the same style so that the structure of the document is clearly visible. Look at the different types of heading in this book (for example, unit titles, main headings, paragraph headings, etc.). You will see that they all use a consistent (standard) style.

You can add styles by formatting each heading separately. However, in Word®️ you can add styles more easily and much faster by using **Styles** (see Figure 13.15).

Figure 13.15: The Styles toolbar

To apply a particular style to a heading, highlight the heading and then click on the appropriate style (for example, 'Title', 'Heading 1', 'Heading 2' etc.). If you use the same style for all headings of that type, your document will look much more professional. It will also be easier for readers to find the information they are looking for.

3 Use word processing tools to format and present documents

Microsoft® Word® includes many tools for formatting document in different ways, such as to emphasise particular words or sections. This will help you present information more clearly and effectively.

Many organisations use set or standard layouts for different types of document. This way they can make sure all their documents are consistent and professional in appearance. Standard documents include letters, memos, reports, invoices and newsletters.

3.1 Format text

To format a word or section of text, highlight it and then click on the appropriate icon in the **Home** toolbar (see Figure 13.16). For example, you can make a key word **bold** or <u>underline</u> it to show that it is important. You can also change the font or the font size to emphasise particular words or phrases.

Allows you to change the font of the highlighted text. Click on the 'down' arrow to see the different fonts you can choose from.

Use this menu to change the size of the font

Use these buttons to make the font larger or smaller

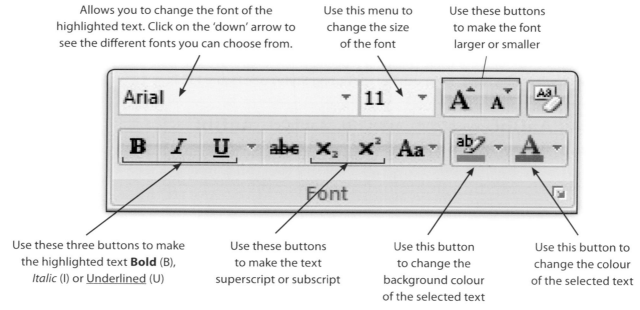

Use these three buttons to make the highlighted text **Bold** (B), *Italic* (I) or <u>Underlined</u> (U)

Use these buttons to make the text superscript or subscript

Use this button to change the background colour of the selected text

Use this button to change the colour of the selected text

Figure 13.16: The formatting icons

Activity: Formatting 1

1 Open a new blank document and type in the following text.

> Difference between word processing software and spreadsheet software
>
> Spreadsheets and word processing programs are similar in look and feel but a spreadsheet application is better for working with number data while a word processing program is better for working with text.
>
> Spreadsheets allow the user to enter number data into a document known as a 'workbook' and to use this data to do calculations. Text can also be entered into spreadsheets and is often used to give headings to columns of data.
>
> A word processing program lets you compose letters, memos and other documents quickly. It will also let you format your document with a variety of fonts, graphics and charts.
>
> Both spreadsheet and word processing programs will let you transfer data to other applications. They will also allow you to save completed files in a variety of formats. Both programs come with spelling and grammar checking tools, find and replace tools, and page formatting and justification options.

2 Save the document as 'WP and spreadsheets' with your initials (e.g. 'WP and spreadsheets AK').

3 Print your document and check the printout very carefully. Correct any errors.

4 Make the title bold and centred.

5 Change the word 'number' to 'numeric' throughout the document.

6 In the last paragraph, emphasise the words 'spelling' and 'grammar' by formatting them in italics.

7 Add your name and date to the bottom of the document, then save and print this new version.

3.2 Format paragraphs

You can also format whole paragraphs to control, for example:

- alignment
- use of bullet points and numbered lists
- line spacing
- borders and shading.

To learn more about these topics, see the section *Formatting paragraphs* in *Unit 10 Presentation software*, pages 215–217.

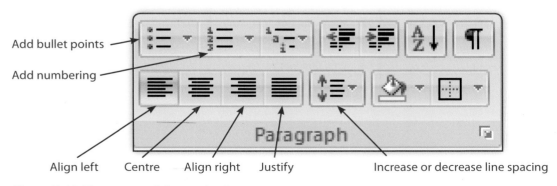

Figure 13.17: The paragraph formatting buttons

Borders and shading

You can draw attention to particular words, phrases or sections of your document by adding borders or changing the shading (the colour of the background behind the text).

How to add a border to a section of text

1. Select the text you would like to put a border around.

2. Click on the **Borders and Shading** icon in the **Home** toolbar.

3. Select the type of border you would like from the drop-down menu that appears (see Figure 13.18).

For example, this sentence has an **Outside border** around it.

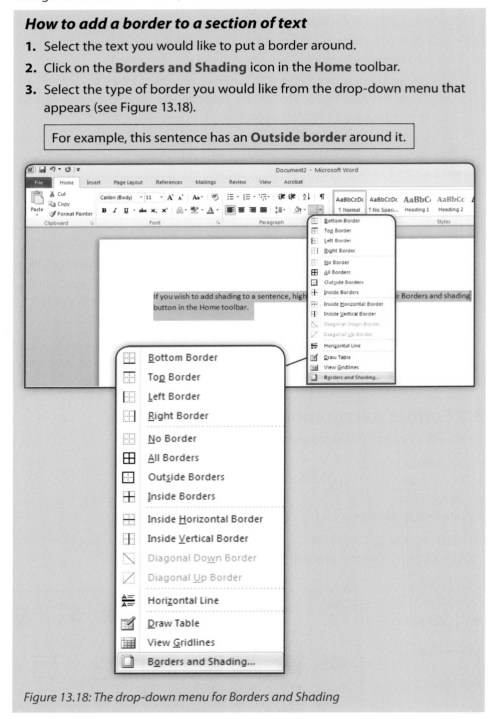

Figure 13.18: The drop-down menu for Borders and Shading

How to add shading to a section of text

1. Select the text you would like to add shading to.
2. Click on the **Borders** and **Shading** icon in the **Home** toolbar, as before.
3. Select **Borders** and **Shading** from the menu that appears (see Figure 13.18).
4. From the dialog box, open the **Shading** tab, choose the colour you would like and then click **OK** (see Figure 13.19).

For example, this sentence has been shaded in pale blue.

Click here to choose the colour for your shading.

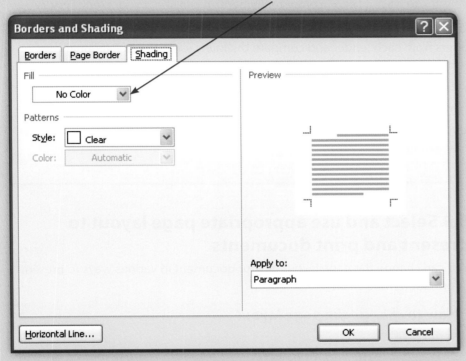

Figure 13.19: The Borders and Shading dialog box

1 Your friend has asked you to proofread a document they have created. You realise that you need to make lots of detailed notes. Explain which formatting options you could apply to the document to make it easier for you to add detailed comments by hand, on a printout. (You will need space to write your comments.)

2 Create a new Word® document and type in the text below. Apply different character formatting options (e.g. bold, italic, etc.) to help the reader understand the content.

Tips on taking out a loan

Here are some hints on what to look out for when arranging a loan. Borrowing is a part of everyday life. However, there are many factors to take into account when taking out a loan so that you borrow sensibly. If you do not keep up your repayments it can affect your credit history.

Do your research

Gather together the offers from each lender and compare the loans using the APR (annual percentage rate), length of the loan and the TAR (total amount repayable).

Make sure you understand the costs, charges, and terms and conditions of the loan agreements.

Check for penalty charges

Read the small print carefully and check you know about any penalties for late or missed payments or for early repayment of the loan.

Figure 13.20: Set paper size

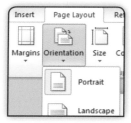

Figure 13.21: Set page orientation

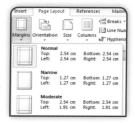

Figure 13.22: Set page margins

3.3 Select and use appropriate page layout to present and print documents

You can change the page layout of your document in various ways to present information more clearly.

How to change the page layout

Paper size

1. Open the **Page Layout** toolbar.

2. Click on **Size** and choose the setting you would like (see Figure 13.20).

Page orientation

1. Open the **Page Layout** toolbar.

2. Click on **Orientation** and choose portrait or landscape (see Figure 13.21).

Margins

1. Open the **Page Layout** toolbar, click on **Margins** and choose a setting (see Figure 13.22).

continued

Page breaks

1. To start a new page before the current one is full (for example, to keep sections separate), open the **Insert** toolbar.
2. Select **Page Break** (see Figure 13.23).

Page numbers

1. Open the **Insert** toolbar.
2. Select **Page Number** and choose an option (see Figure 13.24).

For more information, see section *2.4 Page layout* in *Unit 7 IT software fundamentals*, page 139.

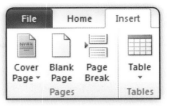

Figure 13.23: Insert page break

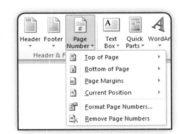

Figure 13.24: Insert page numbers

Activity: Page layout

1 Open the file you saved earlier for the Activity: Formatting 1 (page 291). This will be a useful test to check whether you used a sensible name for the file.
2 The document will probably be in portrait on A4 paper. Find out how to change the orientation to landscape, and reprint the document. Decide or discuss with another learner whether you think it looks better in portrait or landscape.
3 Make both side margins much bigger. Again, print the new version.
4 Put a page break after each paragraph. You can use the menus, but a shortcut is **Ctrl+Enter**.
5 Add automatic page numbering.
6 Save this document under a different name and print the new version.

3.4 Check documents meet needs, using IT tools and making corrections as necessary

You can check your documents in many ways to ensure that they are grammatically and visually correct. These checks are particularly important in business. A letter with spelling mistakes, factual errors or inconsistencies will look very unprofessional. It may also cause a business to lose customers or clients.

Spell check and grammar check

As mentioned earlier, Microsoft® Word® comes with a spelling and grammar check program. First you need to make sure that this is set to the right language.

How to set the checker languge

1. Open the **Review** toolbar, click on **Language** and select **Set Proofing Language**.
2. Choose your language and click **OK**.

The spelling and grammar check program will flag up possible errors in different ways.

1. **Red wavy line** under a word. The word is not in the built-in dictionary. This may be because you have misspelled it or because it is a name or specialist term. If you right click on the word, a list of suggestions appears, from which you can choose.

2. **Green wavy line** under a phrase or sentence. This means there may be a grammatical error. Right clicking on the phrase or sentence will tell you what the problem is or suggest an alternative.

You should also proofread your work carefully because the spell checker will not spot some mistakes – for example, if you have typed 'won' instead of 'own'. Also proofread to make sure that the facts in your documents are correct.

Checking content and layout

When checking your document, think about its purpose and make sure that the content is appropriate for that purpose. In particular, you should think about the following.

Font style	Is the style you have used suitable for the document's purpose and intended audience? In a formal report, you should use a simple, traditional font such as Times New Roman. In a poster, however, you may choose to use a more exciting font, to catch people's attention and encourage them to read the poster.
Font size	Is the size appropriate? In a poster, the text must be large for people to read it at a distance. Similarly, in a document for young children or older people, you could use a larger font size.
Font colour	If you have changed the text colour, you must make sure you can still read it clearly. For example, yellow text on a white background will be difficult to see.
Page layout	People usually use the standard layouts provided in Word® because they look reasonable and print correctly in most situations. If you change the layout (margins, orientation, etc.) you must check that the document still prints correctly.

The print preview will allow you to check for problems before you print your document. You can also use it to make sure that tables are displayed correctly and page breaks appear in the right places (see *Printing a file*, page 286).

ASSESSMENT ACTIVITY

Task 1

You are asked to produce two documents about the planning of a group day visit to London. The group will visit two attractions, one in the morning and one in the afternoon.

Document 1

This will be a report about four places of your choice suitable for the visit, such as the Science Museum, Greenwich Observatory, the Tower of London, the London Dungeon, Tate Britain or Churchill's War Rooms.

The document should have a section on each of the four places you choose. For each place you need to give an overview of what you might see and do.

At the end, produce a summary in the form of a table. Headings for the table should include the name of the attraction, best travel option, entry fee, gift shop (Yes/No) and food available (Yes/No).

The document should include the following:

- page numbers
- at least two different fonts
- at least one image of each attraction
- a number of different text formats.

Document 2

This should be a memo to your teacher, tutor or supervisor explaining which two attractions you recommend and why. Use the memo layout that is provided in Figure 13.2 (page 275) or an alternative provided by your teacher, tutor or supervisor.

For both documents it is important that you have checked them carefully and that there are no spelling or grammar problems. Correct any problems you find.

Task 2

After the group visit, you will be asked to plan a meeting with the other learners to review the visit and then write up a report that explained what you did and saw. You must also find the opinions of the students about different aspects of the visit. You should develop a simple set of questions for a survey that could be summarised in the report.

Choose and describe layouts for the survey and the final report. Note what types of information you would expect to use in each. You do not need to produce the documents themselves. You also need to create an agenda for the meeting – your tutor will provide different ones for you to choose.

Note: You will be asked to meet your tutor at the end of the assessment to talk through the formatting and layout choices you made and your reasons for choosing them. Your tutor may also need to confirm and record that you have chosen sensible filenames and saved the files in the right place.

Glossary

.exe – is an executable file, i.e. one with instructions for a computer to carry out. Often this is a program but it could be a virus.

A

Administrator – someone whose job it is to maintain (look after) and operate a computer or IT system. They will have permission to access most or all parts of the system and make changes if necessary.

Agenda – list of items or matters to be discussed in a meeting.

Alignment – the position of text in a document: on the left, in the centre or on the right.

Attributes – settings on documents that control what can be done to them and by whom.

Audience – the people who a presentation, performance or document is meant for. The audience might be a specific group, such as women over 60 or young men, or it might include different types of people.

Authority – a reliable and trustworthy source of information.

Avatar – an icon or animated image, which is sometimes movable, that represents a person in cyberspace or on a games console.

B

Bias – liking or prejudice for or against something or someone.

Brute force program – a computer program that will try different 'solutions' until it finds the right one; for example, a password.

Bugs – errors in the code of a piece of software.

C

CAD – computer-aided design, often used for producing very accurate graphics such as engineering or architectural drawings.

Case sensitive – where uppercase (capital) letters and lowercase (small) letters are treated differently (for example, PC, Pc and pc would be treated as three different words). If you use the wrong case in your password, you will not be able to log in.

Cellular network – a mobile phone system. It is called 'cellular' because the country is divided into cells. Whichever cell you are in will automatically connect to your phone.

Clip art – ready-made pictures and symbols used to illustrate a range of subjects. They often appear as small cartoons.

Clipboard – when you cut or copy an image or a piece of text, it is stored on the clipboard. You can then paste the contents of the clipboard into a different place in the same document or into a different document in any Microsoft® Office® application.

Colour balance – the colours in digital images are made up of combinations of red, green and blue (RGB); by adjusting the levels of these colours you can change the overall look of the image.

Compression – reducing the size of the file needed to store an image. Compression can reduce the quality of the image as well, but in most cases this is not very noticeable.

Confidentiality – keeping something secret, such as private information.

Composite – made up of several parts or elements.

Cookie – a small file which is saved to your hard disk by a website you have visited.

Copyright – legal ownership of and rights over material that you have created yourself. Copyright covers not only printed material (books, magazines, etc.) but also films, music, paintings, images and so on.

Cores – independent processors which read and execute program instructions.

Corrupt – programs or files that have become unreliable because of damage, errors or changes.

Criterion – a rule or standard used to judge or decide on something (criteria is the plural).

Cross-check – use different sources or methods to check information or details.

Currency – how up to date something is.

Customise – change/modify to suit particular purposes or tasks.

D

Dataset – a database store of information in tables. This information or data can be made into a dataset in many ways; for example, by running a query, joining tables together or reducing the number of fields. The original data in the tables will not be changed and the dataset can then be used by forms or in reports.

Data validation – when a table checks that data is valid using techniques such as the size of a data entry. For example, a mobile phone number can be validated to ensure it has 11 characters.

Deadline – the final date for completing a task.

Dedicated – created or used for a specific purpose.

Default – a standard setting or option that comes with an IT system but may be changed to suit each user.

Default settings – the settings put in place when the computer was built and that remain if you do not change them.

Delete – to remove or erase, such as text in a document or a file or folder you no longer need.

Desktop publishing – or DTP, is the use of application software (e.g. Microsoft® Publisher®) to create complex printed documents which combine text, graphics and other features. Examples of documents that might be produced using DTP software include magazines, brochures and newsletters.

Disable – to turn off or disallow. If you 'disable' a feature, you turn it off (for example, you do not allow cookies to be stored on your computer).

Distort – to twist or pull something out of shape.

Download – copy anything from the Internet to your computer.

E

Easter Egg – a secret put into a computer product, such as a website or a computer game. Easter Eggs are hidden but

designed to be found by users. They usually contain bonus content (often something funny).

Enable – to turn on or allow. If you 'enable' a feature (such as cookies), you turn it on (for example, you allow cookies to be stored on your computer).

Email filter – this is a program which filters emails by looking at keyword content, who the sender is and file size. It automatically screens incoming messages and decides whether the email has come from a legitimate source or whether it is spam. Outgoing messages are also filtered.

Embedded – part of a document or file itself.

Extension – letters added to a file or document's name (after a full stop) to show what type of file/document it is.

Evaluate – work out how useful or worthy something is.

External storage – movable devices such as USB memory sticks, CDs or DVDS for storing data.

F

Font – typeface of a particular style; for example, Arial or Times New Roman.

Formal – according to official or recognised, rules, standards or structure.

Formula – used to carry out a calculation in a spreadsheet. A formula must start with an equals sign (=). Formulas can use actual values (numbers) or cell references.

G

Graphics tablet – an input device which allows you to draw images by hand, just as you would using pen and paper. You can also trace over existing artwork by taping it to the top of the tablet. This is also known as a digitising tablet.

H

Hard drive – a disk inside a computer that permanently stores important software or files that must be kept.

I

Icon – an image or graphic that represents a software program, application, folder or file.

Impersonate – to pretend to be someone or something else. A person who pretends to be someone else is an impersonator or impostor.

Imported – brought in from another source.

Intranet – an internal Internet which can only be viewed within an organisation such as a company, school or college.

Instant messaging – or IM is a form of communication which involves sending and receiving short text-based messages in real time.

L

LAN – a local area network (LAN) connects computers so they can share information and use resources such as printers and the Internet.

M

Macro – a set of codes that carry out a series of functions or repeated actions in software applications.

Meaningful filename – one which will help you find a file again quickly and easily.

Microblogging – social networking on websites where people can discuss any topic or update people on what they are doing. Posts are limited to short messages. For example, on Twitter™ a message (known as a 'tweet') is limited to 140 characters.

N

Netiquette – guidelines on how to be thoughtful and polite when using email and other IT communication methods; general good behaviour online. For example, typing in capitals is considered to be SHOUTING, which is impolite and should only be used to make something stand out when really needed.

O

Objective knowledge – factual information that can be verified (confirmed). For example, 'This hard disk has a capacity of 500 GB' can be confirmed.

Open source – software which is available to the public at no cost; often developed outside a mainstream software company.

Operating system (OS) – a vital set of programs that control and manage computers, such as Microsoft® Windows®. Your IT system will not work without an OS.

Operators – describe a calculation or comparison. Arithmetical operators such as + work with numbers. Logical operators such as OR work with words. Relational operators such as > (greater than) work with both numbers and words.

Orientation – whether a document or image is portrait (longer at the sides) or landscape (longer at the top and bottom).

P

PDF – stands for Portable Document Format and was developed by Adobe® Systems. PDF documents use a standard format that any system can read, no matter what hardware, software or operating system it uses.

Peer-to-peer networks – this is when computers in a network

work together to facilitate shared access to files and services without the need for a central server.

Persona – the part of a person's character that is presented to or perceived by others.

Phishing – this is a technique used to obtain individuals' personal details. Phising emails are designed to look like official emails (e.g. from your bank) and will ask you to click a link and provide personal information (e.g. your name, address and online banking login passwords). If you enter you details on the fake page then your details will become available to the people behind the phising email, who could use them to steal money from your account.

Planning – breaking down a large or complex task into several smaller tasks; identifying the resources you will need to complete each task and in what order you should complete them.

Plagiarism – using someone else's work and pretending it is your own. This is taken very seriously and can lead to poor marks or even exclusion from college courses. You could also be sued (taken to court) by the copyright owner of the work. Not all plagiarism is intentional. Simply forgetting to say what the source of your information or images is could be considered plagiarism and could get you into trouble.

Piggybacking – this term is used to describe several things in computing. Here it describes a situation where someone connects to the Internet via someone else's unsecured WiFi connection.

Pixelated – pixelation happens when some images are made too large. The pixels become visible and the picture looks blocky and unclear.

Pop-ups – online advertisements to attract customers to other websites or to obtain email addresses.

Portal – a gateway or entrance.

Posture – how you position or hold your body.

Primary key – a database table usually has a primary key which is used to make sure every record is different. The primary key can also automatically sort the table into order. Microsoft® Access® sets a default primary key ID to every new table which has an autonumber data type. This automatically enters a number for each new record.

Privacy – not being watched by or disturbed by others; keeping things private.

Privileges – the permissions given to users to set their level of access.

Pseudonym – a made-up or false name.

R

RAM – or random access memory is a form of computer storage.

Recipient – the person receiving an email or other message.

Relational database – uses more than one table to hold different types of information and uses queries to combine this data and produce reports.

Relevant – closely connected/linked to a specific matter in hand.

Repetitive strain injury (RSI) – may be caused by repetitive actions such as holding and clicking a mouse or typing on a keyboard. The main symptom is pain in the hands, wrists or arms.

Rollover – a type of button which changes when the mouse pointer passes over it. Usually, the image will change to show interaction. Buttons can also change when they are clicked.

Rotate – to move a whole image or part of an image in either a clockwise or anit-clockwise direction.

S

Scan – a digital version of artwork or photographic prints.

Scanner – an input device which digitises artwork or photographic prints. The item to be scanned is placed under the lid of the scanner, on a glass plate. A light source then moves across the glass plate and scans the item. Light sensors detect the colours in the item and convert them into digital data.

Screensaver – an animated image (or slideshow of multiple images) which will appear on your display screen after a period of no user activity.

Spam – also known as junk email, is unwanted or unsolicited email.

Sponsored links – companies that have paid a search engine, such as Google™, to put their websites at the top of the search results list.

Streamed – audio or video content which is presented live over the Internet.

Structured data – information that is organised so that each item (record) has the same type of content.

Subscribe – sign up for a product or service; for example, a newsletter or news of upcoming game releases.

Subjective knowledge – information based on opinion that depends on different people's thoughts and feelings about different things. For example, 'That is the most beautiful painting I have ever seen' might be one person's opinion, but another person might think the same painting is really ugly.

Surge protector – a device to protect electrical equipment from voltage surges or 'spikes' (sudden increases); for example,

in a storm. Power surges can damage or destroy computer hard drives.

Synch (synchronise) – updating data in different places at the same time so that files always match: for example, on a home computer and a smartphone.

T

Theme – a set of backgrounds, colours, fonts and effects that can be used in a presentation to give a consistent (standard) feel to all the slides; a set of features that are applied to elements in a file.

Troubleshoot – identify, analyse and solve problems.

Typos – typographical errors (typos) are mistakes made when setting out text.

U

Unauthorised – not having permission or approval to do something, such as access a computer or file.

USB – universal serial bus or USB is a common standard for connecting external devices to a computer. You can connect all sorts of devices to a USB port: a mouse, keyboard, printer, memory stick, digital camera, etc.

USB port – a slot in computers and other devices that you can plug a USB cable into to connect the devices. Most PCs will have several ports – for

example, to connect printers, scanners, keyboard, etc.

V

Vector shape – a mathematical description of a form that includes features, such as line thickness and type (e.g. dotted) and fill colour, shading, etc.

W

WiFi – uses radio waves rather than wires or cables to send data to and from a laptop or other IT device. Many laptops and smartphones have a WiFi link built into them. WiFi only works over quite short distances, usually 100 m or less.

Wizard – a software 'assistant' that helps you through certain IT tasks.

WYSIWYG – 'What You See Is What You Get'. This is where what you have designed on your screen is what the final product will look like. This is good for website creation software as what you see when you are designing will be what the users will see when the site is on the Internet.

X

X-axis – the horizontal scale along the base of a graph.

Y

Y-axis – the vertical scale along the side of a graph.

Index